ISLAMIC MODERNISM IN INDIA AND PAKISTAN

The Institute gratefully acknowledges the comments and suggestions of the following who read the manuscript on behalf of the Research Committee: Canon Kenneth Cragg, Professor Bernard Lewis, and Professor Hugh Tinker.

ISLAMIC MODERNISM IN INDIA AND PAKISTAN
1857-1964

AZIZ AHMAD

Professor of Islamic Studies
in the University of Toronto

Issued under the auspices of the
Royal Institute of International Affairs

OXFORD UNIVERSITY PRESS
LONDON BOMBAY KARACHI
1967

Oxford University Press, Ely House, London W.1
GLASGOW NEW YORK TORONTO MELBOURNE WELLINGTON
CAPE TOWN SALISBURY IBADAN NAIROBI LUSAKA ADDIS ABABA
BOMBAY CALCUTTA MADRAS KARACHI LAHORE DACCA
KUALA LUMPUR HONG KONG TOKYO

Printed in Great Britain
by Ebenezer Baylis and Son, Limited,
The Trinity Press,
Worcester, and London

TO
GUSTAVE E. VON GRUNEBAUM

CONTENTS

CONTENTS

PREFACE

THIS work has been undertaken primarily to introduce to the western student the landmarks of religious and political thought in Islamic India and Pakistan from 1857 to the present day. It is not planned as a comprehensive or detailed survey; consequently it deals mainly with individual thinkers and their works. The principal chapters deal with the long struggle between modernism and orthodoxy, which continues unabated to the present day. The problem is whether Islamic law, which also shapes political institutions, should continue to reject all extraneous stimuli and confine itself to the four traditional orthodox sources, the Qur'ān, *ḥadīs̱*, or the dicta attributed to the Prophet, the *ijmā'*, consensus of the *'ulamā'* (theologians), and *qiyās*, juristic reasoning by analogy,[1] or whether it should reinterpret the first two sources, either apologetically or otherwise, and transform the last two to become the vehicle of modern legal, and later, political notions.

The most forceful challenge to traditionalism came in the wake of the devastating consequences of the 'Mutiny' of 1857–8. It is epitomized in the thought, analysis, and apologetics of Sayyid Aḥmad Khān (1817–98), his movement, and the variations of emphasis in the modernist trends of his associates, Chirāgh 'Alī and Mahdī 'Alī Khān Muḥsin al-Mulk. The problem of legal and political reform led to varying reinterpretations of Islamic history in the writings of Shiblī Nu'mānī (1857–1914) and Amīr 'Alī (1849–1928) and to an emotional involvement with the contemporary world of Islam reflected in the Caliphate movement.

The traditionalist response to modernist challenges entrenched itself behind the bastions of orthodoxy, the great theological schools, as well as in the neo-traditionalist movement of the Ahl-i Ḥadīs̱.[2]

[1] The last principle has been largely replaced in modern Indian Islam by that of *ijtihād*, or the use of individual reasoning.

[2] See below, pp. 113–22.

The key figure in twentieth-century modernism is that of the poet and thinker Muḥammad Iqbāl (1875–1938), as in the nineteenth century it was that of Sayyid Aḥmad Khān. In the complex of his metaphysical approach to the redefinition of Islam in terms of modern values, a middle-of-the-road position emerges. Much more significant in the history of Islamic India was his political thought, which equated the Islamic notion of *ijmāʿ* with parliamentary democracy and worked out a new theory of Muslim nationalism which marked the theoretical beginning of the Pakistan movement. This view was given a more tangible shape in practical politics in Muḥammad ʿAlī Jinnāḥ's two-nation theory, which regarded Hindus and Muslims of the sub-continent as two separate nations.

The figure of Abu'l-Kalām Āzād (1888–1958) is partly complementary and partly antithetical to that of Iqbāl. Āzād's exegetical eclecticism leads him to some extent towards religious pluralism, making it easier for him to develop, sometime later, a theory of composite nationalism, as opposed to the two-nations theory.

Islamic socialism, which makes its first appearance in Iqbāl's verse, developed as an eccentric growth in the Islamic modernist thought of ʿUbayd-Allāh Sindhī and others; and is represented in this book by three of its theoreticians.

In Pakistan the polarization of traditionalist and modernist thought has been studied in the principal works of Mawdūdī (b. 1903) and Parwīz (b. 1903). Both of them base their arguments on the data of exegetical fundamentalism, in the interpretation of which they diverge in the antithetical directions of rigid externalism and speculative extravagance. The heritage as well as the conflict of these cross-currents is reflected in the processes of constitution-making, legislation, and reform in Pakistan, where the trend has been, and still is, to find a middle-of-the-road solution of an Islamic pattern of state on the one hand, and its development and adjustment in accordance with the challenges and requirements of the modern world on the other.

In the case of India since 1947, specimens of the varieties of religious and political adjustment of Islam in diaspora have been studied in a society which is predominantly non-Muslim, and in a state where certain measures offer and may continue to offer challenges of religio-cultural identification.

I have tried as far as possible to summarize the views of religious and political thinkers rather than offer judgements of my own, which have been reduced to the minimum. My objective has been to place in the hands of the western Islamist or student of international affairs a handbook of religious and political thought, as faithfully as possible rendered into English from primary sources, leaving him to draw his own conclusions and relate the problems raised to his own particular field of study. This purpose will be complemented to some extent in an anthology, *Readings in Muslim Self-Statement in India and Pakistan*, which I am editing in collaboration with Professor Gustave E. Von Grunebaum for the Columbia University Press.

An omission which may strike the reader in this book is the Aḥmadiyya movement. My reasons for omitting it are that a great deal of literature published by and on the movement is easily available in the west; that its theological messianism is heterodox, whereas in its political thought and in its modernist posture it is not clearly distinguished from the works of other institutions and groups studied. The position of the Aḥmadiyya in the 1953 Punjab riots has, however, been discussed.

Most of the quotations from the Qur'ān are from Professor A. J. Arberry's lucid version *The Koran Interpreted.*

A.A.

ACKNOWLEDGEMENTS

I AM deeply grateful to the Royal Institute of International Affairs for sponsoring this study. My thanks are due specially to Mr A. S. B. Oliver and Miss Hermia Oliver of the Institute for the help I have received from them.

I am grateful for the generous financial help extended in the way of travel and research grants during 1963 and 1964 by the Canada Council, the University of Toronto, and for supplementary grants to the American Council of Learned Societies and the Royal Institute of International Affairs, providing me with the opportunity of collecting material in the libraries of the United Kingdom.

I am grateful to Professors Bernard Lewis and Hugh Tinker and to Canon Cragg for reading the MS. and for very helpful suggestions. I am most grateful to Mr John Burton-Page and Mr C. Shackle, of the School of Oriental and African Studies, University of London, who have made themselves responsible for the system of transliteration and have also made other helpful corrections.

Parts of this book are based on matter previously published in the forms of articles in the *Archives de sociologie des religions*, *Journal of World History*, *The Middle East Journal*, and *Saeculum*. I am obliged to their editors for agreeing to its use in this work.

SYSTEM OF TRANSLITERATION

THE letters of the Urdu alphabet—that is to say, the Perso-Arabic alphabet as further modified for certain Indian usages—are in this work transcribed as follows, in Urdu alphabetical order:

a b p t ṭ s̱ j ch ḥ kh d ḍ ẕ r ṛ z zh s sh ṣ ẓ t̤ z̤ ʻ gh f q k g l m n w h y

The vowels used are a i u ā ī ū; e and o, which are always long; and, for the diphthongs, ay and aw. *Hamza* is written with ʼ. It has not been felt necessary to underscore those transcriptions which involve two roman letters, as is done in some scientific work; theoretically there might thus be some confusion possible between the Urdu fricatives kh and gh and the aspirated k and g, but in the present work such confusion does not arise. It is, however, necessary to avoid confusion of the aspirated t and d with two letters frequently transcribed *in Arabic* by t̲h̲ and d̲h̲: hence in this work s̱ and ẕ, which represent their pronunciation in Urdu, Persian, and Turkish and in some dialects of Arabic itself, replace them. Such words familiar to readers of Arabic as *hadit̲h̲* and *d̲h̲ikr* therefore appear here as *ḥadīs̱* and *ẕikr*.

The convention used in the *Encyclopædia of Islam* is followed for the Arabic article, which is everywhere transcribed al; thus we write ʻAbd al-Raḥīm, not ʻAbdur-Raḥīm. Note also Abu'l-Faẓl, not Abūl-Faḍl.

The following table shows the differences between the *Encyclopædia of Islam* transliteration and our own:

Islamic modernism	*EI*	*Islamic modernism*	*EI*
ṭ	t́	ṛ	ŕ
s̱	t̲h̲	ẓ	ḍ
j	d̲j̲	t̤	ṭ
ch	č	z̤	ẓ
ḍ	d́	q	ḳ
ẕ	d̲h̲		

J. B-P. C.S.

ABBREVIATIONS

Ameer Ali, *SHS* & *SI*:	Ameer Ali, *Short History of the Saracens* and *Spirit of Islam*.
Āzād, *TQ*:	Abu'l-Kalām Āzād, *Tarjumān al-Qu'rān*.
Blunt, *SH*:	Wilfrid Blunt, *Secret History of the English Occupation of Egypt*.
Cheragh Ali, *Proposed . . . Reforms*:	Cheragh Ali, *The Proposed Political, Legal and Social Reforms in the Ottoman Empire and Other Mohammedan States*.
EI:	*Encyclopaedia of Islam*.
Ḥālī, *HJ*:	Alṭāf Ḥusayn Ḥālī, *Ḥayāt-i jāwīd*.
IBLA:	*Revue de l'Institut des belles lettres arabes* (Tunis).
Maududi, *ILC*:	Sayyid Abdul Ala Maududi, *Islamic Law and Constitution*.
Munīr Report:	Punjab, Court of Inquiry constituted . . . to inquire into the Punjab Disturbances of 1953 [Pres.: M. Munīr], *Report*.
Parwīz, *NR*:	G. A. Parwīz, *Niẓām-i Rubūbiyyat*.
TA:	*Tahẕīb al-Akhlāq* (periodical founded by Sayyid Aḥmad Khān).
TD:	Maḥbūb Riẓwī, *Ta'rīkh-i Deoband*.

CHAPTER ONE

INTRODUCTION

EARLY CONTACTS AND INFLUENCES

IN 1497 Vasco da Gama sailed round the Cape of Good Hope and discovered the sea route to India. This led to the discovery of the Europeans by the Indian Muslims. The first Portuguese ships to operate off India were regarded as a menace to the maritime trade conducted mainly by the Arabs between India and the Arabian coast, East Africa, and Egypt. Naval wars of the kings of Gujarāt in alliance first with the Mamlūks and later the Ottomans did not succeed in dislodging the Portuguese from their Indian coastal strongholds or shake their power in the Indian Ocean.

The emperor Akbar evolved a political and commercial *modus vivendi* after his incorporation of Gujarāt as a province of the Mughal empire in the sixteenth century. Insular and continentally compact India had no great maritime or naval tradition which could supply the powerful Mughal emperor with an alternative. He made from time to time empty gestures in the direction of an alliance with Philip II against the Ottomans, and even went through the motions of dispatching an embassy to Spain which, however, never sailed.[1] He saw the maritime trade interests of his empire served best in maintaining and morally supporting the *status quo* of the Portuguese command of the Arabian sea, and tried to turn it to his economic and political advantage. To these policies the Portuguese response was pragmatically correct and affirmative. Portuguese sea captains relegated their crusading prejudices to the background in the profitable

[1] B. M. Ord. MS. 1702, ff. 202–a–b; Abu'l-Faẓl 'Allāmī, *Akbar nāma* (Calcutta, 1848), ii. 497–501; *The Commentary of Father Monserrate SJ on his Journey to the Court of Akbar*, Eng. tr. Hoyland and Banerjee (Cuttack, 1922), pp. 163–91; Aziz Ahmad, *Islamic Culture in the Indian Environment* (London, 1964), pp. 31–33.

enterprise of offering sea transport to the Muslim pilgrim caravans to the Hijāz and back. Indirectly they played a cohesive role in providing the facility of a renewal of direct contact between Mughal India and the holy cities of Islam. The land route to the Hijāz had become unsafe since the collapse of the Tīmūrid empire of Central Asia, and had been blocked from time to time by the Shīʿite Ṣafavid empire of Persia. From the sixteenth to the twentieth centuries Indian Muslim contact with the Hijāz has remained possible thanks to western navigation.

This change of the pilgrim route from land to sea made a considerable impact on the theological development of Muslim India. Islamic religious movements which had travelled overland from various Muslim lands until the middle of the sixteenth century had been heavily tinged either with Ṣūfism (mysticism) or rationalism. Since then the focus of the point of contact came to be fixed on the Muslim holy cities of the Hijāz which had remained impregnable fortresses of traditionalist and later fundamentalist orthodoxy. During the sixteenth century Indian schools of *ḥadīs̱* came to be established in the Hijāz by the Indian émigrés Sayyid ʿAlī Muttaqī and ʿAbd al-Wahhāb Muttaqī, and were transplanted thence to India by the latter's disciple, ʿAbd al-Ḥaqq Dihlawī. The fundamentalism of Shāh Walī-Allāh, who spent some years studying in the Hijāz in the early eighteenth century, heralded the first thaw which melted, to some extent, the frozen and rigid mass of traditionalist orthodoxy in Indian Islam and pointed the way simultaneously to two mutually incompatible directions, revivalistic conservatism and rationalist modernism.[2]

In the sixteenth century the intellectually eclectic court of Akbar was not interested in the beginnings of these religious movements, but in two other elements of western civilization brought to India by Jesuit missionaries and cultivated merchants: the Christian religion and Renaissance painting. In the religious disputations held in Akbar's 'Chamber of Worship'

[2] ʿAbd al-Ḥaqq Dihlawī, *Zād al-Muttaqīn*, B.M. Ord. MS. 217 and *al-Makātīb wa'l-Rasā'il* (Delhi, 1879): Shāh Walī-Allāh, *Ḥujjat Allāh al-bāligha* (1953).

(*ʿIbādat khāna*) under the influence of some of his intimate intellectual associates like Abū'l-Faẓl and Faiẓī, Akbar gradually turned from orthodoxy to heterodoxies within Islam, and finally to a comparative study of world religions—Hinduism, Jainism, Zoroastrianism, and Christianity—and to a quest of the inter-religional element in all faiths, a rare development in Islamic history. The study of Christianity was a part of this general intellectual and spiritual quest, and occupied no position of primacy as a discipline of study. The Bible was translated into Persian. There is an odd verse or so in Faiẓī's *Dīwān* which must be a free rendering of the first lines of a hymn. The next undertaking in comparative religion, two generations later, is Muḥsin Fānī's *Dabistān-i maẕāhib*, which contains a short section on Christianity.[3] But perhaps the most significant influence of this early intellectual contact with Christianity was an attitude of tolerance towards the Christians which lasted in Muslim India until the later decades of the eighteenth century.

Under Akbar Mughal painting had moved from the traditional impress of the parent Tīmūrid and cognate Ṣafavid schools towards cross-fertilization with indigenous Hindu techniques. It was at this juncture that religious painting of the European Renaissance was introduced at Akbar's court. Stchoukine's analytical researches, even if one disagrees with some of his sweeping conclusions, throw interesting light on the possible technical influences of western painting on the Mughal school from the sixteenth century onwards.[4] More balanced is the assessment of this influence under Akbar's son and successor, Jahāngīr, as summed up by Lubor Hajek:

> Jahāngīr's albums are not infrequently adorned with European engravings presented to the Emperor by the Jesuit missionaries of Goa. Most of these engravings are copies of the Dutch mannerists after Dürer, Rottenhammer, and Beham. The Mughal painters often copied these engravings, as well as pictures brought as gifts to Jahāngīr by the British ambassador Sir Thomas Roe.[5]

[3] Eng. tr. D. Shea and A. Troyer (Paris, 1843), ii. 305–21.

[4] Ivan Stchoukine, *La peinture indienne* (1929).

[5] *Indian Miniatures of the Mughal School* (London/Prague, 1960), p. 20.

No doubt other visitors to the Mughal court must have brought similar gifts.

Acceptance of the technical influences of western painting on Mughal miniatures was imitative and decorative rather than integral. European elements of colour, form, and scriptural content and motif are hospitably accommodated, as exoticisms preserved and not interfered with in the miniature framework, set but not entirely blended in a landscape, context, and technique that remains inalienably Mughal. Among typical instances of this composite texture is a portrait of Ibrāhīm ʿĀdil Shāh, the musician-king of Bījāpur, by Jahāngīr's court painter Farrukh Beg who has incorporated two European engravings intact, surrounded by a decorative margin of golden flower-tendrils, at the top of his miniature.[6] The exotic engravings do not blend with the composition of the rest of the painting, but they do not introduce a discordant note. Another interesting specimen is a miniature of Madonna and Child in Jahāngīr's 'Gulshan' album,[7] in which the Virgin and Child are exact replicas of a possible Florentine original, but the Three Wise Men have been transformed into two Mughal courtiers of inferior rank presenting a water-fowl and a bird in a cage, an obvious concession to Jahāngīr's love of birds and plumage. It is safe to conclude that on the whole Renaissance influence on Mughal painting remains an occasional frozen gesture of aesthetic eclecticism.

Italian craftsmen, as well as others from Persia and Turkey, were employed in the construction of the Tāj Maḥal by Shāh Jahān. In this great architectural monument, which is a cross between indigenous and foreign architectural and decorative elements, the Italian technique of *pietra dura* was adapted and thoroughly acclimatized, and the technically western inlay work was transformed in Islamic themes and artistic styles. Thus in Mughal architecture of the earlier seventeenth century there was a far more evident absorption of western techniques than in painting.

[6] Original folio of Jahāngīr's Album in Náprestek Museum, Prague; reproduction in Hajek, colour plate 10.

[7] Original in Tehran Imperial Library; reproduction ibid. pl. 31.

During the seventeenth century European gentlemen-adventurers were sometimes employed in the lower cadres of the Mughal artillery. Manucci, the author of *Storia do Mogor*, which is largely a *journal scandaleux*, was employed by Dārā Shikoh during the Mughal war of succession. Bernier was employed at Aurangzeb's court as a physician, since medical disciplines other than *Yūnānī* (Greco-Arab), including the indigenous Hindu Ayurvedic, were generally patronized by the Mughals on a minor scale. Despite the impression of their importance at the Mughal court, which Manucci, Bernier, and others like them try to convey to their readers at home, it seems that their positions were insignificant enough to be totally ignored in Mughal chronicles and all other surviving documents of the period. In the case of Bernier one might safely regard some of his observations on the intellectual situation of Mughal India as reflecting a lack of intimate or effective contact and as misinformed, and his report of the famous 'lament' of Aurangzeb over the inadequacy of the curricula and methodology of Muslim education compared with European as Bernier's own well-intentioned fabrication.[8]

The appointment of Europeans to higher military posts became a common practice of the successor states of the Mughal empire during the period of Mughal decline in the early eighteenth century on the eve of the beginnings of the territorial empire of the British East India Company. This was an overt acknowledgement of European technical mastery in the manufacture and use of the implements of artillery, as of European techniques of the strategy of war.

The pioneer civil servant of the East India Company adopted a style of living in India which was not very different from that of the Muslim aristocrat. Before the large-scale use of the steamship he treated India as his permanent or semi-permanent home. He could seldom marry into the Muslim élite or the Hindu higher castes, but like the local nobility he kept concubines, patronized dancing girls, frequently relaxed at home in

[8] *Travels in Mughal India* (Eng. tr.) (London, 1891), pp. 155–61 and *passim*.

baggy oriental dress, joined hunting parties and relished the Indo-Muslim cuisine. To this phase of the British nabobs belongs the large number of Urdu loan-words that found their way into the English language, certain adaptations of Indian recipes which the austere British diet has retained to this day, and certain comforts used extensively by the British in India.

With the advent of the steamship and the memsahib, the situation was basically altered. It became possible for the British civil or military officer to visit Britain frequently on furlough, to bring his own womenfolk to India, and to live in racial isolation from all elements of the local population. The pressure of Englishwomen seems to have been a major determining factor in this direction. In India where sexes were segregated and well-born women were veiled, reciprocal social mixing was in any case out of question. To this was added the famous Anglo-Saxon insularity. Towards the end of the eighteenth century, as Percival Spear has so aptly pointed out,

> the gulf which Mussulman nawwābs and English *bon viveurs*, diplomatic pundits and English scholars had for a time bridged over began ominously to widen again. With it the attitude of the average Englishman changed also . . . into one of contempt for an inferior and conquered people'; and later, 'as the new century advanced, things grew worse rather than better, until the time of Bentinck . . . By that time, in contrast with their attitude to the feasts of Warren Hastings' days Mussulmans considered dining with Europeans degrading.[9]

EARLY IMPRESSIONS OF WESTERN CIVILIZATION: ABŪ ṬĀLIB KHĀN

The monumental assessment of Anglo-Saxon civilization by an Indian Muslim, Mirzā Abū Ṭālib Khān, is a landmark of the first phase of interracial and intercultural contact. Others before him, no doubt, such as I'tiṣām al-dīn, who visited England in 1767 as an emissary of the Mughal emperor Shāh 'Ālam II, had visited Europe and recorded their impressions, but I'tiṣām

[9] *The Nabobs* (London, 1932), pp. 236, 240.

al-dīn's account of his travels does not compare with that of Abū Ṭālib Khān and remained unpublished until 1827.

Abū Ṭālib Khān had contacts with the court of Awadh (Oudh) and was a personal friend of several Britons. He recorded his impressions of travel in Europe during 1799–1803 in an intelligent and entertaining work, *Masīr-i Ṭālibī fī bilād-i Afranjī*,[10] which is one of the first introductions to modern western civilization written by a Muslim. It was written nearly a quarter of a century before the impressions of the Egyptian scholar and educationist al-Tahtāwī.[11]

Abū Ṭālib Khān spent most of the four years of his sojourn in England but he also visited Ireland, France, Italy, and Turkey. In London he was known as the 'Persian prince', a misunderstanding arising out of his first name, Mirzā, and his Persian lineage, which enabled English society to 'place' him and treat him more or less as an exotic equal. He received frequent visits and occasionally generous gifts in cash and kind from members of the British nobility. He moved with complete ease in salons and social receptions and in the company of aristocratic ladies. He was received by the British sovereign and Queen Charlotte. He met orientalists like Wilkins and Ouseley and was the first Muslim on record to show a distrust for western orientalism. He criticized Sir William Jones's Persian Grammar as occasionally inaccurate, and accused the British orientalists in general of false pride.[12] He had a lively and curious mind as he visited London coffee-houses, taverns, clubs, literary societies, theatres, masquerades, charity shows, the Bank of England, the royal exchange, and the British Museum. He received some information about the Freemasons though he did not join a lodge. He noted the difference between the individual charity enjoined by Islam and the large-scale social charity in England which served to create and support educational and other humanistic institutions.

[10] *Travels in Asia, Africa and Europe*, tr. by C. Stewart (London, 1814); see also C. A. Storey, *Persian Literature* (Cambridge, 1953), 1/2, 878–9; Humayun Kabir, *Mirzā Abū Tālib Khān* (Patna, 1961).

[11] Rifā 'a Badawī Rafī' al-Tahtāwī, *Takhlīs al-ibrīz ila talkhīs Barīz* (Cairo, 1905).

[12] *Travels in Asia* etc. 1. 197, 206, 227–42; ii. 142–3.

He noticed some curious resemblances between the architecture of the Oxford colleges and some ancient Hindu temples. Western love for antiques, sculpture, and the plastic arts was incomprehensible to his iconoclastic Muslim mind and seemed to verge on idolatry, but he admired the realism of the western theatre.[13]

In his assessment of the British character he was critical of their want of faith in religion and 'great inclination towards philosophy'. This he thought had left the lower classes of British society without any moral supervision. He deplored English snobbery and self-complacency; but he made a clear-cut distinction between the growing bureaucratic and racist arrogance of the English in India and the aristocratic or intellectual class snobbery of the British in Britain. He gave warning to his friends that a high standard of living and a leisurely routine were conducive to apathy, which in turn could expose a nation like Britain to the risk of being superseded by her rivals. His disapproval of the English passion for money and complete preoccupation with worldly affairs struck a note comparable to the attitude of the 'romantic revolt' in English poetry of that age. 'If the English as a nation have not suffered because of these vices, it is because of the strength of their constitution, both of individuals and of the Government', and because their neighbours possessed these vices in a greater proportion.[14]

On the credit side he complimented the English for being honourable, law-abiding, disciplined, courteous, anxious to do good, sincere, straightforward, and hospitable. His remarks on English womanhood were specially interesting. He admired the checks and balances under which they were given liberty and equality with men. He weighed, like Lady Mary Wortley Montagu, this chaperoned freedom favourably in comparison with the lack of surveillance behind the veil in Ottoman Turkey.[15]

Abū Ṭālib Khān was perhaps the first modern Muslim to pay a fearless tribute to monogamy. Single marriages as among the

[13] Ibid. i. 143–4, 205, 263, 288; ii. 127.
[14] Ibid. ii. 156–7.
[15] Ibid. pp. 32–81.

Christians could be more conducive to domestic peace: 'where the progeny being all of the same stock, no room is left for the contentions and litigations which too often disturb the felicity of a Mohammedan family'. On the other hand Muslim family life had its points. For instance, as it was organically patriarchal, it did not suffer from the emotional distance between near relations which characterized the life of a European family.[16] In describing the virtues of the British social or family life he distinguished clearly between the idealized norms of the conservative élite which he defended, and the absence of sexual morality in the lower and, as a frequent exception, in all classes. In another context he did not hesitate to castigate the British nation for its 'want of chastity', citing instances of elopements, cohabitation before marriage, frequency of sex vices in London, and the multiplying number of public houses and bagnios.[17]

Of the values of the Anglo-Saxon civilization the one which struck him as the most outstanding was its passionate respect for individual freedom fully protected by British law. But he was also aware that certain classes were less equal than others. 'After all this equality is more in appearance than in reality; for the difference between the comforts of the rich and the poor is, in England, much greater than in India.'[18] But it was precisely in this overstatement that he failed to recognize the future direction of western civilization towards a levelling of the standards of living between classes; whereas in India under British rule during the subsequent century and a half the gulf between privileged and under-privileged classes yawned wider and wider, ominously accelerated by a population explosion.

Coming from a medieval feudal background in India, Abū Ṭālib Khān showed a remarkable awareness of the impact and potentialities of the industrial revolution. He attributed the military and economic superiority of Britain over even the monolithic resources of Napoleonic France to greater advancement in industrial technology. In his visits to mills, iron foundries, and hydraulic machines he was impressed by the order, discipline,

[16] Ibid. pp. 40–42. [17] Ibid. pp. 31–35. [18] Ibid. pp. 2–23.

regularity, and precision which the mechanical and industrial processes imposed upon men. He recognized the procedures of credit and trust in banking and trade as logical by-products of the evolution of an industrial society. To industrial civilization, to the discipline imposed by machines, he attributed the regular and hard-working habits of the British middle classes.[19]

Describing his first visit as an observer to watch the proceedings of the British House of Commons he remarked, 'the first time I saw this assembly they reminded me of two flocks of Indian parakeets sitting upon opposite mango-trees scolding each other; the most noisy of whom were Mr Pitt and Mr Fox'. And in describing the working of the British parliamentary system he did not fail to notice the occasional high-handedness of the ruling party. Explaining the workings of British public finance, the assessment of taxation, government loans, and international debts, he offered some facetious advice to his English hosts in the good old medieval Muslim *Fürstenspiegel* tradition on the question of the liquidation of the national debt by persuading the creditors to agree to reduce it by 50 per cent, to secure their own long-term interests against a possible revolution.[20]

He explained to his fellow Muslim readers that in England law and religion are distinctly separate institutions, and that unlike the *'ulamā'* in contemporary Islam, the duty of the clergyman was limited to watching over the moral and spiritual welfare of his flock, to burying the dead, visiting the dying, uniting persons in marriages and christening children. He had no soft spot for the Anglican clergy and entered into argument with the Bishop of London on the familiar question of the advent of the Prophet being foretold in the 'original' New Testament before it was interpolated. The British secular law fascinated him. He paid frequent visits to English courts. There he was impressed by the right of every British subject to trial by jury and by the integrity and sense of honour of the English judiciary. He could develop no corresponding respect for the British bar, and deplored the 'manipulations and intimidations' of British lawyers

[19] Ibid. p. 44.

[20] Ibid. i. 299–301; ii. 55, 124–5.

which would often unnerve an honest man sufficiently to lose his case. Very different were British courts of law in India at that time, which were 'converted to the very worst of purposes'.[21]

He travelled through France when Napoleon Bonaparte was at the height of his powers, but his accounts of Paris are disappointing. He may have been over-cautious to avoid giving any possible offence to his British patrons; in any case he knew no French and his contacts were indirect. He did not stay in Paris long enough to form detailed impressions, but he complimented the French on their almost oriental courtesy, and noted that their language was more circuitous than English. And he did not fail to meet the French orientalists Langlois and de Sacy.[22]

After some mishaps in Italy he reached Turkey, nearly three-quarters of a century before the generalized Turcophilia of Muslim India. Thus Abū Ṭālib Khān landed in Smyrna without any pan-Islamic sympathies, considering himself a British protected person, and he was received as such by the British ambassador, Lord Elgin.

After Europe he found the Turks indolent and noisy; their inns horrid; their cafés filthy and 'common to both sexes'; their dress extravagant; their cuisine inferior to that of India and Persia; but he liked Turkish books, horses, fountains, and bazaars. He admired the Turkish élite and carefully noted the first signs of westernization. He complimented the Turks for being persons of strict honour, intrepid, liberal, hospitable, friendly, and compassionate; and 'their government is conducted with greater attention to justice than any other Mohammedan States'. He found the Turkish upper classes religious and pious. He observed that the Turkish women enjoyed greater freedom than their Persian or Indo-Muslim sisters, while upper-class women went out unveiled or partly veiled.[23]

He was received by the Turkish foreign minister (*reis-efendi*) at the request of the British ambassador and presented to the Grand Wazīr, Yūsuf Pasha, and to Sultan Selīm III, who bestowed upon him a robe of honour. Of Turkish politics he

[21] Ibid. ii. 63–65; 103–14. [22] Ibid. pp. 247–61. [23] Ibid. iii. 28–64.

formed the impression that the wazīrs had excessive power at the expense of the Sultan. After the English judicial institutions he found the Turkish *qāẓīs* (judges) corrupt and arbitrary. In Baghdad, which he regarded as inferior to Indian cities, he complained of the Turkish oppression of the Shīʿite pilgrims to Najaf and Karbala, where the first and the third of the Shīʿite *Imāms* were buried. But Abū Ṭālib Khān was no Shīʿī bigot. He did not hesitate to praise the character of Muḥammad b. ʿAbd al-Wahhāb and the fundamentalist promise of the Wahhābī movement, despite its iconoclastic zeal and insolent disregard of Shīʿī susceptibilities.[24]

THE IMPACT OF THE BRITISH JUDICIAL SYSTEM[25]

A charter of Queen Elizabeth I issued on 31 December 1600 had brought the East India Company into existence. By it certain limited powers of legislation were conferred upon the Company, which was authorized to make, ordain, or constitute laws, orders, and constitutions, provided they were 'reasonable' and not contrary or repugnant to the laws, statutes, or customs of the realm of England. These legislative powers were confirmed by James I in his charter of 31 May 1609. Sir Thomas Roe, the ambassador of James I to the court of the Mughal emperor Jahāngīr (1605–27), obtained certain concessions from the Mughal court which were to some extent similar to those granted by the Ottoman Porte to the French which later developed into the 'Capitulations'. The British were permitted to live according to their own religion or laws without interference; disputes among them were settled by their own tribunals, though any disputes that arose between them and Mughal subjects came under the jurisdiction of Mughal

[24] Ibid. pp. 60–79, 168–9.

[25] I am grateful to Professor A. Gledhill for information and advice for this section. For sources see M. P. Jain, *Outlines of Indian Legal History* (1952); A. A. A. Fyzee, *Outlines of Muhammedan Law* (1964); W. H. Morley, *The Administration of Justice in British India* (1858); A. Rahim, *Muhammedan Jurisprudence* (Madras, 1911); W. H. McNaghten, *Principles and Precedents of Moohomuddan Law* (Calcutta, 1825); S. C. Sircar, *Muhammedan Law* (Calcutta, 1875); Ameer Ali, *Mahommedan Law* (1929); R. K. Wilson, *Anglo-Muhammedan Law* (London, 1930); N. J. Coulson, *A History of Islamic Law* (1964).

officials. From the Mughal point of view, this must have been quite a logical and convenient decision, as then in India personal Hindu law was being applied to Hindu subjects, and Muslim law only to the Muslims.

The legislative powers of the East India Company were enhanced by James I in 1623. By the charter of 1661 Charles II extended these powers to include Indian elements of the Company's settlements. By the second half of the seventeenth century the Company's courts were dealing with criminal as well as civil cases in Madras and Bombay, while the Mughal empire was still at the zenith of its power. But since the introduction of the British judicial system was marginal and hardly came in contact or conflict with the Mughal judicial system—based largely on the *sharīʿa*—its foothold on the Indian soil was scarcely noticed in the Mughal imperial records.

In 1698 the East India Company was given a landholding (*zamīndārī*) of three villages in the vicinity of Calcutta by the Mughal governor of Bengal, Prince ʿAẕīm al-Sha'n. In this area, like other tenants of the Mughals, the Company obtained a legal and constitutional status within the framework of the Mughal administration. It established a criminal court and an *ʿadālat* (civil court). Appeals were sent, as by other landlords' courts of that area, to the Mughal Court of Appeal at Murshīdābād. But since the East India Company had derived its legal powers from two separate sovereign sources, the British Crown and the Mughal court, an anomalous situation soon developed. In death sentences and in certain civil cases appeal was made to the Company's governor and Council in Calcutta and not to the Indian Court of Appeal. In 1726, by a charter of George I, Crown Courts were established in the British commercial ports of Calcutta, Bombay, and Madras. Mayors' Courts were formed in these three presidencies to deal with civil cases, whereas criminal cases were dealt with by governors and their councils, with provision for trial by jury. The *Zamīndārī* (landlord's) Court of Calcutta, which had been functioning since 1698, became in 1853 the native Court of Appeal.

In the power vacuum which the rapid disintegration of the Mughal empire had caused after 1707, and which had been aggravated during half a century's predatory civil strife between its successors, creating complex and shifting patterns of anarchy, the East India Company began its phase of imperial expansion in 1757 with large-scale acquisitions of Indian territory. Its *de facto* jurisdiction now covered the provinces of Bengal, Bihar, and Orissa. In 1764 it obtained a legal executive status in the three provinces when the nominal and powerless Mughal emperor Shāh 'Ālam II appointed the Company as his Revenue Commissioner in return for an annuity of 2½ million rupees. The British thus found themselves heir to a judicial system which was based on the Islamic *sharī'a*, adapted by the Mughals to local conditions. Under the Mughals, the governor or *nāẓim* of a province was its civil and military executive head, was responsible for law and order, and, therefore, also for the administration of criminal justice. The *dīwān* of a province, who ranked next to a governor, collected revenue and was in charge of the administration of justice. Though, technically, only the *dīwān's* functions, i.e. revenue administration, had been granted to the East India Company by the Mughal emperor in 1765, in fact the Company gained full control of judicial departments.

Outside its own presidency towns, the Company retained the Mughal judicial machinery at first; and former Mughal functionaries were confirmed in the newly acquired provinces. In 1772 Warren Hastings remodelled the local judicial system, though entirely on the traditional Mughal pattern, reorganizing the district *dīwānī* (civil) and *fawjdārī* (criminal) courts, the former presided over by the British Collector assisted by Muslim *muftīs* and Hindu *paṇḍits*. These district courts decided all cases of personal law and custom, such as inheritance, marriage, caste, and other religious usages and institutions, according to the laws of the *sharī'a* for the Muslims and *Dharmashāstras* for the Hindus. Appeals in civil and criminal cases could be made to the provincial Supreme Civil (*Ṣadar Dīwānī*) and Criminal (*Ṣadar Fawjdārī* or *Niẓāmat*) Courts. The former consisted of the

Company's governor and his Council; the latter of an Indian *dārūgha*, appointed technically by the pensioner Nawwāb of Murshīdābād, but actually by the British governor.

In 1773 Warren Hastings was appointed Governor-General. In 1774 a Supreme Court of Judicature was established under a Royal Charter with Sir Elijah Impey as its first Chief Justice. It had jurisdiction over British residents, the servants of the Company, and Indian residents of the provinces of Bengal, Bihar, and Orissa in case of dispute with a British citizen. It used a grand jury and a petty jury composed of British residents in the town of Calcutta. Its judges were professional lawyers who held office during His Majesty's pleasure. It operated on the basis of the British common law as well as of equity jurisdictions.

Two distinct and independent judicial systems thus began to operate quite separately, while their jurisdiction overlapped. One of these derived its authority from the British Crown and parliament and the other from the East India Company as the Revenue Commissioner of the Mughal emperor. This anomaly was partly resolved when in 1780 Impey was also appointed the sole judge of the native Supreme Civil Court.

The next major step in judicial reorganization was taken by the Governor-General, Cornwallis, who in 1790 described the administration of civil justice in Indian courts as 'entirely useless, futile and rotten to the core' and pinned the blame on two assumptions: 'the gross defects of the Muhammedan law of crimes; and defects in the constitution of the courts'.[26] The *sharīʿa* law was modified by the Governor-General-in-Council as Anglo-Muhammadan law. According to the new procedure of appeals, decisions of lower Indian courts were examined by the Chief Qāẓī and the *muftīs* and submitted with their comments to the Supreme Civil Court for the Indians, which consisted of the Governor-General and his Council, to pass the final judgments. District criminal courts were abolished and courts of circuit were set up at four major towns on a similar pattern. Cornwallis's reorganization of the judiciary had certain drastic features; the

[26] Jain, pp. 152–3.

pattern of law was anglicized and controlled by the central authority of the Governor-General, while the only concession made to Indian interests was at the lower levels, where in subordinate courts in the districts Indian *munṣifs* (magistrates) were appointed. On the other hand the regular profession of *wakīl* (lawyer), which was to provide the subcontinent with much of its political leadership a century later, was thrown open to Indians.

Further structural reorganization took place under Wellesley, Cornwallis (Governor-General for the second time), and Amherst. Instead of functioning as the Supreme Civil and Criminal Court for the Indians, the Governor-General-in-Council appointed three judges and a Chief Justice, who were British covenanted servants of the Company, as the personnel of the bench. With the territorial extension of the Company's empire in India, this judicial structure was extended to other provinces with minor modifications. The Chester Act of 1833 and the legal reforms of 1836 and 1843 placed Europeans and Indians under procedural equality in civil cases. In British Indian criminal law the Europeans managed to retain a privileged position, despite the hardly contested reforms of 1872, the Ilbert Bill of 1884, and the Criminal Procedure Amendment Act of 1923. It was not until India and Pakistan gained independence in 1947 that racial discrimination was finally removed from the sphere of criminal law in the subcontinent.

The *modus vivendi* which the British judicial system evolved with what it considered to be the politically explosive strata of Hindu and Muslim personal law were summed up in the Regulation enacted by the Bengal government for the administration of justice, which laid down that in all suits regarding inheritance, marriage and caste, and other religious usages or institutions, 'the laws of the Koran with respect to Mahomedans, and those of the Shaster with respect to Gentoos, shall be invariably adhered to'.[27] Where the parties differed in religion, the law of the defendant was applied.[28]

[27] Cited in Morley, pp. 177–8.

[28] G. Rankin, *Background to Indian Law* (Cambridge, 1946), p. 9; Fyzee, *A Modern Approach to Islam* (1963), p. 60.

Muslim personal law continued to be applied to the Muslims in cases of inheritance, succession, gifts, *waqfs* (settlements to safeguard property for a charitable use), pre-emption, marriage, divorce, parentage, guardianship, and maintenance. In the case of Muslim personal law the British 'tried to maintain the policy of non-interference perhaps much more tenaciously than they did in the case of Hindu law'.[29] Interference with *waqf* laws was an exception which was regarded by the westernized political leadership of Muslim India as a blow to the economic security of Muslim gentry, and led to protests which began with Sayyid Aḥmad Khān and ended with Muḥammad ʿAlī Jinnāḥ's success in steering the Waqf Act through the Indian legislature in 1913, which restored to the Indian Muslims the right to make valid *waqfs* to their families.

The main sphere of British interference with the *sharīʿa* law was therefore principally in criminal law. In practical application Muslim criminal law formed four broad categories. Specific penalty, or *ḥadd*, prescribed scourging or stoning or amputation of a limb for such crimes as larceny, slandering a virtuous woman, or adultery. Cruel by modern standards, these punishments reflected the norms of a tribal society and were pronounceable only in face of undeniable evidence. In view of their severity, the medieval ecumenical caliphate of the ʿAbbāsids had also instituted semi-secular parallel courts, the *maẓālim*, which prescribed lighter punishments. The second category was *taʿzīr* (discretionary punishment), dealing with such crimes as did not strike at the root of the moral fibre of the society, and imposed exile, imprisonment, or lighter corporal punishments. The third category, *qiṣāṣ* (chastisement, retaliation), involved the death penalty for capital murder, but it could be substituted by the fourth category, *diya* (blood-money), if the dependants and relatives of the victim were prepared to accept blood-money from the murderer in compensation, foregoing personal vendetta. The last two categories reflect the customary law of the ancient Arabian blood feuds making accommodation for economic stresses.

[29] Jain, pp. 152–3.

British reaction to Muslim criminal law changed over the years from *laissez-faire* to toleration and finally to repugnance. To Warren Hastings it seemed 'founded on the most lenient principles and an abhorrence of bloodshed'.[30] In 1832 official British opinion still regarded it as mild,

> for though some of the principles it sanctions be barbarous and cruel, yet not only the infliction of them is rarely rendered compulsory on the magistrate, but the law seems to have been framed with more care to provide for the escape of the criminals than to found conviction on sufficient evidence and to secure the adequate punishment for offenders.[31]

The Muslim legal view of homicide or murder as a private injury rather than a social crime was repugnant to British legal thinking from the outset.[32] From the viewpoint of law and order lacunae in the Muslim law of evidence made the conviction of offenders difficult. Cornwallis's legal reforms of 1790, which made the first inroads into Muslim criminal law, operated by selection and rejection of rulings from various jurists in the Ḥanafī school of traditional law, inherited through the Mughal empire.[33] But these reforms emphasized the importance of circumstantial evidence and regarded capital crime as a public rather than private injury.[34] *Diya* was abolished; such extreme corporal punishments as mutilation or physical injury were replaced by hard labour. In 1803 the law of *ta'zīr* was modified to be applied more strictly against anti-social crimes. In 1817 the punishment for adultery was reduced and confined to the infliction of thirty stripes and imprisonment.

In its early stages Anglo-Muhammadan law followed a policy of circumspection and circuitous gradualism. Regulation VI of 1832, however, marked the end of the universal applicability of Muslim criminal law to non-Muslims. Certain ancient Hindu legal features such as the *panchāyat* (village assembly) system were revived. Trial by jury was introduced.

[30] Ibid. p. 396.
[31] *Parl. Papers*, 1931–2, xii. 696.
[32] *Bengal Revenue Consultations*, 11 Nov. 1789.
[33] Coulson, pp. 154–5.
[34] Jain, pp. 154–5.

This early dissemination of British concepts and institutions of jurisprudence facilitated the growth of modernist trends in Indian Islam and set the legal thinking of Muslim India on a course of development slightly different from that of other Muslim countries in the Middle East and North Africa.[35]

RELIGIOUS REACTIONS AND THE 'MUTINY' OF 1857

After centuries of Muslim rule and a certain amount of liberalization by the Mughals, the traditional Ḥanafī *sharīʿa* law was compiled under the auspices of the emperor Aurangzeb (1658–1707) in the *Fatāwā-i ʿĀlamgīrī*. It had not been interfered with by the Hindu Marāṭhās, who had been the most dominant and the most turbulent power during the Mughal period of decline in the eighteenth century. They had devised no alternative legal system for the areas they dominated. It is in this light that one has to examine the two conflicting rulings of the great theologian Shāh ʿAbd al-ʿAzīz (the son of Shāh Walī-Allāh), declaring India as still *dār al-Islām* (the land of Islam) under the Marāṭhās, but pronouncing it *dār al-ḥarb* (land of war, enemy territory) under the British.[36]

'In this city [Delhi]', runs his famous injunction denouncing Anglo-Muhammadan law and British rule,

> Islamic Law does not prevail at all; and the law of the Christian overlords is current without check or hindrance in the sense that in administrative and civil cases, in the prescription of punishments, the non-Muslims are in complete authority. It may be that they do not interfere with such Muslim rites as Friday or *ʿId* prayers, or call to prayers or ritual killing of eatable animals. But their chief principle is profit and sovereign control. . . . From this city to Calcutta Christian rule prevails.[37]

[35] Cf. M. Khadduri and H. J. Liebsny, eds., *Law in the Middle East* (Washington, 1955); J. N. D. Anderson, *Islamic Law in the Modern World* (London, 1959); G. H. Bousquet, *Du droit musulman et de son application effective dans le monde* (Algiers, 1949).

[36] *Fatāwā-i ʿAzīziyya* (1904), pp. 16–17; Urdu tr. (Cawnpore, n.d.), pp. 35–37; W. W. Hunter, *The Indian Musalmans* (London, 1871), p. 140.

[37] Hunter.

This verdict is not purely a legal one. Its overtones are broadly political. A ruling by his disciple, Shāh ʿAbd al-Ḥayy, is even more explicit: 'Calcutta and its dependencies are Country of the Enemy'.[38] These rulings are the angry reactions of the orthodox *ʿulamā*' to what they considered to be undue interference with the inherited tradition and practice of Ḥanafī law.

Lively controversy has raged since 1870 as to whether the militant objectives of the fundamentalist-reformist movement of the Mujāhidīn (holy warriors) led by ʿAbd al-ʿAzīz's dynamic disciple Sayyid Aḥmad Barelwī, whose chief supporters ʿAbd al-Ḥayy and Muḥammad Ismāʿīl were scions of the house of Walī-Allāh, was directed primarily against the British as much as against the Sikhs on India's north-western frontier.[39] Twentieth-century Muslim historiography in India and Pakistan invests Barelwī with an anti-imperialist role, basing its case mainly on his unpublished correspondence with the rulers of Afghanistan and Bukhara without fully evaluating the diplomatic latitude and import of these letters.[40] There is little doubt, however, that after the liquidation of the Sikh state in the Punjab, the British inherited from it the problem of the persistent hostility of the Mujāhidīn.

In fact the attitude of ʿAbd al-ʿAzīz and his disciples, including the Mujāhidīn, to the British was ambivalent. A ruling of this divine permitted Muslim students to enrol in British schools.[41] The preachings of his nephew Muḥammad Ismāʿīl recommending a loyal *modus vivendi* with the British as long as they did not interfere with the religious freedom of the Muslims stood in sharp contrast to earlier rulings.[42] Even ʿAbd al-Ḥayy had at one stage served under the British East India Company with the

[38] Ibid.

[39] Ibid. *passim*; cf. Sayyid Aḥmad Khān's letters refuting Hunter's views in the *Pioneer* (Allahabad, 1907); E. Rehatsek, 'History of the Wahhabys in Arabia and India', *JAS* (Bombay), 1880, pp. 274–401; Jaʿfar Thānesarī, *Tārīkh-i ʿAjība* (Lahore, 1890), pp. 175, 189–90; Mirzā Ḥayrat Dihlawī, *Ḥayāt-i ṭayyiba* (Lahore, 1958), pp. 119–30.

[40] B. M. Ord. MS. 6635; also quoted from another unidentified MS. in Ghulām Rasūl Mihr, *Sayyid Aḥmad Shahīd* (Lahore, 1952), i. 259–60.

[41] Thānesarī, p. 35; Mirzā Ḥayrat Dihlawī, pp. 127–8.

[42] Sayyid Aḥmad Khān, *Asbāb-i baghāwat-i Hind* (1903), p. 8.

permission of his mentor ʿAbd al-ʿAzīz.[43] Other eminent *ʿulamāʾ* who participated in the Uprising of 1857, like Ṣadr al-dīn Khān Āzarda and Faẓl al-Ḥaqq Khayrābādī, had accepted judicial appointments under the Company at one time or another.[44]

Neither was the Muslim rejection of western institutions in the later eighteenth and early nineteenth centuries as rigid as it is generally supposed. The pleasure-loving rulers of Awadh showed some interest in modern sciences. Under the patronage of Āṣaf al-dawla (1778–92) Newton's *Principia* was translated into Arabic. His successor, Saʿādat ʿAlī Khān, founded an observatory in Lucknow. A laboratory was constructed in the same city by Ghāzī al-dīn Ḥaydar (1814–27), who was also a patron of western and oriental philological studies.[45]

Receptiveness of the impact of British institutions is especially reflected in the intellectual career of Karāmat ʿAlī Jawnpūrī (d. 1873), who forms a bridge between the fundamentalist Mujāhidīn and the modernists. Though a Shīʿī, he was a disciple of ʿAbd al-ʿAzīz, and supported Barelwī's movement of reform in Bengal between 1820 and 1824. At the same time he seems to have developed a trend in his own fundamentalist views towards the assimilation of western sciences and a personal loyalty to the East India Company. By 1931, he was in close contact with the Company's administration and received gifts from its Directors. Later he joined the Muhammedan Literary Association, founded in Calcutta by ʿAbd al-Laṭīf Khān, and endeavoured to keep politics out of religion. Among his pupils was the famous Amīr ʿAlī, on whose mind he seems to have exercised a lasting influence.

Karāmat ʿAlī's *Maʾākhiẓ al-ʿulūm*, through written in the post-'Mutiny' phase in 1865, reflects a mental approach he had developed long before the political and cultural watershed of 1857, which divides modern from medieval Islam in India and

[43] A. S. K. Sherwani, introd. to Faẓl al-Ḥaqq Khayrābādī, *al-S̲awra al-Hindiyya*, Urdu tr. (Bijnore, 1957), p. 39.

[44] Ibid. p. 50.

[45] Abdullah Yusuf Ali, *A Cultural History of India* (Bombay, 1940), pp. 73–75, 95–97.

may, therefore, be mentioned here. He develops the thesis that the Divine Creator is the original source of all knowledge which He caused to be revealed to His creatures through His Prophets, especially Muḥammad and his descendants the *Imāms* (infallible guides, according to the Shīʿite creed). Modern scientific discoveries have mainly resulted from and coincide in principle with the declarations of the Qur'ān and the *ḥadiṣ*. Science passed from the Greeks to the Arabs, and from the Arabs through modern Spain to Europe in a historical continuity. This process of cultural diffusion is still operative, and the Muslims of India can derive much benefit from intercourse with Europeans. Luther is blamed by the author for lack of historical honesty in suppressing the evidence of the Islamic contribution to iconoclasm and the actual Islamic influence on Leo the Isaurian.[46]

Karāmat ʿAlī is not satisfied with the Trinitarian version of monotheism and emphasizes that Islam alone has succeeded in developing a purely unitarian concept of the Deity. He regards all knowledge as good in itself, but its application can be useful or harmful. Knowledge can be demonstrable or otherwise; religious knowledge belonging to the second category. Since the Qur'ān is the infallible source of all knowledge, it is valid to compare the themes of exact sciences with its text. Also 'the principles of every false doctrine are mentioned there, with the most satisfactory arguments for confuting them'. Guidance towards modern physics can be obtained from the Qur'ān and the *ḥadīṣ*, which mentions that 'the planets and the stars are inhabited, and that they contain all that this earth contains in more excellent form'. There are pointers in the Qur'ān to the modern principles of 'optics and perspectives'.

> The whole Koran is full of passages containing information on physical and mathematical sciences. If we would but spend a little reflection over it we should find wondrous meanings in every word it contains. The Koran has most satisfactorily confuted all the systems of ancient philosophy; it plucked up from the root the physical sciences as

[46] Karāmat ʿAlī Jawnpūrī, *Ma'ākhiẕ al-ʿulūm*, Eng. tr. ʿUbaydī & Amīr ʿAlī (Calcutta, 1867), pp. 1, 12, 15–22, 69–71.

prevalent among the ancients. What a strange coincidence exists between the Koran and the philosophy of modern Europe.[47]

Whereas the Europeans did not disdain to learn Greek and Arab sciences during the period of the Crusades or in Spain, modern Muslims, 'on whom tables are now turned', have contracted a dislike for all sorts of learning, and 'have forgotten that knowledge will not come to any person unless wooed with the utmost assiduity.' He is happy about the receptivity of Egypt under Muḥammad 'Alī and of the Ottoman empire under Maḥmūd II at least to some western institutions, and as a Shī'ī regrets Persia's backwardness on that score. He emphasizes the necessity of learning European languages as a first step in the direction of the acquisition of scientific knowledge. Scientific works can then be translated into Arabic, Persian, and Urdu.[48] His views provide a theoretical basis for a favourable response to the educational, cultural, and economic institutions introduced by the British in the early nineteenth century such as the study of modern sciences in English begun in 1835, the establishment of the first engineering college at Roorkee in 1847, and the first medical college in Bombay in 1845.

For the Muslims the most vital of these institutions was Delhi College, originally a school of classical Islamic studies, which came to be subsidized by the British in 1827, in which Urdu was used as the medium of instruction and English taught as a subsidiary discipline. It attracted such outstanding theologians as Mamlūk al-'Alī, of the Walī-Allāhī school, to its staff; and produced the first crop of semi-westernized intellectuals, including the historian Zakā-Allāh, the poet Alṭāf Ḥusayn Ḥālī, and the novelist Naẕīr Aḥmad. Delhi College unjustly became a casualty of the aftermath of the 'Mutiny' of 1857 and was closed by the British administration.

Apart from Delhi College and the schools in Calcutta, Muslim adaptability to and inclination towards westernized institutions was less positive than that of the Hindus. This general repugnance stemmed from a psychological, social, and economic

[47] Ibid. pp. 25, 29–42. [48] Ibid. pp. 76–77, 121–2.

discontent and a sense of injustice, consummately analysed in Sir William Hunter's classic study, *The Indian Musalmans.* Hunter, a high ranking civil servant, assigns the greater part of responsibility for this situation to several British administrative decisions taken inadvertently or with a view to immediate expediency but which had a disastrous impact on the economic resources and the cultural foundations of the Muslim élite. Revenue reorganization, known as the Permanent Settlement, enforced by Cornwallis and Sir John Shore in Bengal in 1793, reduced the Muslim peasantry to the status of serfdom, and created a class of Hindu landlords as middlemen.[49]

Unlike the Hindus the Muslims, who for several centuries had constituted the ruling class in India, were psychologically unprepared for the economic upheavals bound up with the switch from Persian to English as the language of public instruction in 1835. The western educational system which had replaced theirs made no provision for their religious instruction, whereas it was providing opportunities for religious education in England through the divinity faculties in universities. Feelings were further embittered by the effect of the abrogation of the *waqf* laws on private Muslim schools and misappropriation of funds of these schools by British officials. Muslim reluctance to make use of the new educational facilities contributed to the vicious circle brought about by their lack of qualifications for government services and so to their lack of proportionate representation in them. Between 1835 and 1870 the proportion of Muslims to Hindus in the government service was less than one-seventh.[50] British racial exclusiveness eclipsed from the view of the Indians, Hindu and Muslim alike, much that was commendable in the English character and attractive in the western civilization.[51] Even more disturbing to Muslim religious susceptibilities was the patronage of Christian missionary activities by some officials of the East India Company, and the close identification of these missions with British rule. In 1813 the revised Charter of the

[49] Hunter, pp. 158–9.
[50] Ibid. pp. 147, 166–7, 181–6.
[51] Abid Husayn, *Indian Culture* (1963), p. 56.

East India Company had provided facilities to the Christian missionaries for the 'moral improvement' of the Indian people. In the decades preceding the 'Mutiny' of 1857 British administrators of the predominantly Muslim provinces of the Punjab and Sind, Sir Henry Lawrence and Sir Robert Montgomery, provided moral and financial backing for the missionaries, in their efforts of conversion.[52] Bentinck's legislation in another province with a Muslim majority, Bengal, had no doubt extended the right of conversion and reconversion to all religions, but it also provided a special safeguard for converts to Christianity from Islam by protecting their right of inheritance, contrary to the *sharīʿa* law. In 1853 Sir Herbert Edwardes, Agent to the Governor-General for the Muslim North-Western Frontier Areas, declared that the 'Divine plan' of entrusting the rule of India to the British was that 'England had made the greatest efforts to preserve the Christian religion in its purest Apostolic form . . . Our mission, then, is to do for other nations what we have done for our own.'[53]

Though it may be argued that the government of the East India Company had functioned on the whole as a secular state interfering as little as possible with the religious freedom of the indigenous peoples, the impression grew in India that its aim, slow but sure, was the Christianization of the land. This impression was confirmed by such measures as the official encouragement of the conversion of orphaned and destitute children to Christianity during the famine of 1837. The situation was exacerbated by the fact that Christian missionary denunciations of other religions still continued in the mid-nineteenth century in the medieval tradition of virulence and abuse,[54] which was directed especially against the Prophet of Islam.

The climax came in 1855 when Father E. Edmund sent a circular to all government employees suggesting that as the whole of India had come under the rule of the British and was linked

[52] R. Clark, *The Punjab and Sindh Missions* (1885), pp. 4–9; J. Richter, *A History of Missions in India*, trs. S. H. Moore, (London, 1908) pp. 137–8.

[53] Clark, pp. 162–4.

[54] Sayyid Aḥmad Khān, *Asbāb*, pp. 21–22.

by a unified system of communications, it would be desirable if it possessed a single religion, namely Christianity. Sensing a gathering storm, the Lieutenant-Governor of Bengal issued a Gazette Extraordinary dissociating the government from Edmund's views, affirming Bentinck's policy of recognizing the right of conversion and religious disputation as equally applicable to all religions, assuring the Muslims especially that though the government had abolished the Hindu rite of *satī* for humanitarian reasons, it had no intention of interfering with the Muslim passion play of Muḥarram (commemoration by the Shīʿīs of the martyrdom of the Prophet's grandson), or the rite of circumcision, or the practice of purdah. The introduction of western education in English, the Gazette affirmed, was not meant to overthrow the 'older' religions but 'to free the people of this land from ignorance, to open for them intellectual vistas of progress, and thus to root out gradually the backwardness and poverty of the country'.[55]

The years 1855–7 also mark the consolidation and counter-offensive of Muslim theologians against missionary polemics. This took the form of treatises and, more enlivening, of public disputations refuting the arguments of the missionaries and emphasizing that Trinitarianism was a travesty of the 'real' Christianity. One of the most outstanding of these disputations took place between a famous polemicist, C. G. Pfander, and the Muslim theologian Raḥmat-Allāh Kīrānawī, assisted by a westernized scholar Wazīr Khān.[56] In this disputation, which was held in the presence of a number of British officers including the scholar-polemicist Sir William Muir, Hindu, Christian and Muslim scholars and the general public, and which raged for three days, Pfander was worsted on the crucial Muslim argument that the text of the New Testament contains contradictions which can only be explained as 'interpolations', whereas the

[55] Persian text ibid. pp. 63–66.

[56] C. G. Pfander, *Mīzān al-Ḥaqq* (1862); among other anti-Islamic polemics were his *Miftāḥ al-asrār* (London, 1861); al-Kindī [pseud.], *Risāla* (Urdu tr., Mussoorie, 1888); Ram Chander, *Iʿjāz al-Qurʾān* (Lahore, 1895); C. H. Spurgeon, *Faẓl-i Ilāhī* (Ludhiana, 1893), and numerous publications of the Religious Book Soc., Lahore.

contradictory injunctions in the Qur'ān could be satisfactorily explained in the light of the Qur'ānic doctrine of *naskh* (abrogation).[57] On the invitation of the Ottoman 'Abd al-Ḥamīd II, Kīrānawī and Pfander had another exchange at Constantinople, where Pfander settled after his 'retreat from India'.[58]

The causes of the composite Uprising of 1857–8, referred to as the 'Sepoy Mutiny' in the British records and as the 'War of Independence' by modern Hindu and Muslim historians (borrowing the expression from a tract by Marx and Engels), fall outside the scope of this work except for such features as are related to religious and broadly political orientations of Indian Islam. Religious sentiments of the Muslim and Hindu soldiers who mutinied at Meerut were outraged as they imagined respectively that the cartridges they had to bite off before use contained pork or beef fat, violating their respective religious taboos and sentiments. To this extent the Uprising can be terned a mutiny. But this beginning merely triggered off an explosion of discontent and unrest which these soldiers shared with the élite and the masses of great sections of people in northern India. This discontent and unrest had features which make it necessary to redefine the Uprising as a confused, abortive revolution, if not quite the 'First War of Independence'.

Sir Sayyid Aḥmad Khān, by far the most objective analyst of the causes of the Uprising of 1857, discounts some of the official theories such as an incitement by Russia or Persia, though there might have been some correspondence between Bahādur Shāh (Ẓafar) II, the nominal Mughal emperor of Delhi, and the Shāh of Persia.[59] The participation of Muslim theologians in the Uprising has a more interesting background. In the Walī-Allāhī school, those followers of his grandson, Muḥammad Isḥāq, who had accompanied him in his immigration to the Hijāz, were in

[57] Text of proceedings of the disputation in Wazīr al-dīn, *al-Baḥs̱ al-Sharīf fī is̱bāt al-tansīkh wa'l taḥrīf* (Delhi, 1853); 'Abd-Allāh Akbarābādī and Muḥ. Amīr, *Mubāḥis̱a-i maẕhabī* (Agra, 1853) and *Murāsilāt-i maẕhabī* (Agra, 1853); Raḥmat Allāh Kīrānawī, *Iẕhār al-ḥaqq* (1899).

[58] Muḥ. Miyān, *'Ulamā'-i Hind* (1957–60), iv. 395–6.

[59] *Asbāb*, pp. 4–5.

favour, and those who had stayed behind in Delhi were initially opposed, to participation in the Uprising.[60] The first clear ruling proclaiming the Uprising as a *jihād* was made in Delhi after the arrival of the mutineer Bakht Khān from Meerut and on his insistence.[61] The argument of the ruling was that 'the obligation for *jihād* depends necessarily on the capacity of waging it'. Since the people of Delhi had sufficient strength (consisting partly of the Muslim soldiery from Meerut) and a supply of arms and ammunition, *jihād* against the British overlords was binding on them, as on Muslims of other regions in the country who had similar means.[62]

Those scholars of the Walī-Allāhī school who later founded the great theological seminary of Deoband were persuaded to participate in the Uprising by the most dynamic member of their group, Muḥammad Qāsim Nānotawī; they drove the British officials out of the small township of Thana Bhawan and founded a miniature theocracy there, which was, however, soon overthrown by a British counter-attack. Their leader, Imdād-Allāh, escaped temporarily to the Hijāz while another leader, Rashīd Aḥmad Gangohī, was discharged after a short term of imprisonment because of insufficient evidence.[63]

Faẓl al-Ḥaqq Khayrābādī (1797–1861), the author of interesting memoirs on the Uprising which he wrote in Arabic, was a scholar of the same theological school but his views were influenced by medieval 'rationalist' trends. For a while he had served under the British, but later broke with them, signed a ruling denouncing them, and took up service under Bahādur Shāh II during the Uprising. Caught by the British, he was deported to the Andamans where he died in 1861. He accused the

[60] 'Ubayd-Allāh Sindhī, *Shāh Walī-Allāh awr unkī siyāsī taḥrīk* (1952), p. 201.

[61] Zakā-Allāh, *Tārīkh-i 'urūj-i 'ahd-i Inghlishiyya* (Agra, n.d.), pp. 301, 675.

[62] Text in *Ṣādiq al-Akhbār* (Delhi, 26 July 1957); facsimile of the document published by S. A. A. Riẓwi in his articles in *Swātantra* (Delhi) and *Nawā-i Āzādī* (Bombay) in their War of Independence centenary nos. in 1957. The document was regarded as a forgery by Sayyid Aḥmad Khān (*Asbāb*, pp. 8–9).

[63] Miyān, iv. 275–307; Ḥusayn Aḥmad Madanī, *Naqsh-i Ḥayāt* (1953), ii. 42–43.

British in his memoirs of a policy aimed at the eradication of Islamic scholarship and at the imposition of suffocating poverty on the Muslim gentry, interpreting it all as a traditional manifestation of Christian hostility to Islam. He accused the British administration of an agricultural policy that had impoverished the peasant and reduced him to a status of enslaved serfdom. He protested, like numerous Hindu and Muslim historians after him, that in the aftermath of the Mutiny the brunt of British punishment fell far more heavily on the Muslims than on the Hindus. Like Sayyid Aḥmad Khān, he explained that the Muslims resented the official interference with their religious and educational institutions more bitterly than the Hindus, as in Islam, unlike Hinduism, religious beliefs had a revelatory significance.[64]

According to Sayyid Aḥmad Khān, the principal causes of the Uprising were the misconceptions and misinterpretations of the government's policies by the people of India, certain legislative and administrative measures that ran counter to Indian traditions and which were in actual fact harmful to the Indian population, the monumental indifference of the government of the East India Company to the economic plight of the masses of the people, its failure as *de facto* sovereign authority in India to fulfil certain welfare obligations which had devolved upon it, and the disorganized state of its Indian army. In its hundred years of rule the Company's record was empty of any genuine affection for the Indian people. Indians were subjected by its British officials to insufferable humiliation, a situation which was resented more bitterly by the Muslims, the former rulers of the country, than by the Hindus. In the last analysis the 'Revolt' of 1857 was a result of the extraordinary political situation that a country as vast as India was ruled by a commercial concern which exploited its people without any qualms of Christian conscience. Things might have been different had it been ruled directly by the British Crown and parliament. Indians could then have had a voice and some form of parliamentary or advisory

[64] *al-Ṣawra al-Hindiyya*, pp. 91–92, 255–60, 377, 384.

representation in the government of India, apprising it of their problems and explaining in turn to their masses the benevolence or reformist intent of some of the government's well-intentioned policies.[65]

[65] *Asbāb*, pp. 11–15, 27–30, 31–42, and *passim*.

CHAPTER TWO

SAYYID AḤMAD KHĀN AND THE ALIGARH MOVEMENT

LOYALISM AND POLITICAL SEPARATISM

THE East India Company turned out to be the principal casualty of the 'Mutiny' of 1857–8. The destinies of India passed from the hands of the Board of Directors of the Company to those of the British parliament and the British electorate. In a Speech from the Throne in 1859 Queen Victoria proclaimed a general amnesty and a vague promise of gradual political representation for the Indian people. On 28 July 1859 15,000 Muslims gathered in a mosque in Delhi to thank her. As he addressed them, Sayyid Aḥmad Khān found himself the leader of a defeated and demoralized community which had waged a conservative, 'archaic' struggle against the impact of foreign rule and its alien but dynamic institutions, and had failed. There was only one way of survival left open, loyalism in politics and modernism in institutions.

Sir Sayyid Aḥmad Khān (1817–98), scion of a noble family of Delhi, joined the service of the East India Company in 1839, but remained attached also to the court of the nominal Mughal emperor of Delhi who conferred upon him several honorific titles. During the 'Mutiny' he remained strictly loyal to the British. His three works on the Uprising, his history of the Mutiny in Bijnore (1858), *Asbāb-i baghāwat-i Hind* (Causes of the Indian Mutiny, 1858) and the *Loyal Mohammedans of India* (1860), are indispensable source material for any serious study of its background. From 1859 until his death in 1898 he came to be more and more preoccupied with the problems of Muslim education in India. In 1868 he adopted a westernized way of living, developed cordial social contacts with British officialdom, and visited England in 1869–70. In 1876 he retired to devote his time entirely to the institutions of modern education he was building up at Aligarh. In 1869 he became a Commander of the Star of India and was awarded a knighthood in the same Order in 1888. In 1878 he was appointed a member of the Viceroy's Legislative Council, an appointment which was a fulfilment of a suggestion he was the first Indian to make, as early as 1859. In 1883 he resigned from the Council to meet the opposite challenge, that of the inevitable dominance of the Hindu majority over the Muslim minority in the representative or parliamentary institutions in India which Gladstonian liberalism had begun to introduce.

Apart from the political problems that faced him from 1859 onwards, there was also the intellectual problem of a better evaluation of western civilization, and the theological problems of the rationalization of the basic data of faith which was bound to be challenged by the findings of the new sciences,[1] and of meeting the challenge of Christian missionary polemics and its heritage in the more scientific study of Islam by western orientalists. Well equipped with a consummate theological scholarship in the tradition of Shāh Walī-Allāh, he also turned to the study of Christian apologetics in the writings of the Unitarians,[2] to a reorientation of Islam in terms of a rationalist scholasticism in the tradition of the Muʿtazila,[3] and an appreciation of Christianity in terms of what is now generally described as religious pluralism.[4] In one sense his entire intellectual energy was devoted to trying to resolve the conflict between religion and science and to reconcile the best of both for the younger generation of the Muslim élite whom he wished to attract.[5]

[1] Alṭāf Ḥusayn Ḥālī, *Ḥayāt-i jāwīd* (*HJ*) (1901), ii. 133–4.

[2] A detailed study of the nineteenth-century Unitarian influences on Indian Islamic modernism, as on such liberal religious movements in Hinduism as the Brahma Samāj, may yield interesting results.

[3] The great theological school which created the speculative dogmatics of Islam.

[4] Cf. Egyptian Coptic trends in the direction of religious pluralism, especially Christopher Jabbāra, *Waḥda al-adyān wa waḥda'l-īmān fi'l-Tawrāt wa'l-Injīl wa'l-Qur'ān* (Cairo). For a Coptic tribute to Sayyid Aḥmad Khān's Commentary on the Bible see Jurjī Zaydān, *Ḥayāt-i Sayyid Aḥmad*, Urdu tr. Q. M. Farīq (Aligarh, 1903), pp. 1–17.

[5] Similar problems were dealt with by a Tripolitan scholar, Shaykh Husayn, in his *Kitāb Ḥamīdiyya* (cited in *HJ*, ii. 210).

His loyalism can be measured in three stages. From 1859 to 1870 it was essentially a politically stabilizing factor, its object being to wean his own community 'from its policy of opposition' to one of acquiescence and participation, and to wean the British government 'from its policy of suppression to one of paternalism'.[6] This objective was more or less achieved in 1870. His argument was that as long as the Muslims of India enjoyed liberty to conform to their religious rituals publicly and, to propagate and defend their faith, there could be no theological case for them to rise against the British or even to aid a Muslim invader, though their emotional reaction in such an eventuality would be difficult to calculate.[7] On the controversial question, whether India under the British remained *dār al-Islām* or *dār al-ḥarb*, he did not commit himself. The second phase of his loyalism, from 1870 to 1884, will be discussed in some detail in a later chapter. It was mainly a response to the infiltration of pan-Islamic ideology, which Sayyid Aḥmad Khān considered dangerous political adventurism. In this phase, championing the security of the loyalist *status quo*, he went to the extreme of defining the British rule in India 'as the most wonderful phenomenon the world has ever seen', with the argument that loyalty to it 'springs not from servile submission to a foreign rule, but from genuine appreciation of the blessings of good government'.[8]

In the third phase, from 1887 to 1898, his loyalism was employed to emphasize Muslim political separatism, with the advent of elective institutions and the rise of the Indian National Congress founded in 1885. Earlier he had been one of the first to assess the implications of the Urdu-Hindi controversy as the ultimate factor of cultural division between Muslims and Hindus. As early as 1867 he had told a British civil servant that the linguistic and cultural gulf between the two communities was widening so sharply that they were unlikely to co-operate in the

[6] W. Cantwell Smith, *Modern Islam in India* (1946), p. 16.

[7] C. F. I. Graham, *Syed Ahmad Khan* (London, 1885), pp. 238–9.

[8] Address presented to the Viceroy, Lord Lytton, in *Speeches and Addresses relating to Muhammedan Anglo-Oriental College* (Aligarh, 1888), pp. 24–31.

composite development of a single nationhood.[9] In 1884 he proposed a political pattern based on triangular unity and loyalty between Hindus, Muslims, and British: 'In India peace cannot be maintained if either Hindus or Muslims rule the country. It is therefore inevitable that another nation should rule over us. . . . We should take full advantage of these times of peace.'[10]

Sayyid Aḥmad Khān's active opposition to the Indian National Congress did not begin until 1887 when a Muslim, Badr al-dīn Tayyibjī, was elected its president. From Sayyid Aḥmad's viewpoint this was the beginning of an erosion in Muslim political solidarity, disastrous for the future of the Muslim community, which was numerically much smaller than the Hindu population, educationally backward, politically immature, and in economic resources and enterprise far behind the others. A political alliance with the Hindus could therefore lead only to one inevitable result, the eventual domination and the subjugation of the weaker by the stronger.[11] On the question of pan-Islamism his lead was not entirely followed by the Muslim intelligentsia, and was later subjected to vigorous criticism, but on the question of political separatism the vast consensus of Muslim India followed him.[12]

OCCIDENTALISM

Realpolitik loyalism was only a fraction of the far more significant approach towards a closer understanding of western civilization. Sayyid Aḥmad Khān's journey to England in 1869–70 'to study the culture and institutions of Europe for the progress and betterment of India' is the outstanding landmark of his 'occidentalism'. Compared with the travels of Abū Ṭālib Khān seven decades earlier, Sayyid Aḥmad's impressions of the west present interesting parallels and contrasts. On the steamship during his voyage through the Mediterranean he met de Lesseps

[9] Ḥālī, *HJ*, i. 140; Sayyid Aḥmad Khān, *Makātīb*, ed. Mushtāq Ḥusayn (1960), pp. 267–74.
[10] *Lectures*, ed. Sirāj al-dīn (1892), pp. 24, 275–6.
[11] Ibid. pp. 240–58 and *Ākhirī Maẓāmīn* (1898), *passim*.
[12] *Lectures*, pp. 240–8; *Speeches and Addresses*, p. 133; Ḥālī, *HJ*, i. 247, 276.

and was profoundly impressed by his idealism and patriotism. He admired the elegance of the architecture of Versailles, and in the art galleries of Paris and Versailles he enjoyed the work of the French Romanticists. He was distressed by a painting depicting the capture of ʿAbd al-Qādir's *dā'ira* in Algeria and the rape of his harem by French soldiers. He regarded ʿAbd al-Qādir as a great soldier who resisted the French without guile and with honesty and chivalry until he was overwhelmed, and the theme and the exhibition of the painting of the dishonour of his *dā'ira* as a disgrace to the French traditions of honour and chivalry. He admired another painting in which Napoleon III is shown releasing ʿAbd al-Qādir from an unjust and treacherous imprisonment and shaking hands with his mother. Napoleon III, whom he never met, is for Sayyid Aḥmad Khān an image of humanity and honour, enlivened by the glitter of his smart army and the 'glamour and array' of Paris where the Indian traveller admired the Arc de Triomphe, the Bois de Boulogne, the great boulevards, and the exterior of Notre-Dame.[13]

He was favourably impressed by London, by the tasteful décor of the London hotels, by the impeccable dignity of English butlers, and by the good manners of British housemaids. He was impressed by the extent of equality of opportunity for both sexes during his visit to the observatory of Mt St Vincent at Clifton which worked under the direction of a woman, and he wrote back, to the annoyance of orthodox theologians in India, that 'European women were as shocked to hear that Indian women were generally illiterate as Indians would be if they saw a woman walking naked in the bazaars'. He recorded his satisfaction that at least in Turkey and Egypt there had been some progress in female education and no absolute complacency in 'compound ignorance'.[14]

In England his contacts included Lord Lawrence, Lord Stanley of Alderley, and Sir J. W. Kay, the Under-Secretary of

[13] Impressions of his travels published in the *Scientific Society Gazette* (Aligarh, 1869–70); collected travel records in *Musāfirān-i Landan*, ed. Ismāʿīl Pānīpatī (1961).

[14] Ibid. pp. 167–90.

State for India; and he was presented at the levées of the Prince of Wales (later Edward VII) and Queen Victoria. He was elected a fellow of the Royal Asiatic Society and a member of the Athenæum Club. He attended the last reading given by Charles Dickens, and met Thomas Carlyle, whose 'Hero as a Prophet' he admired and with whom he discussed the project of his own life of Muḥammad.[15] He visited the University of Cambridge and carefully studied its structure, government, and syllabus as the model of the educational institution he was planning to set up in India.

His contacts with the British ruling bureaucracy in India were even more extensive and influential. To the growing racial snobbery of the British in India and to the first signs of a growing racial prejudice in Britain his attitude was ambivalent, critical when it was openly discriminatory, tolerant in the perspective of the western cultural advancement.[16] With the adoption of the western style of living since 1868 he and some of his friends had chosen a bicultural social life, which gave rise to some biting satire from friend and foe, such as a novel by his protégé Naẕīr Aḥmad, *Ibn al-waqt* (The Time-Server), and some facetious verses by the brilliant conservative poet Akbar Allāhābādī. The theologians frowned and the majority looked askance at his eating with the English masters meat killed contrary to the prescribed Muslim ritual, a position for which he offered a scholarly apologetic defence in his treatise on eating with the 'People of the Book'.

EDUCATION AND CULTURE

Sayyid Aḥmad Khān's educational programme which was to change the intellectual, political, and economic destiny of Muslim India had its humble beginnings in the critical year of 1859. From that date onwards the inescapable emphasis on the use of English as the medium of instruction was one of the main planks

[15] Ḥālī, *HJ*, i. 137–9; Graham, p. 99.
[16] *Musāfirān-i Landan*, pp. 120, 183–5; cf. Ḥālī, *HJ*, ii. 43–46.

of his programme. In 1864 he founded a Scientific Society for the introduction of western sciences primarily among Muslims in India. The Society translated works on physical sciences into Urdu and published a bilingual journal.[17] In 1864 he founded a modern school at Ghazipur, and in 1868 promoted the formation of educational committees in several districts of northern India. He prepared his blueprint for the higher education of Muslims during his visit to England in 1869–70. In 1874 the scheme of his Anglo-Muhammadan Oriental College at Aligarh assumed a concrete shape, the school classes were opened in 1875 and college classes in 1878. The institution, intentionally modelled on Cambridge University, soon assumed a form and personality of its own. Meant primarily for Muslims, it was interdenominational, providing for Sunnī as well as Shī'ī theological education, and included a fair percentage of Hindu students. It aimed at the liberalization of ideas, broad humanism, a scientific world view, and a pragmatic approach to politics. It strove for a steady increase of educated Muslims in the government services. It smoothed the transition of the younger generation of Muslim élite from almost medieval conservatism to at least superficial modernism. And, finally, it was to produce the leadership for Muslim political separatism in India as a counter-balance to the growing influence of the Indian National Congress.

In 1886 he founded the Muhammadan Anglo-Oriental Educational Conference for the general promotion of western education in Muslim India, for the enrichment of Urdu through translations of indispensable scientific works, to exercise political pressure for the acceptance of Urdu as the secondary language in all government and private schools, to emphasize the necessity for educating women as essential for the balanced intellectual development of future generations, and to formulate a policy for the higher education of Muslim students in Europe, who were discouraged from marrying abroad in order that they should remain

[17] Prospectus in Mawlawī 'Abd al-Ḥaqq, *Sayyid Aḥmad Khān* (1959), pp. 138–9. List of some of the works on physical and social sciences trans. under the auspices of the Scientific Soc., ibid. pp. 147–9.

involved with the problems of their own land of origin.[18]

The question of religious education at the Muhammadan Anglo-Oriental College (MAO College) at Aligarh was complex. Personally opposed to denominational education, and disapproving of the existence of denominational colleges even in the great universities of England as anachronistic and a heritage of medieval obscurantism in the west,[19] Sayyid Aḥmad Khān left the direction of the compulsory theological studies to a committee which included some of his fiercest orthodox critics.[20] He thus succeeded in his objective, that however unpopular his own religious radicalism was, it should not interfere with the popularity of the College among all sections of the Muslim upper classes. But the chasm between the pragmatic premiss of modern physical sciences and the data of revealed religion alarmed him as tending to a vacuum threatening to engulf the younger generation of Muslims whom he was leading from the past to the present. The motive and the entire methodology of his speculative modernist theology was intended to bridge this chasm.

With this end in view he began the publication of a journal, *Tahẕīb al-akhlāq*, named after the famous ethical treatise of Ibn Miskawayh, but apparently modelled on Addison and Steele's *Spectator* and *Tatler*. It covered articles on a wide range of subjects from public hygiene to rationalist speculation on religious dogma. It revolutionized Urdu journalism, simplified Urdu prose, and gave it a plasticity and a capacity to convey novel intellectual concepts in easily readable language. It raised storms of bitter controversy. In its brilliant pages modernism emerged as a potent force and considerably changed the course and the direction of Islam in India.

[18] MAO Educational Conference, *Majmūʿa-i rezolūshanhā-i dihsāla 1886–95* (1896), pp. 10–14, 20–21, 43, 48; *Musāfirān-i Landan*, pp. 100–11, 197–8; ʿAbd al-Ḥaqq, pp. 100–15 for documents on the proposal to set up an Urdu university.

[19] Letter in *Aligarh Inst. Gazette*, 26 Nov. 1869.

[20] *Scientific Society Gazette* (Aligarh), 24 July 1874.

[21] 1st ser. 1870–6; 2nd ser. 1896–8.

METHODOLOGY OF HISTORIOGRAPHY

Sayyid Aḥmad Khān's intellectual accession to the western *Aufklärung* led to the realization of the principle of change, flux, and movement in history, including Islamic history. He turned to history fairly early in his intellectual career. Though not a trained archaeologist, inspired by the archaeological work undertaken by the British in India, he wrote in 1847 *Āṣār al-ṣanādīd*, a work of considerable pioneer importance on the monuments of Delhi, covering the history of the monuments, their measurements and decorative details. He studied and discussed inscriptions. In 1855 he edited Abu'l-Faẓl's *Ā'īn-i Akbarī*, collating various manuscripts, explaining the terminology of Mughal administration, analysing its linguistic borrowings from Arabic, Turkish, and Sanskrit, adding photographs of numismatic data and appendices on Akbar's taxation policies. This edition served as the basis for Blochmann's scholarly translation of this sixteenth-century historical classic.[22] In 1862 Sayyid Aḥmad Khān collated four manuscripts of another great historical work of medieval India, Ẓiyā al-dīn Baranī's *Tarīkh-i Fīrūz Shāhī*, to edit it for the Asiatic Society of Bengal.

By 1870 he began to apply something like a westernized methodology, partly scientific and partly speculatively apologetic, to the history of Arabia at the birth of Islam and to certain aspects of the *sīra*, or the traditional biography of the Prophet. For this work, which was the starting-point of modern Indian historiography of Islam, published as *Essays on the Life of Mohammed* (1870) in English and as *Khuṭbāt-i Aḥmadiyya* (1870) in Urdu, he consulted manuscript sources in the British Museum and in the India Office Library in London, and collected Arabic works on the *sīra* published in the Near East as well as some rare Latin commentaries. This work was undertaken to refute Sir William Muir's scholarly but highly polemical *Life of Mahomet*

[22] Vols. i and ii published in Delhi, 1855; MS. of vol. ii lost during Uprising of 1857 (Ḥālī, *HJ*, i. 54–57); cf. Blochmann's trans. of Abu'l-Faẓl, *Ā'īn-i Akbarī*. As. Soc. of Bengal, 1873.

(1858); nevertheless it received inspiration and documented support from other western scholars sympathetic to Islam, including Carlyle and Godfrey Higgins; and it influenced in turn other western Islamists like John Davenport, Garcin de Tassy, and Sir Thomas Arnold. Negatively it also set the pattern of modern Muslim apologetics as dialectically and technically different from the pattern of Judaeo-Christian apologetics in the west. But whatever inroads the necessities of polemics or apologetics made into Sayyid Aḥmad Khān's historiography, he remained to the end committed to a theoretical concept of accurate and scientific methodology.

One of the basic programmes assigned to the Muhammadan Educational Conference between 1886 and 1895 was to investigate, collect, edit, and print Persian manuscripts, records, archives, and other source material for a correct assessment of the history of Muslim India, and to promote research and dissemination of general information on Islamic history and institutions in general. At the same time the Conference also emphasized the necessity of publishing in English and in Urdu, in Europe and in India, books and articles to correct the misinterpretations of Islam in the writings of some European scholars, as these writings were adversely affecting the western view of Islam.[23]

THEOLOGICAL SPECULATION

Sayyid Aḥmad Khān's Islamic reformism has some fundamentalist data as its starting point, originating in the school of Shāh Walī-Allāh, in which he received his early theological training.[24] Walī-Allāhī fundamentalism had already mitigated the influence of the watertight compartmentalization of Muslim jurisprudence by permitting a believer to choose on any point the ruling of any of the four great Sunnī juristic schools; it had rejected *bidaʿ* (innovations) and accretions borrowed from extraneous and alien cultural contacts by Islamic traditionalism. It

[23] *Majmūʿa-i rezolūshanhā*, pp. 35–44. [24] Ḥālī, *HJ* i. 16.

had reiterated Ibn Taymiyya's significant anti-traditionalist thesis that the *bāb al-ijtihād* (the gate of individual reasoning) was still open and should not be considered closed. Of the three disciplines of Islamic theology, the Qur'ānic *tafsīr* (exegesis), the science of *ḥadis̤*, and *fiqh* (jurisprudence as worked out by the four great juristic schools), the last had already been subjected to some anti-traditionalist dialectics by Shāh Walī-Allāh. This break-through had been absolutely unconnected with any western influences, and was inspired by internal spiritual and historical forces that had led to a stock-taking of theological data in the early eighteenth century during the period of the decline of the Mughal and the Ottoman empires.

Sayyid Aḥmad Khān's first theological work, *Rāh-i sunnat wa radd-i bid'at* (1850), is directly in this tradition. Since then, and specially after 1870, he turned to Walī-Allāhī fundamentalism again and again, but only to transfer and reinterpret it in terms of his own revolutionary modernism. The key phrase of Shāh Walī-Allāh: 'The time has come for Islamic theology to be brought in the field fully armed with dialectics',[25] actually referred to the need of a reorientation of the classical methodology of disputation. But Sayyid Aḥmad Khān used it as the starting point for limitless rationalist speculation.

Though no other writer has been quoted and discussed more frequently in Sayyid Aḥmad Khān's writings than Walī-Allāh, and though he often returns to anti-traditionalist sources within Islam, such as the views of the Mu'tazila and of the Ikhwān al-Ṣafā (Brethren of Purity), some features of his speculative system show the unmistakable influence of Unitarianism. He regards religion as a discipline essentially for the establishment of ethical criteria. Its essence is truth rather than faith, which distinguishes a true creed from a false one. Faith is one of the ingredients of this essence. Truth, in so far as it is cognizable by human reason, is identical with nature and its laws, which determine the organizational causality of all material and non-material phenomena. These natural laws also posit moral criteria which

[25] *Ḥujjat*, i. 4.

constitute the basis of human social ethics. And the logic of the natural laws points necessarily to a Final Cause, a Prime Mover, God.[26]

He interprets Islam, freed from the traditionalist accretions it has accumulated in its long history, according to his own criteria and on the basis of a rationalist reinterpretation of the Qur'ān.[27] As he analysed the corpus of traditional exegetical literature, he found it almost solely preoccupied with such secondary problems as the relation of the Qur'ān to the theological sciences of *fiqh* and *kalām* (scholasticism), or with the 'miraculous' nature of its *i'jāz* (style), or with minutiae of differences of interpretations among the classical exegetes. There was hardly any material available on the chronological order or classification of the verses of the Qur'ān, on its underlying principles of guidance for future ages in widely different climes, or on its position as the ultimate source for the resolution of any problems that the Muslim community might face in circumstances very different from those of the Arabs of the early seventh century.[28] This led him to formulate his own principles of exegesis. He accepted in principle the thesis advanced by his associate and critic, Muḥsin al-Mulk, that the Qur'ān can only be interpreted given an accurate understanding of the Arabic idiom in the Prophet's time, but reserved for himself or any individual Muslim the right not only of a literal but also of a symbolic or analytical interpretation. The bases of interpretation were to be the underlying principles (*uṣūl*) and not the minutiae or details (*furū'*) derived therefrom or the verses in the Qur'ān referring to specific historical situations.[29]

He outlined fifteen basic principles for his own exegesis: God is omnipotent, omnipresent, and the Creator of the universe; He has sent prophets, including Muḥammad, for the guidance of mankind from time to time; the Qur'ān is the authentic *waḥy* (revelation), the Word of God; it was conveyed to Muḥammad's mind by a process of *waḥy*, and it is immaterial whether it was

[26] *Khuṭbāt-i Aḥmadiyya* (1870), i. 1–5.
[27] Ibid. pp. 7–8.
[28] *al-Taḥrīr fī uṣūl al-tafsīr* (1892), p. 4.
[29] Ibid. pp. 8–9 and 29.

conveyed to him by the Archangel Gabriel, or whether its sense as well as its words were received directly by Muhammad's prophetic intuition; the Qur'ān contains nothing which could be wrong or incorrect or anti-historical; the attributes of God mentioned in it exist only in their essence; they are identical with His Self and are eternal; these attributes can have no limitations, but in His wisdom and freedom God has created the laws of nature and maintains them as the disciplines of creation and existence; therefore there can be nothing in the Qur'ān contrary to the laws of nature; the present text of the Qur'ān is complete and final without any interpolations or additions. The verses of every *sūra* in their present sequence follow a chronological order: *naskh*, accepted as a textual and exegetical reality in classical Islam, is a doctrine which must be rejected in the study of the Qur'ān; the *waḥy* of the Qur'ān has developed in gradual stages; Qur'ānic eschatology, angelology, demonology and cosmology cannot be contrary to scientific actuality and must be interpreted in its terms; and, finally, linguistic research is necessary to study the sociological *mores* and possibilities of development of human society contained in the direct and indirect expressions of the Qur'ān.[30]

It follows from these fifteen principles that *waḥy* and natural law are identical.[31] *Waḥy* operates as natural instinct in lower forms of life. Man's problem in relation to *waḥy* is much more complex. Unlike most animals he is compelled to live in society; through social organization alone he survives and overcomes the hostile forces around him. The natural necessity of social organization imposes upon him another necessity, that of an ethical code, without which society cannot hold together as an entity. For the human individual and society revelational law is necessarily in consonance with human rationality. In human society *waḥy* and reason are therefore identical. Reason as a natural revelational instinct operates in man's scientific investigations as much as in his concept of the deity, his distinction

[30] Ibid. pp. 32–56; also in *Taṣfīyat al-ʿaqāʾid* (1901), which contains their detailed refutation by the Deoband traditionalist, Muḥammad Qāsim Nānotawī.

[31] *Tafsīr al-Quʾrān* (1880–95), iii. 9; cf. Qur'ān, 16:170.

between good and evil, his views on divine judgment and retribution, and his belief in life after death. With the passage of history these revelational instincts are imprinted as clear and fixed images upon the human mind.[32]

The capacity of revelational cognition of rational reality is not possessed by all men in equal degree. Certain individuals, for whom Shāh Walī-Allāh has used the term *mufahhimūn* (the understanding ones),[33] are endowed with this faculty to a much higher degree than certain others. These former leaders of men include philosophers, statesmen, founders of classical juristic schools, and outstanding mystics, and culminated in the prophets. The natural revelational instinct of a prophet is the highest form of its development in man. It comes as a sudden flash, often unconnected with any immediate causation. The impact of this flash has received many names in theology including that of Gabriel. The more highly developed the instinctive flashes of a prophet, the more consistent they would be with divinely ordained laws of nature. Reason revealed through prophetic intuition is the most developed form of true faith in God. Prophets can be true or false. False ones are those in whose intuitional cognition the message of divine reality has gone astray and is therefore contrary to human rationality and the norms of human ethics. But they may also attract followers and create societies which are, however, inclined towards evil.[34]

The term 'nature' is used by Sayyid Aḥmad Khān in the sense in which the nineteenth-century scientists interpreted it,[35] 'as a closed system of the universe which obeys certain laws of mechanics and physics and which is invariably characterized by a uniformity of behaviour in which there cannot be any excep-'ion'. Analysing this point further B. A. Dar aptly comments: the grafted the purely theistic view of Nature on its totally antitheistic interpretation current during his days. . . . It was a totally illegitimate transition from a mechanical to a teleological

[32] *Tafsīr*, iii. 9–12.
[33] Walī-Allāh, *Ḥujjat*, *passim*.
[34] *Tafsīr*, iii. 14–18, 35–36.
[35] *Khuṭbāt*, p. 287; *Tafsīr*, iii, *passim*; cf. Qur'ān, 30: 29.

view of nature.'[36] But, partly at least, his 'naturalism' was an orthogenetic heritage of the Muʿtazila, especially Naẓẓām, and other Muslim speculative thinkers, including al-Jāḥiẓ and Ibn Ṭufayl.[37]

A 'naturalistic' commentary on the Qur'ān raised certain problems. One of these was to explain the 'folklore' which is encrusted in it, as in the scriptures of other religions. To meet this difficulty Sayyid Aḥmad Khān redefines the familiar classical distinction between two kinds of Qur'ānic verses, the 'clear' and the 'ambiguous', as 'essential' and 'symbolic', the former constituting the irreducible minimum of Islamic faith and creed, the latter being open to two or more interpretations, permitting deductions appropriate to other ages and circumstances different from those of Arabia in the early seventh century.[38]

Another problem, basically of considerable textual, legal, and historical significance, was that of *naskh*, or the supersession of one Qur'ānic injunction by another, a principle affirmed in the Qur'ān itself.[39] On this question Sayyid Aḥmad Khān takes the view that a single scripture like the Qur'ān is a monolithic eternal reality. The principle of *naskh* can only be valid in terms of comparative religion, where a later prophetic religion abrogates an earlier one. Thus Christianity abrogates Judaism, and Islam Christianity. But the principle is quite irrelevant to the Qur'ān. The Qur'ān abrogates the Old and the New Testament with chronological finality.[40]

The first in modern Islam to experience the impact of Darwinian evolutionism, Sayyid Aḥmad Khān was also the first to search for a formula to reconcile it with the Islamic tenets of Creation and the Fall of Adam. The Qur'ān affirms that the law

[36] *Religious Thought of Sayyid Ahmad Khan* (1957), pp. 150–2.

[37] Ibid. p. 155; J. M. S. Baljon, *Reforms and Religious Ideas of Sir Sayyid Ahmad Khan* (1949), pp. 91–92.

[38] *Khuṭbāt*, pp. 97–99.

[39] cf. Qur'ān, 2:99–100:

And for whatever verse we abrogate
or cast into oblivion, We bring a better
or the like of it.

[40] *Tab'īn al-kalām* (1862), i. 203, 265–8, ii. 66; *Tafsīr*, v. 130–2; *Ākhirī Maẓāmīn*, p. 29; *Khuṭbāt*, pp. 439–40.

of evolution is observable in relating one species of created beings to another. The 'symbolic imagery' of 'semen' or 'seed' as the nucleus of life refers to the primeval movement of life emerging out of inert matter. The literal reference in the Qur'ān, as in the Old Testament, to the genesis of the universe is the use by God of a popular belief for the sake of argument. For the scripture must necessarily approach and address the people among whom it is revealed in terms of their folklore, store of knowledge, and understanding, and within the conceptual framework comprehensible to them. The legend of the Fall of Adam is likewise metaphorical. Adam connotes human nature.[41]

Sayyid Aḥmad Khān views the soul as a pragmatic reality which is 'proved' in animal as in man, though human reason cannot grasp its exact nature. The animal soul is primarily circumscribed by instinct. The human soul is capable of unlimited action. It can evolve or suffer decline, and can range from scientific research to gross inhumanities. It is incapable of absorbing or rejecting good or evil at its choice. It exists in essence and is therefore immortal.[42] In its immortality it is accountable for the good or evil it has chosen to absorb. This account it will have to render on the Day of Judgment which begins for each individual at the moment of his death. There is also a final and collective Day of Judgment, on which all humanity will be resurrected, but in a different physical sense, with a physical personality which would be different from the human body in this life.[43]

Prophets are the promulgators of the divine law of nature. The concept of a miracle contradicts this law wrongfully and anarchically. Miracles mentioned in the scriptures have therefore to be interpreted as either symbolical or metaphorical or legendary. The laws of nature are immutable. They are 'pledges' of God to his creation and cannot be broken. To believe in a miraculous suspension or reversal of these laws amounts therefore to repudiation of faith in the divine 'pledges' and to accuse God of falsehood.

[41] *Khalaq al-insān*, pp. 1–3, 7–12; *Tafsīr*, iii. 76 ff., 121–2.

[42] I am grateful to Prof. M. Marmura for the suggestion that this concept might be a borrowing from Avicenna's view of the soul as an individual essence.

[43] *Tafsīr*, iii. 90–119.

True, we do not know all the laws of nature. Every day new laws are revealed to us. But known to us or unknown these laws do exist independent of our knowledge, and by analogy we may perceive that they exist in regularity and harmony, and are not contradicted by miracles.[44]

The only miracle attributable to the Prophet of Islam is his great prophetic role, which is revelational in nature but thoroughly consonant with reason. The great miracle traditionally attributed to Muḥammad, the *isrā'* (his ascension to heaven and vision of God on a night of beatitude), was neither a physical nor a spiritual experience but a dream.[45] On the question of man's capacity to perceive the vision of God, Sayyid Aḥmad Khān accepts the orthodox Ṣufistic view of Shaykh Aḥmad Sirhindī that it can only be a mystical and spiritual and not a physical experience.[46]

A similar process of rationalization is applied to Islamic angelology and demonology. Angels are the 'properties' of created things like hardness in stone, fluidity in water, and intuitive cognition of reality in man. In Qur'ānic terminology a secondary sense of the 'concept' angel is the divine moral support which encourages man in his struggle against overwhelming odds.[47] Satan, the fallen angel, is metaphorically mentioned in the Qur'ān as created of fire. This signifies the dark passions of man.[48]

In Muslim demonology, commenting on the identity of jinn whom the Qur'ān has mentioned on several occasions, Sayyid Aḥmad Khān tries to determine their position in the comparative data of animistic folklore: 'Not only the pagan Arabs but medieval Jews and Zoroastrians believed in supra-human invisible creatures, created from fire, with attitudes benevolent or malevolent towards men.' Then he argues that on five occasions the word 'jinn' used in the Qur'ān is synonymous with 'jānn' and refers to the pagan belief in these creatures without actually

[44] Ibid. pp. 22–29. In his denial of miracles he is inspired by Isfarā'īnī, Hishām b. 'Amr al-Fuwātī, and Walī-Allāh.

[45] *Tafsīr*, iii. 22, 204; *Khuṭbāt*, pp. 658–714.

[46] *Tafsīr*, ii. 204–8.

[47] Ibid. i. 49; iii. 37–38; iv. 812.

[48] *TA*, Lahore reprint, ii. 191.

recognizing their existence. In the Qur'ān they are projections of evil, diseases, and other calamities. On certain other occasions the Qur'ān uses the term for 'wilder men living in forests, hills and deserts'.[49] This later theory of the historicity of the jinn is based upon the biblical researches and apologetics of Sayyid Aḥmad Khān's more radical associate, Chirāgh 'Alī.[50] The devils referred to in the Qur'ān are evil human beings who misinterpret divine decrees 'and inhibit free will by astrological calculations'.[51]

References in the Qur'ān, as in the Bible, to natural calamities as visitations of divine punishment on sinful peoples have roots in popular superstition, and have been restated in the scriptures not as historical verities but with an ethical motive borrowing the popular legendary framework.[52] This bold exegetical approach should have been enough for Sayyid Aḥmad Khān, but he vitiates it in detail when he indulges in apologetics explaining away the 'folklore' of the Old and the New Testament and of the Qur'ān in terms of untenable historical hypotheses. Thus the Seven Sleepers of Ephesus are interpreted as members of a ' "Unitarian" Christian sect persecuted by Diocletian. They did not remain literally asleep for several years but were dead and mummified by the temperature and soil of the caves they lived in.'[53] Rejecting al-Rāzī's identification of the Qur'ānic *Ẕu'l qarnayn* (the two-horned one) with Alexander the Great, Sayyid Aḥmad Khān advances a theory identifying him with the Chinese emperor Chī Wāng Tī (*c.* 247 BC), and Gog and Magog with the races of Chinese Turkestan (Mongolia?); and he makes the interesting but rather anachronistic observation that a number of legends are common to Chī Wāng Tī and the *Alexander Romance* of the Muslim poets, showing that the two had become confused and telescoped together in the medieval Muslim mind.[54]

[49] *al-Jinn wa'l-jānn* (1892), pp. 2–19; *Tafsīr*, iii. 59–67; v. 115.
[50] See Ch. III below.
[51] *Tafsīr*, v. 109–10.
[52] Ibid. *passim*.
[53] *Tarqīm fī qiṣṣa Aṣḥāb-i Kahf* (1890), pp. 8–18, 50.
[54] *Izālat al-ghayn* (1890), pp. 12–20, 34.

However startling his speculative rationalization of Muslim faith and dogma, on the question of prescribed ritual he was conformist and a conservative. The prescribed form of the Muslim ritual prayer (*ṣalāt*) he considered logically perfect and structurally immutable.[55]

Of the four sources of Islamic law, the question of a modernist interpretation of the first, the Qur'ān, was by far the most difficult. It is not surprising therefore that by far the greater part of Sayyid Aḥmad Khān's theological work concerns itself with exegetics. The next most important source of law, the *ḥadis̱*, was easier to deal with. To begin with, by all traditional accounts it was well recognized that during the first three centuries of Islam a vast corpus of apocryphal traditions was fabricated and attributed to the Prophet; and that two sciences, that of the study of *ḥadis̱* (*'ilm al-ḥadis̱*) and of biographical verification (*asmā' al-rijāl*), had to be developed by the classical discipline of the ninth and tenth centuries to sift truth from falsehood. Sayyid Aḥmad Khān's views on the doubtfulness of even the six great classical collections of *ḥadis̱* are not very different from the conclusions arrived at by western orientalists like Goldziher and Schacht.[56] Among motives for the fabrication of *ḥadis̱* attributed to the Prophet, he advances the loss of the focus of reality with the passage of time, popular credulity for the unusual and the extraordinary, uncritical faith in the narrated word, confusion between the incident and the injunction, political manipulations in the context of dynastic rivalries, mischief-making by the dissemblers (*munāfiqūn*), and fabrication as a purely psychological phenomenon. Supernatural incidents were woven in, in consonance with the credulity common to all ancient and medieval cultures.[57] He objects to the methodology of classical *ḥadis̱* criticism, including that of Bukhārī and Muslim, on the same ground as did the western Islamists later, that it is based entirely on the personal reliability of the individuals in the

[55] *Makātīb*, pp. 142–3.

[56] I. Goldziher, *Muhammedanische Studien* (Halle, 1889–90); J. Schacht, *Origins of Muhammadan Jurisprudence* (Oxford, 1950).

[57] *Ākhirī Maẓāmīn*, pp. 128–33.

isnād (chain of narrators) and not on a logical or rational criticism of the text (*matn*) of a *ḥadīs̱* itself.[5] The *ḥadīs̱* in the great classical *ḥadīs̱* collections, therefore, constitutes, generally speaking, not so much an infallible source of law as a historical reflection of the ideas and attitudes of the first few generations of Muslims.[59]

Sayyid Aḥmad Khān's own theory of *ḥadīs̱* criticism, later more elaborately developed by Chirāgh ʿAlī, postulates that the greater part of the classical *ḥadīs̱* which is repugnant to human reason should be rejected forthwith. One should also reject a *ḥadīs̱* which is repugnant to the dignity of prophethood. Authentic *aḥādīs̱* can only be of three varieties; those which are in consonance with the Qur'ān and repeat its injunctions; those which explain or elucidate these injunctions; and those which deal with basic legal formulations not touched upon in the Qur'ān. Any *ḥadīs̱* which contradicts an injunction of the Qur'ān is necessarily a fabrication. Even in the *aḥādīs̱* which are accepted at their face value as genuine statements of Muḥammad, a distinction has to be established between those which he made as the Prophet of God and those which reflect his personal views or his likes and dislikes as a human being.[60]

Much of the modern method of re-explanation and reinterpretation of such points of sensitivity to western criticism among traditional Islamic institutions as *jihād* or the permissibility of polygamy and slavery begins with Sayyid Aḥmad Khān, his associates, and his critics including Jamāl al-dīn al-Afghānī and Shaykh Muḥammad ʿAbduh, partly as genuine historical research, partly as apologetics. Even T. W. Arnold's view of *jihād*[61] as purely defensive is inspired by Sayyid Aḥmad Khān, whose basic theory regarding the Prophet's *maghāzī* (militant expeditions) is that in the historical context of pagan Arabia, as indeed in the international code of war in all times, reconnaissance forays and raids against the enemy have been a recognized institution

[58] Ibid. p. 97; *Khuṭbāt*, p. 353.
[59] *Tafsīr*, iv. 118–23.
[60] *Khuṭbāt*, pp. 334–5; *Ākhirī Maẓāmīn*, pp. 132–4.
[61] *The Preaching of Islam* (1896), Introd.

of defensive warfare. Hebrew prophets occupied themselves in similar warfare without any apologies.[62]

On the question of slavery, his argument is based on the principle that freedom and slavery are mutually exclusive; they cannot co-exist or evolve together. Therefore both of them cannot be in accordance with divine approval. Man has been created free, endowed with reason, consciousness, and organs, mental and physical, over which he has been given full control. If he is his own master, he cannot be anybody else's slave. His soul is free and cannot be enslaved under any circumstances. Most societies based on religion or philosophy, Jewish, Christian, and Greco-Roman, however, sanctioned slavery. Islam alone limited and rejected slavery, condemning it on moral grounds. Historical Islam has indeed, like Greco-Roman, Hindu, the Byzantine, and American societies, patronized the institution of slavery in disobedience to divine injunctions. Some contemporary Muslim states failed to abolish it when the west decided to do so. In such cases the institution has its roots in history and not in Islamic religion. Ideal Islam has no place for slavery, judging from the famous *ḥadīs̱* that there is nothing more pleasing to God than the manumission of slaves, and the Qur'ānic injunction in verse 47: 5 laying down that all prisoners of war should be set free gratuitously or for a ransom.[63]

Historical Islam came in the wake of two cultures, pagan Arab and Judaeo-Christian, both of which sanctioned and maintained slavery as an institution. Islam's solution of this problem was a gradual mitigation of the lot of the slave, and to recommend his manumission as one of the greatest acts of piety. A loan was made available to a slave from the state treasury to purchase his freedom. The injunctions in the Qur'ān refer only to the slaves then existing; there is no evidence in its text that fresh enslavement was encouraged or even permitted.[64] The entire corpus of reference to slavery in the Qur'ān refers to the slave-owning social

[62] *Tafsīr*, iv. 45, 106, 110.

[63] Qur'ān, 47:5: 'Then set them free, either by grace or ransom'.

[64] *Ibṭāl-i ghulāmī* (1893), pp. 26–40.

order inherited from pagan Arabia, which could only be gradually abolished 'within a generation'. The verse 47:5 of the Qur'ān:

> Then set them free, either by grace or ransom

marks therefore the watershed and the point of prohibition of fresh enslavement for the future. This verse is termed by Sayyid Aḥmad Khān and Chirāgh 'Alī as the 'verse of liberation' (*āya ḥurriyya*), and its revelation dated to 629, the year of the occupation of Mecca. This view stands in opposition to the general opinion of classical jurists, who date the verse to the occasion of the Battle of Badr (622), and therefore regard it as abrogated by other verses in the Qur'ān referring to slavery as an institution.[65]

In the later decades of the nineteenth century the question of slavery in Islam was a burning political issue and one of the principal points of British propaganda against the Mahdī of the Sudan. The stand taken by the Indian modernists was to argue that the theory of Islam was innocent of the guilt, which should be laid at the door of the historical inheritance of the Muslim states.

The institution of polygamy had been one of the main bastions of Sir William Muir's polemics against Islam. Sayyid Aḥmad Khān examines it from three points of view: in terms of natural law; in the context of its social use and abuse; and as a religious dogma. He sees no biological objection to the permissibility or practicability of polygamy in terms of natural law, as a male is naturally equipped to fertilize several females. As a social problem he argues that in certain societies remarriage is a necessary evil, either after divorcing one's first wife or without a divorce, to safeguard her economic, though not her psychological or emotional, interests.[66] Coming to the third point, he and Chirāgh 'Alī advanced the famous theory based on a liberal and modernist interpretation of the Qur'ānic verse 4:2–3:

[65] Ibid. pp. 44–50, 79–86, 132–52. [66] *Khuṭbāt*, pp. 238–40.

If you fear that you will not act justly
towards the orphans, marry such women
as seem good to you, two, three, four;
but if you fear you will not be equitable,
then only one, or what your right hands own;
so it is likelier you will not be partial.

This argument, which has formed the basis of family law reforms in several Muslim states, contends that justice in a man-woman relationship can only be synonymous with love; and since a man is emotionally incapable of loving more than one woman equally at any given time, in fact polygamy has been prohibited by demonstrating its underlying shortcoming. In these arguments he ignores the problem of concubinage. Sayyid Aḥmad Khān then takes the counter-offensive by arguing, unlike the Qur'ān, that polygamy as an unjust institution is forbidden neither in the Old nor clearly in the New Testament. Christ's celibacy, he argues, was not based on any moral or theological principle but was due to the fact that the Jews regarded him as illegitimate and therefore not an eligible husband for a Jewish girl; and in any case he died young.[67]

Interest on loans (*ribā*) is categorically forbidden in the Qu'rān. On this question, which has been one of the greatest significance in relation to the development of an Islamic state in modern times, involving the future of banking and finance, Sayyid Aḥmad Khān's interpretation is that compound interest might be considered forbidden, but simple interest, specially bank interest or interest on government bonds, should be considered permissible.[68]

In the final analysis, Sayyid Aḥmad Khān's modernism can be discerned as grappling with two broadly distinct problems; the rationalization of the minutiae of non-essential dogma, and the liberalization of Islamic law. In regard to the first of these he shows signs of psychological pressures which occasionally result in some easily avoidable apologetics as well as certain extreme

[67] Ibid. pp. 246–7.
[68] *Ākhirī Maẓāmīn*, pp. 143–5; *Tafsīr*, i. 298–313; *Lectures*, p. 79.

rationalist positions which were repugnant to the traditionalists. In regard to the second, in spite of some slight apologetic residue, his work is dynamic and constructive, and as such it has made a tremendous impression on modern Islam in general and on Indian Islam in particular. It contains an undercurrent of juristic change, facing the question of the adjustment of law to the contemporary as against the historical context. He tried to resolve the difficulties inherent in the four traditional sources of Muslim law by a dialectical rationalist exegesis of the Qur'ān; by historical scepticism in scrutinizing the classical data of the *ḥadīs̱*; by an almost unlimited emphasis on *ijtihād* as the inalienable right of every individual Muslim; and finally by rejecting the principle of *ijmā'* in the classical sense which confined it to the *'ulamā'*.[69]

COMPARATIVE RELIGION

Chronologically Sayyid Aḥmad Khān's Commentary on the Bible (1862) precedes his exegesis of the Qur'ān (1880–95). He seems to have turned to comparative religion within five years of the Uprising of 1857, primarily to understand the religious *mores* of the rulers of his country, and secondly to pursue the counter-offensive against the Christian missionaries into their own territory. In this he chose the path of understanding and eclecticism. He made some effort to learn Hebrew and to study the Old Testament in the original, though he relied largely on the Persian translation.[70]

His exegetic thesis of the Bible turns on the crucial argument that revelation is a secret disclosure to man of the will and purpose of God. It can be either prophetic or non-prophetic. In the latter sense the Apostles could also be considered as inspired, though their inspiration is neither perfect nor accurate.[71] The difference between the revelational character of the Qur'ān and

[69] Ḥālī, *HJ*, ii. 256 ff.
[70] Ibid. i. 97; ii. 450.
[71] *Tab'īn*, i. 2–16; ii. 30–43, 124–5, where the view is less orthodox. It is more so in *Tafsīr*, ii. 15–43.

the New Testament is that whereas the latter includes a number of non-revelatory traditions narrated by the Apostles, the former contains nothing except the authorized Word of God.[72] The corpus of the Old and the New Testaments has therefore to be tested for veracity by comparison with the indisputably divine message in the Qur'ān.

On the question of *taḥrīf* (corruption and interpolation) in the Bible, Sayyid Aḥmad Khān's views are at this stage closer to Muslim orthodox theory. He divides the totality of the Old Testament into three broad categories: genuine revelation, the sections that have been lost, and the sections which have been deleted by later Christian or Jewish compilers. The New Testament could likewise be divided into an authentic canonical part and an apostolic apocrypha. In the Commentary on the Bible he applies the classical Muslim technique of *isnād* criticism (examination of the reliability of persons involved in a chain-link narrating a *ḥadīs̤* of the Prophet) to distinguish what he considers genuine revelatory passages from the apocrypha. He interprets the classical Muslim theory of *taḥrīf* as referring essentially to exegetical interpretations rather than actual verbal corruption of the text.[73] On textual criticism of the Bible he draws attention to the historical fact of the multiplicity of earlier manuscripts, to the accumulated errors that might have crept in through centuries of copying, and to the complicated problems of translation.[74]

The Commentary itself is guided by the basic principle, which he later followed in his Commentary on the Qur'ān, that between the work of God (nature) and the word of God (revelation) there can be no contradiction. His biblical apologetics has therefore to rely equally on his exegetical subtlety.

In his identification of biblical and Qur'ānic concepts of monotheism, he asserts that he could find no trace of the Trinitarian dogma in the New Testament itself, and that by emphasizing the humanity of Christ the Qur'ān simplifies Christian dogma, reducing it to a consonance with the laws of nature. Revelational

[72] *Tab'īn*, i. 22. [73] Ibid. 32–58, 58–71; ii. 96–148; *Khuṭbāt*, pp. 581–93.
[74] *Tab'īn*, i. 156–255.

reference to Christ in Matthew iii, 17 as 'My beloved Son' leads to his equating the biblical term 'Father' with the Qur'ānic term ***rabb*** (the provider), a paternalistic concept of the deity,[75] which is interesting in view of the later development of the theory of ***rubūbiyyat*** (divine providence) in its relation to man's economic and social life in the subsequent exegetical speculations of Āzād and Parwīz.

More methodically than some medieval Muslim scholars, but in their tradition, Sayyid Aḥmad Khān interprets certain passages in the Old Testament as referring specifically to the advent of Muḥammad, and in the case of the New Testament he follows Godfrey Higgins in interpreting John xiv, 25–26 and xvi, 7 as also referring to the Prophet's advent.

The study of Christianity in the Commentary is essentially sympathetic. It is groping its way towards a religious pluralism in an age in which the western theologians had taken no significant step in that direction. It is all the more regrettable that Sayyid Aḥmad Khān's *expérience interreligionale* should have died out not only in Indian Islamic speculation but also in his own later writings.

[75] *Tab'īn*, i.4 ; ii. 4.

[76] *Khuṯbāt*, pp. 592–650.

CHAPTER THREE

THE CONSOLIDATION OF SPECULATIVE MODERNISM

RADICALISM: CHIRAGH 'ALĪ

CHIRĀGH 'Alī, one of Sayyid Aḥmad Khān's principal associates and a civil servant in Hyderabad state, developed some of his ideas with consummate scholarship. But his mind was no pale reflection of Sayyid Aḥmad Khān's. It is most probable that both influenced each other. Of the two Chirāgh 'Alī had a more scholarly knowledge of Hebrew and the Old Testament. As early as 1870 Sayyid Aḥmad Khān paid tribute to his exegetical speculations on passages in the Bible which they both believed referred to the advent of Muḥammad,[1] and followed Chirāgh 'Alī in his explanations of jinns as a primitive people. Like Shiblī Nu'mānī, Chirāgh 'Alī learnt some French and had at least a working knowledge of it.

Modernist trends from other parts of *dār al-Islām* converged in Chirāgh 'Alī's writings. In an article written in 1880 he cites works of the Egyptian traveller to the west and educationist, Rifā'a Rafī' al-Tahtāwī, of Ṣayf Efendī of Beirut, of the Tunisian modernist and statesman Khayr al-dīn Pasha, and of the Syrian journalist and literary critic Aḥmad Fāris al-Shidyāq.[2]

His own modernist approach develops the basic point that the Qur'ān is full of references to nature and the laws of nature, and points the way to a natural theology.[3] Islamic culture is

[1] *Khuṭbāt*, p. 607.

[2] *TA*, iii. 87; Khayr al-dīn Pāsha's *Aqwām al-masālik* (Tunis, 1867–8) also exercised a powerful influence on Sayyid Aḥmad Khān's mind in its dual thesis: there is nothing in Islam which could be considered contrary to modern science; and without adaptation of a modernist form and psychology Muslim society would disintegrate and cease to exist. Shaykh Aḥmad Effendī's favourable account of England and the English way of life was prescribed in the syllabus of the NWP Education Dept.

[3] *TA*, ii. 74–75.

distinguishable from other cultures in having evolved certain intellectual disciplines like the scrupulously investigated biographical dictionary, the principles of rational criticism (*dirāya*) in the study of religious tradition, and a scholasticism which reinterpreted Greek science and presented Europe with that dialectical methodology on which the modern European civilization is based. Within Islamic culture itself this methodology was stultified by orthodox traditionalism, which he regards as fed by the pious frauds (*ḥiyal*) of the jurists throughout the centuries.[4]

Like Sayyid Aḥmad Khān, he turns to examine the four sources of Muslim law, *waḥy*, *ḥadīṣ*, *ijmā*ʿ, and the rights and methods of *ijtihād* to overcome the mental fossilization which he thinks the traditional theologian is still imposing on modern Islam. He shows a fairly creditable acquaintance with Qur'ānic studies in Europe from the twelfth to the nineteenth centuries. He is critical of the monotony and the impression of an artificial confusion which translations of the Qur'ān in western languages tend to produce. He takes every opportunity to correlate, confirm or refute incorrect deductions of western Qur'ānic scholarship with similar or contrary deductions in classical Islam, feeling his way towards a composite methodology of scholarship.[5] Like Nöldeke, he believes in classifying the *sūras* as belonging to Meccan or Medinan period; but his own classification of them, guided by the necessities of modernist arguments, differs considerably from Nöldeke's.[6] In determining his own chronological sequence of the *sūras*, he made considerable use of the classical exegetical works of Bayẓāwī and Zamakhsharī. His interpretation of the principle of *naskh* in the Qur'ān differs from that of Sayyid Aḥmad Khān, and aims at arriving at a legal ruling by identifying the abrogating (*nāsikh*) and the abrogated (*mansūkh*) verses as absolute (*muṭlaq*) and conditional (*muqayyad*) respectively. The principle as it finally emerges demands that an 'absolute' verse should be interpreted in the light of a 'conditional' one when the situation and the ruling are parallel. This helps

[4] *Rasā'il* (1918–19), pp. 224–6.
[5] *TA*, ii. 105–24 and *passim*.
[6] *Taḥqīq al-jihād*, pp. 202–12.

him to explain, for instance, the defensive nature of *jihād*.[7]

His exegetical apologetics is based firmly, if not soundly, on a comparative study of the Old Testament and the Qur'ān. On the question of the existence of jinn, for instance, whereas Sayyid Aḥmad Khān was satisfied with the primarily psychological position that they were projections of the forces of evil, Chirāgh 'Alī offered the quasi-historical explanation that they were also a primitive Semitic tribe living in the hills of Jordan whom Solomon employed to build his temple.[8]

This unrestrained enthusiasm for a pseudo-historical exegetical trend had serious dangers. For example, at least in one place Chirāgh 'Alī has quite unconsciously regarded the Qur'ān not as the divine word but the work of Muḥammad:

> But the final and effectual step taken by Muhammad towards the abolition of this leading vice [polygamy] of the Arab community was his declaring in the Kor'an that nobody could fulfil the condition of dealing equitably with more than one woman . . .[9]

In his modernist re-examination of the second source of Muslim law, the *ḥadīs̱*, he shows a far greater critical acumen. He proceeds from Shāh Walī-Allāh's position to argue that a narrated *ḥadīs̱* sometimes conveys the sense but not the exact words of the Prophet, and is therefore liable to a mutation or alteration of meaning. This thesis is advanced by Chirāgh 'Alī not as a possibility but as a fact, covering, in principle, the entire corpus of *ḥadīs̱*.[10] So reluctant is he to accept the evidence of classically recognized *isnād* to concede the authenticity of a *ḥadīs̱* which would be considered anti-liberal today, that Chirāgh 'Alī does not hesitate to make use of this very classical methodology of criticism when it suits him to reject a particular tradition. His restatement of the role of the Prophet in historical perspective is essentially not very different from that of sympathetic scholars such as Sir Hamilton Gibb writing in the west today: he regards

[7] *Rasā'il*, pp. 42–43, 112.

[8] Sayyid Aḥmad Khān, *Tafsīr*, ii. 67; Chirāgh 'Alī, *TA*, ii. 137–45.

[9] *Proposed Political, Legal, and Social Reforms in the Ottoman Empire* (1883), p. 128.

[10] Walī-Allāh, *Ḥujjat*, pp. 281–3; Chirāgh 'Alī, *Rasā'il*, p. 99.

the Prophet primarily as a reformer who supplanted ancient Arabian superstition by monotheism, elevated the moral standard of Arabs and other peoples, and improved the lot of women by restricting polygamy, discouraging slavery, and abolishing infanticide.[11] Even more striking is his instinctive rejection of much of the classical *ḥadīs̱*, in which he forecasts the methodology and the conclusions reached by Goldziher in the west.[12]

The two other sources of classical Muslim law, *ijmā'* and *ijtihād*, were more easily assailable; and Chirāgh 'Alī finds them easier to demolish in his efforts to lay the foundations for an anti-classical basis for Muslim law. *Ijmā'* of the *'ulamā'* could hardly be regarded as a finally binding source of law, for it is rejected alike by jurists such as Aḥmad b. Ḥanbal, by theologians such as Ibn Ḥazm, and by mystics such as Ibn al-'Arabī. *Ijtihād* is in itself not an independent source of law, but is dialectically related to the other three sources. Its rulings can therefore be neither final nor immutable.[13]

Rejecting all classical sources of law except the first, the Qur'ān, which is to be reinterpreted, Chirāgh 'Alī proceeds to investigate the possibilities for a new basis of Muslim law. This basis has to be essentially humanistic, for man is born free and sinless, though he can later acquire sin in his social environment. Islam is capable of progress, and possesses sufficient elasticity to enable it to adapt itself to the social and political changes going on around it. Not the Islam of Muslim common law, but the faith as preached in the Qur'ān itself constitutes progress and a change for the better. It has the vital principle of rapid development, of advancement, of rationalism, and of adaptability to new circumstances. Muḥammad did not compile a code of law, civil or canonical; nor did he enjoin the Muslims to do so. He left it to them in general to frame any code of civil or canon law and to

[11] *Taḥqīq al-jihād*, p. 78.

[12] Chronologically Chirāgh 'Alī's work precedes that of Ignaz Goldziher, who pays him a tribute on this point (*Muhammedanische Studien* (1889–90), p. 132); see also A. Guillaume, *The Traditions of Islam* (Oxford, 1924), pp. 94–97.

[13] *Proposed . . . Reforms*, pp. xxi–xxiii.

found systems which would harmonize with the times and suit the political and social changes going around them. Classical Muslim law is essentially not canonical but common law. It includes and mainly consists of the survivals of pagan Arab institutions, of oral *aḥādīṣ* attributed to the Prophet which are mostly spurious, and of 'consideration of humanity, reason, common sense, and also the principles of moral fitness and public convenience. . . '.[14]

Islam exists as a religion distinct from a social system, though Muslims in various phases of their history confused the individual or cumulative experience of their social systems with the Qur'ān.[15] Neither the four traditional sources of Muslim law, nor the authority of the four Sunnī schools of jurisprudence which make use of them, can be regarded as legally infallible or immutable. Certain sections of Muslim civil law require re-writing. The codification of Islamic jurisprudence was a reflexion of the historical situation of Islamic society in the ninth and tenth centuries. Traditional Islamic law might still be practicable in fossilized Muslim societies which have refused to change. But some of its features are out of date in Muslim countries which have come in contact with or experienced the impact of the west, such as Turkey, India, or Algeria. In such countries a new legal theory has to be evolved to effect thorough-going legislative changes in the inherited traditional law, to eliminate outdated, and by modern standards inefficient, unprogressive, and in-human features in legal institutions. In the only free Muslim state of any considerable importance, the Ottoman empire, marriage and divorce laws have to be reformed. The equality of all citizens, Muslim and non-Muslim, has to be established in theory as in practice. Rulings in Muslim common law prescribing legal disabilities against non-Muslims are disowned by Chirāgh ʿAlī as having no real theological basis.[16] Recognizing that the reforms initiated in the Ottoman empire between 1839 and 1876 were inadequate to enforce equality of legal status between

[14] Ibid. pp. 10–12.
[15] Ibid. p. xxxiv.
[16] Ibid. pp. xxvii, 95–100.

Muslim and non-Muslim citizens, he develops the argument that political and legal institutions of the western empires in which Muslims live also needed far more liberalization.

> Conformity, in certain points, with foreign laws must be allowed to Moslems, living under the Christian rule, either in Russia, India or Algiers. Political and social equality must be freely and practically granted to the natives of British India. Political inequality, race distinctions and social contempt evinced by Englishmen in India towards their fellow-subjects, the Natives, is very degrading and discouraging.[17]

Having arrived at a dynamic basis of Muslim law, Chirāgh ʿAlī could have relegated such controversial medieval Muslim institutions as the *jihād* and polygamy to a historical perspective irrelevant to the development of a modernist Islam. Instead, under the influence of Sayyid Aḥmad Khān, he chooses the alternative of speculative fundamentalism in trying to explain them away. He regards the *jihād* as permissible only for defensive purposes, and like Arnold he makes extensive use of Lane's *Dictionary* to examine linguistic terms related to, derived from, or cognate with *jihād*.[18] Injecting a modernist vein into the views of Ikhwān al-Ṣafā, he argues that all the *maghāzī* undertaken by the Prophet were essentially defensive.[19] In terms of historical sequence, the offensive had already been taken by the hostile Meccans by torturing and humiliating the followers of the Prophet. Military strategy demanded initiative against the enemy and its Beduin allies after the Prophet's migration to Medina. Punitive measures were taken against the Jews of Medina because of their treachery, and their role as a 'fifth column' within Medina. In any case the Prophet's *maghāzī* should be regarded as historical incidents related to and relevant to specific situations. The Qur'ānic verses referring to them deal only with those specific situations and cannot be regarded as the basis of any subsequent legal theory.[20]

[17] Ibid. pp. xxvii–xxviii.
[18] *Taḥqīq al-jihād*, pp. 187–8.
[19] *Dafʿ-i ilzām fī Ghazwāt al-Islām* (Lucknow, 1874); *Rasā'il*, pp. 3–5.
[20] *Taḥqīq al-jihād*, pp. 1–12, 40–49, 137.

Whereas Chirāgh ʻAlī's views on *jihād* were largely a repudiation of what he considered the misleading arguments of western orientalists such as Muir, Robertson Smith, George Sale, and Sprenger, or of more specifically Christian missionaries like T. P. Hughes, Samuel Green, and others, his writings on slavery in Islam were directed against the traditional theologians in Islamic India, especially against Muḥammad ʻAskarī's refutation of Sayyid Aḥmad Khān's theory that fresh enslavement was categorically forbidden by the Qur'ān (47: 5) at a specific juncture.[21]

In his rejoinder to ʻAskarī's attack, Chirāgh ʻAlī largely endorses and enlarges upon Sayyid Aḥmad Khān's thesis. Slavery is mentioned in the Qur'ān as a practice according with the customary law of the Arab people and does not indicate divine sanction or permission. Manumission of slaves is not merely commendable, it is 'an indispensable duty for a Muslim'. Even in historical Islam, in which slavery persisted as an institution sanctioned as politically expedient by the jurists, though not by the Qur'ān, the treatment of slaves has been more liberal and human than in any other culture.

Islamic personal law should be viewed in the historical context of the pagan Arab practices of that time, which included infanticide, unrestricted polygamy, and exploitation of women in every conceivable way. The Qur'ān gradually raised the status of women by curtailing the unlimited plurality of wives to four, and then making even this concession conditional on justice, which in sexual relationship could only be synonymous with love, thus virtually abolishing polygamy.[22] Justice in love cannot be meted out to more than one woman at a time by a man. Limiting its conditional permission by this psychological impossibility, the Qur'ān gradually and almost imperceptibly prescribes the abolition of polygamy. The jurists have submerged the letter and the spirit of the Qur'ān by legal manipulation, re-enforcing

[21] See Ch. II above and *TA*, iii. 54–56; cf. Sayyid Muḥ. ʻAskarī, *Ḥaqīqat al-Islām* (Cawnpore, 1874), p. 13.

[22] *Tahẕīb al-Kalām* (Hyderabad, 1918); *Majmūʻa-i riwāyāt-i istirqāq wa-tasarri* (Hyderabad, 1918); *Rasā'il*, pp. 32–35, 159, 167–205; *TA*, iii. 51–54.

the earlier oriental customary practices denounced by it.[23]

Similarly, Muslim divorce laws have to be studied as gradualist reforms of the ancient Arabian excesses and taboo-creating vows. All that could be done at that stage was to restrict, at least to some extent, man's primitive freedom of wilful separation, and to provide for woman some economic security through dowry and other obligations binding on the divorcing husband. Compared with paganism, Judaism, or Christianity, Islam gave the woman a fairer deal.

> The Mosaic law fell short of accomplishing any great good for the moral and social elevation of the Hebrew females, and the New Testament did comparatively nothing towards their worldly preferment. Emancipation of the woman in the west is a heritage of Roman law and primitive Teutonic tolerance rather than a Christian element of culture. The dogma of original sin in Christianity explains the unparalleled degradation of women in the medieval west. Islam, on the other hand, changed the attitude towards women to one of respect, kindness, and courtesy. The Muslim law of inheritance, giving a woman exclusive right to her own property, compares favourably with the British law. Man's superiority is recognized by the Qur'ān only in matters relating to his natural physical attributes.[24]

ANTI-TRADITIONALIST MODERNISM: MUḤSIN AL-MULK

Chirāgh 'Alī's speculative position is slightly more radical and perhaps a little more extravagant than that of Sayyid Aḥmad Khān. A cautiously moderate trend is discernible in the speculative writings of Sayyid Aḥmad's associate and later successor, Mahdī 'Alī Khān (1837–1907), commonly known by his title Muḥsin al-Mulk, which he received in the service of the Nizam of Hyderabad. His association with Sayyid Aḥmad Khān dates from 1862. Though he disagreed with some of the views expressed in Sayyid Aḥmad Khān's Commentary on the Bible, Muḥsin al-Mulk nevertheless decided to support him; became a member of the Scientific Society in 1864, helped him collect

[23] *Proposed . . . Reforms*, pp. 112–13; *Rasā'il*, pp. 238–49.
[24] *Proposed . . . Reforms*, pp. 117–18; *TA*, iii. 26–27.

material for the *Khuṭbāt-i Aḥmadiyya*, maintained a life-long correspondence with him which forms the basis of the Aligarh movement; and contributed to Sayyid Aḥmad Khān's journal, the *Tahẕīb al-akhlāq*, in the 1870s. Minor differences of opinion, however, developed between them in 1893 on the question of the administration of the College, and Muḥsin al-Mulk moved to Bombay, where he made contact with the Āghā Khān and collaborated with the nationalist Badr al-dīn Ṭayyibjī in the publication of three Muslim newspapers. In 1899 he was appointed secretary of the MAO College at Aligarh, but he soon had to relinquish a post which had made him the natural successor of Sayyid Aḥmad Khān through the opposition of Sir Anthony MacDonell, the Lieutenant-Governor of the United Provinces, against whose anti-Urdu and pro-Hindi policies he had protested.[25]

Throughout his life he remained a staunch loyalist in the tradition of Sayyid Aḥmad Khān, and was generally opposed to pan-Islamism and to Muslim participation in the Indian National Congress, though his personal relations with the liberal Congress leader Gokhale were quite cordial and he was in sympathy with certain aspects of the nationalist movement. He stood, however, strongly for inter-communal harmony and a peaceful *modus vivendi* with the Hindus.

In 1905 a committee set up by Muḥsin al-Mulk on the problems of religious education reported that the students of modern physical sciences were not generally convinced by traditional theological teaching and recommended the use of the works of the modern Egyptian and Syrian scholars, Shaykh Muḥammad ʿAbduh, Rashīd Riḍā, and other writers of the *al-Manār* group. Muḥsin al-Mulk favoured the instruction of religious education at the primary or secondary school level, and not at the belated stage of the university education when agnostic or atheistic trends had taken a firm root in the student's mind. It was mainly because of this emphasis on the need of a balance between religion and science in education that the opposition of the *ʿulamāʾ*

[25] Muḥ. Amīn Zubayrī, *Ḥayāt-i Muḥsin* (1934), pp. 103–4.

to Aligarh considerably decreased; and divines like Shāh Sulaymān Phulwārwī and ʿAbd al-Bārī of the Farangī Maḥal attended several meetings of the Muhammedan Educational Conference.

The year 1906 marks the culmination of Muḥsin al-Mulk's political career, and a turning-point in Muslim politics in the subcontinent. Morley's budget speech had inspired the influential Muslim élite to define and formulate their community's political demands: separate Muslim electoral bodies, not merely in proportion to their percentage in population but in accordance with their importance as a community. These two principles, separate electoral bodies and 'weightage', remained the basis of all political bargaining between the Muslims, the Indian National Congress, and the British, until the demand for a separate Muslim state, Pakistan, gathered irreversible momentum in Muslim India in the 1940s.

Muslim separatism in politics was undoubtedly 'encouraged' by the government in India, but in the light of the overwhelming evidence of the Minto Papers, recently made available to the public, it is difficult to accept the Indian nationalist thesis that this separatism was 'engineered' or even 'inspired' by the British.[26] It was a direct logical development of the policies Sayyid Aḥmad Khān had stood for and preached, and which had won the adherence of Muslim opinion during his lifetime. As Sayyid Aḥmad Khan's successor at Aligarh, Muḥsin al-Mulk was the focal figure in the representation of the views of the Muslim élite to the British Viceroy, Lord Minto. He naturally used the British Principal at Aligarh to sound Minto's views before giving Muslim representation a concrete form, but that form seems to have been largely a corporate effort of outstanding Muslim minds. One of the chief promoters of this design of Muslim separatism was the Āghā Khān, who had been in touch with Muḥsin al-Mulk for nearly a decade; another was ʿImād al-Mulk (Sayyid Ḥusayn Bilgrāmī), who was a distinguished civil servant in Hyderabad state and who prepared the draft of

[26] The Minto Papers, in the National Library of Scotland, throw new light on the question.

the address which the delegation of the Muslim élite presented to Minto at Simla in 1906. Minto's reply to this monumental address laid the foundations of British policy towards the growth of parliamentary and self-governing institutions in India: 'that any electoral representation in India would be doomed to mischievous failure which aimed at granting a personal enfranchisement, regardless of the beliefs and traditions of the communities composing the population of this continent'.[27] Before Muḥsin al-Mulk's death in 1907 much of the bitterness of his quarrel with MacDonell seems to have been mitigated by direct contacts with Minto, with whom he discussed problems of the organization of Muslim politics and of the administration of Aligarh College.[28]

The religious thought of Muḥsin al-Mulk is interesting primarily for its moderation and its slightly more conservative restatement of some of Sayyid Aḥmad Khān's views. In following Sayyid Aḥmad Khān from *taqlīd* (traditionalism) to *ijtihād*, Muḥsin al-Mulk drew support from his own studies of al-Ghazzālī and his conviction that static traditionalism was leading to the Hinduization of Indian Islam.[29]

The main area of difference between Sayyid Aḥmad Khān and Muḥsin al-Mulk is the concept of natural law. Whereas the former regards it as immutable, admitting of no exceptions, the latter holds exceptions to be within its range. Nature, argues Muḥsin al-Mulk, is still a vague concept even in modern European thought. The same vagueness would therefore apply to any theories based on 'natural law'. His exegetical approach is thus inclined to interpret extra-natural agencies as allegorical. Laws of nature are being perpetually rediscovered and reinterpreted by modern science. The Qur'ān lays down the principle of possible exception to the familiar laws of nature. Miracles, angels, and Satan could be categorized among these exceptions rather than explained away in terms of uncompromising naturalistic rationality. Rejecting the extreme externalism of traditionalist angelology,

[27] Text of Address and Minto's answer in *The Struggle for Independence, 1857–1947* (1958), app. iv.

[28] Zubayrī, p. 189.

[29] *TA*, i. 218–22.

he accepts angels and Satan as vague, undefinable external forms and not internal psychological reflexes.[30]

Muḥsin al-Mulk's fundamentalist modernism starts from the premiss that everything has in itself a reality and a nature. If we are familiar with the reality of a thing, but we find its nature altered, we should find the cause behind this change, which could only be due to mixing or interjection of an extraneous element into the thing. In examining a thing we shall therefore have to examine whether it is in its original condition or mixed. If it is mixed, it has to be analysed and its components isolated and distinguished by reliable criteria. The exercise of these criteria constitutes the principle of *ijtihād*, whereas mere traditional faith is imitative belief which can provide neither any real spiritual satisfaction nor certainty of truth.[31]

The present religious complex which is generally called Islam is not a monolithic religious unity, but a collection of numberless elements. In the collective belief called Islam we can brush aside the extraneous impurities and arrive at the basic minimum of religious faith, law, and experience only by exclusive reliance on the Qur'ān and the *sunna* (practices) of the Prophet. The law of religious interpretation has prevailed in Islam as in every other religion which preserves the purity of its laws for a time and then succumbs to borrowings and intermixture of impurities from other sources. In Islam the phase of interpolation dates back to the generation after the Prophet. In due course the Islamic religion was unrecognizably transformed through a number of causes, such as the attribution of a person's own beliefs or actions to Prophetic authority, dishonest and worldly-wise interpretation of the Prophet's injunctions, esoteric excesses, over-emphasis on the *ijmā*ʿ of the ʿ*ulamā*', intellectual errors of the founders of the great schools of law, and the trend of representing borrowings from other religions and cultures as purely orthogenetic.[32]

This erroneous theological methodology has been the bane of exegetical discipline in Islam. Not a single work of Qur'ānic

[30] Ibid. pp. 240, 320, 344–9, 396–7.

[31] Ibid. pp. 1–3.

[32] Ibid. pp. 4–5, 30–36.

exegesis can be regarded as reliable. The Prophet's *ḥadīs̱* cited in exegetical interpretations are often doubtful even by traditional standards, being based on faulty *isnād*. Pseudo-historical episodes, messianic traditions, far-fetched legal interpretations, which are commonplace defects of classical works of exegesis, have made a study of *waḥy* difficult. Scientific study of the Qur'ān can be subjected to only one criterion: that it should be in consonance with Arabic grammar and syntax, and with the miraculous literary merit of the word of God. Thus interpreted, it would be permissible to explain the verses of the Qur'ān in the light of the ascertained realities of science. To quote the Qur'ān wrongfully in support of one's own argument or purpose is, of course, wrong, but it is not the same thing as rationalist exegesis. The 'ambiguous' verses of the Qur'ān are miraculous in the sense that they were transmitted as mysteries for the contemporaries of the Prophet, but future ages could correctly understand and interpret them. The divine word would become more and more rationally intelligible with the advance of human knowledge and the march of science.[33]

As a source of law, the *ḥadīs̱* can only be accepted with the greatest caution. A dictum of the Prophet may be genuine, but only partly so. Oral communication is a very defective method of transmission; it may omit or forget to transmit a complementary, qualifying, or superseding phrase. Action and the *ḥadīs̱* of the Prophet cannot be regarded as uniformly binding; some of them are no doubt basically theological, whereas the others could be social, or habitual, or accidental. Finally, the law of *naskh* which operates in the Qur'ān must necessarily operate in the *ḥadīs̱*, and the determination of a scientific chronology for distinguishing between the superseding and superseded statements of the Prophet becomes a legal necessity.[34]

The main consideration which has to be stressed in modernist *ḥadīs̱* criticism is that the actual wording of a statement attributed to the Prophet can never be absolutely exact literally. No narrator could be credited with a memory so phenomenal. He

[33] Ibid. pp. 105–57, 228. [34] Ibid. pp. 58–59.

could only convey the approximate sense of a statement. In this process several human factors could change or transform a *ḥadīs̱*.[35]

Under the ʿAbbāsids the science of *fiqh* became more and more independent of *ḥadīs̱*. It came closer to logic and Greek rational sciences, and farther removed from its original theological foundations. If *ḥadīs̱* is to receive primary emphasis as a source of law at the expense of recognized jurisprudence, new criteria for its verification will have to be evolved. These criteria Muḥsin al-Mulk has not been able to evolve or formulate. He ends by adapting Sayyid Aḥmad Khān's thesis of the right of every Muslim to renounce traditionalism and to put forward his own speculative interpretations of theological problems to the well-known Walī-Allāhi view, that *ḥadīs̱* supersedes jurisprudence where a judicial ruling is demonstrably contrary to it, and that the follower of a particular school of law can follow other schools in various matters of belief or conduct.[36]

Muḥsin al-Mulk does not totally reject the *ijmāʿ* of the *ʿulamāʾ* as a source of law, but considerably waters it down. *Ijmāʿ* of the *ʿulamāʾ* cannot be an ultimate or indisputable source of law, as in the last analysis it is the analogical deduction or decision or action of a body of people who do not possess Prophetic intuition, and these cannot be considered infallible. A decision reached by *ijmāʿ* can therefore remain valid only until an error of judgment in it comes to light. A secondary or subsequent *ijmāʿ* supersedes an earlier ruling; but the difference between the operation of the principle of *naskh* in *waḥy* and in the *ijmāʿ* lies in the latter's situation of perpetual changeability. It therefore follows that the rulings of the *ijmāʿ* cannot be accepted in their totality, but only as single items constantly re-evaluated in the processes of historical experience. In modern times they need to be judged in the light of the findings of physical sciences and by the standards of contemporary humanistic ethics.[37]

All the creations of God follow a single principle of reality,

[35] Ibid. pp. 251–3.

[36] Ibid. pp. 63–65, 98–103.

[37] Ibid. pp. 68–69, 159–62.

which man has been given the power and the capacity to understand. Theologians object to rationalism on the grounds of the fallibility of human reason, arguing that knowledge as revealed to human reason is subject to constant adjustment and change. They further argue that since the divine word is the absolute and immutable truth, it need not and should not be exposed to the hazard of parallelisms of fluctuating human knowledge. In reply to these objections Muḥsin al-Mulk points out that modern rationalism is different from the classical, which was based on Greek logic. Modern rationalism has no choice but to face the demonstrable results of scientific truths, which can be suppressed neither by clerical pressure nor by theocratic legislation. The flux and change of human reason grappling with physical sciences to explain and utilize the mysteries of divine creation for the good of mankind does not derogate from the divine word by making any or several interpretations of it. As rational creatures we are bound by unavoidable necessity to accept the realities of physical nature and of the revealed word simultaneously, and merge the knowledge received from both sources into a single and integrated formula of belief.[38]

This might be called *bid'a*, but then *bid'a* has been the foundational basis of finding fresh solutions for new situations in historical Islam since the time of 'Umar, whose laws were original guiding principles dictated by the requirements of expansion of the world of Islam and the incorporation in it of other non-Muslim societies. Our worldly affairs cannot be independent of our relation to our religion. This applies to our politics as well. Our social behaviour has to be conditioned by our faith, which does not teach us asceticism in a hostile milieu. We should therefore be guided in our religious and social philosophy by the example of the orthodox Caliphs, especially 'Umar, to find our own solutions for coexistence with non-Muslims, re-codification of our laws according to the exigencies of the times, and the promotion of the civilization of Islam amidst the challenges and tribulations of this day and age.[39]

[38] Ibid. pp. 45–53, 66–103.

[39] Ibid. pp. 6–7, 113.

MUMTĀZ ʻALĪ AND THE FEMINIST MOVEMENT

Sayyid Aḥmad Khān had felt the necessity of facing the problem of the education and to some extent of the emancipation of Muslim women during his visit to Europe in 1869–70. In his educational programme, however, this problem received only a secondary priority. In 1878 Mumtāz ʻAlī, a scholar of the conservative school of Deoband, came under his influence,[40] learnt some English, and devoted his life to an open championship for women's education and rights in Muslim India. His journal *Tahẕīb al-niswān* was for women the counterpart of Sayyid Aḥmad Khān's *Tahẕīb al-akhlāq*.

In his major work, *Ḥuqūq-i niswān*, Mumtāz ʻAlī preaches complete equality between men and women. He analyses the traditional arguments on which the more privileged position of man is based in Islamic culture: man is physically stronger, more rational, less emotional and superstitious than woman; he is the exclusive recipient of certain divine favours like prophethood; man is God's representative on earth, while woman is his comforter and nourisher; the scriptures permit polygamy but not polyandry, promising houris as a reward to pious men in paradise, but making no corresponding promise for pious women.

Mumtāz ʻAlī then proceeds to refute these arguments. Physical strength can be no criterion of superiority between animal and animal, or animal and man, or man and man, and therefore between man and woman. No doubt women have to perform certain biological functions to which their nervous system and their emotional life is conditioned, but this can neither presuppose nor prove any biological or intellectual inferiority. Vocations like prophethood or the leadership of men require a life of continuous stress and strain and detachment; for this, no doubt, women are not physically well equipped. But this is so because a

[40] I am grateful to his son, the famous dramatist, Imtiyāz ʻAlī Tāj, for the information that between Deoband and his association with Sayyid Aḥmad Khān, Mumtāz ʻAlī had come for a time under the influence of Christian missionaries.

complementary divine favour has been bestowed on them exclusively, that of conceiving, giving birth to, nourishing, and bringing up future generations of mankind. It would be exegetically inaccurate to read the Qur'anic verse 4: 38:

> Men are the managers of the affairs of women
> for that God has preferred in bounty
> one of them over another

as meaning that man has mastery over women. It should be rendered according to Shāh Walī-Allāh's explanation that man works for the benefit of women. The anti-feminist explanations of the classical exegetes reflect the customary law of their times rather than the letter and spirit of the scripture. The whole verse could equally mean that women have precedence over men who work for them.[41] Adam's precedence in creation and his privileged position *vis-à-vis* Eve is a Judaeo-Christian and not a Qur'ānic belief, as the order of their creation is not mentioned in the Qur'ān. The disparity between male and female witnesses in the Islamic law of evidence has been exaggerated due to the misinterpretation of a Qur'ānic verse, which in fact refers only to business transactions, with the technicalities of which male Arab merchants were more familiar than their womenfolk. This disparity does not relate to personal law. On the question of polygamy Mumtāz 'Alī's position is similar to that of Chirāgh 'Alī. Since love for more than one woman is impossible, the strictly conditional formula of the permissibility of polygamy cancels polygamy itself by demonstrating it to be unjust. Similarly the houris promised to pious men in paradise would be their own spouses in this world, who would be restored to them in their youth and in a renewed state of virginity.[42]

In short, if there is any difference between man and woman, it is merely one of biological functions and does not justify any claim of superiority on the part of man who has placed himself in a dominant position by brute force and then tried to rationalize his position by invidious arguments.[43] Female education is a

[41] *Ḥuqūq-i niswān* (Lahore, 1898), pp. 5–7 ff.
[42] Ibid. pp. 7–34.
[43] Ibid. pp. 40–41.

historical necessity. In spite of conservative opposition it has come to be accepted by both the upper and middle classes of Muslim India. Women are receiving some education in any case, though its standards vary from bare literacy to advanced stages. It would be futile to argue that women deserve only the barest minimum of education; this would be a position contrary to the logic of history. Their right to equality of educational opportunities must be recognized, even though they may be kept under some surveillance to save them from the risks of inexperience in a transitional society. Immorality cannot be a direct result of the education or emancipation of women, but rather of the distorted impulses of men who have been used to sexual segregation and who might take time to adjust to the moral standards of a mixed society. Highly educated women would be men's companions in coming generations and provide for them that interest at home which they now lack and seek in immoral intrigues or in red light districts.[44]

Marriages in Muslim India are arranged and loveless, and conform to a detestable pattern of a man's tyranny over his wife, which the uneducated woman accepts grudgingly as the fulfilment of her destiny, but which the educated wife will question as an unacceptable experience of a very unjust situation. For this reason Sayyid Aḥmad Khān is right in assuring that the education of young men has a higher priority; and the education of women has to be adjusted to the ratio and class distribution of male education. Transitional and well supervised private rather than the government schools can serve a better purpose in the early stages of female education.[45] This latter view was also the thesis of Naẕīr Aḥmad, who in his novels advocated a moderately conservative but firm policy of female education, and was later succeeded in the journalistic and institutional development of this view by Rāshid al-Khayrī, who represents the cautious and pessimistic approach of the non-westernized lower middle classes.

On the question of purdah, Mumtāz ʿAlī argues that the

[44] Ibid. pp. 44–52. [45] Ibid. pp. 57–59.

Qur'ān (33: 53) refers to something like it only on one clear occasion. On another occasion it prescribes modesty and the 'concealing of ornament'; other verses refer specifically to the social evils of ancient Arabia and are therefore relevant only to that society and age. They cannot be treated as laying down a general and binding commandment. Qur'ānic verses referring to man-woman relationships merely emphasize propriety and respect. Purdah in its present form in Muslim India seems to be comparatively a fairly recent indigenous development. The monumental collection of Sunnī juristic rulings, *Fatāwā-i 'Ālamgīrī*, compiled by the order of the orthodox emperor Aurangzeb towards the close of the seventeenth century, permits women to uncover their faces and hands in public. Quoting whatever favourable material he could discover in classical works of *ḥadīs̱* or jurisprudence, he argues that forcing the veil on women is an act of flagrant injustice and contrary to religious law as well as morality. If the argument is advanced that women have to go about veiled in India to escape molestation by undesirable elements of society, then the answer lies not in inflicting the virtual imprisonment on the innocent party but rather in punitive measures against the offensive anti-social elements.[46]

It might further be argued that the emancipation of women would lead to a laxity of moral standards, at least in the transitional stages of Muslim society in India. This Mumtāz 'Alī discounts as contrary to the logic of nature and therefore of religion. If God has created woman free and equal, he is bound to regulate and keep morally pure the relationship between the sexes and the sanctity of the institution of the family. An educated woman can take care of herself better than an inexperienced, uneducated, mentally confused bundle of veils which has not been allowed to develop self-confidence and cannot take care of herself.[47]

Marriage laws must be drastically reformed. Arranged marriages are disastrous, and child marriages enforced by parents' feelings of insecurity are inhuman. Marriage can only be based

[46] Ibid. pp. 64–79.

[47] Ibid. pp. 93–94.

on love and natural choice, which is as much the birthright of woman as of man. Any violation of this human principle is tantamount to the exploitation of legal loopholes by jurists to sanctify customary laws of the various societies in historical Islam, and are by the standards of today inhuman and immoral.[48]

[48] Ibid. pp. 105–19.

CHAPTER FOUR

APPROACHES TO ISLAMIC HISTORY

TURNING INWARDS: SHIBLĪ NU'MĀNĪ

THE balance which Sayyid Aḥmad Khān wished to maintain between scientific and theological studies at Aligarh led to the employment of traditionalist Islamists at the College, of whom by far the most outstanding was Shiblī Nu'mānī (d. 1916). Steeped in conservative classical Muslim scholarship, his mind was also open to the challenges and inspirations of western orientalists. Unlike Sayyid Aḥmad Khān, he was more sensitive to the pull of pan-Islamism, visited Istanbul in 1893, received a medal from 'Abd al-Ḥamīd II, came in contact with the Naqshbandī Ṣūfīs at Damascus, who traced their line of inspiration through Khālid al-Kurdī to the Indian mystics, Ghulām 'Alī and Maẓhar Jān-i Jānān; and was the first of Sayyid Aḥmad Khān's associates to establish contacts with the legendary Jamāl al-dīn al-Afghānī's co-worker and disciple, Shaykh Muḥammad 'Abduh, in Cairo. Encouraged by Sayyid Aḥmad Khān he created the tradition of Islamic historiography in Urdu; but he also gave it a strong conservative colour of revivalism. The methodology he developed was a synthesis of the traditional Islamic disciplines of chronicles and hagiography and the western discipline of objective analysis. The greater part of his historical work is essentially biographical. Individuals in historical Islam are for him the focal points of emphasis, luminaries that radiate and bring into relief the patterns of historical growth. In the study of Islamic history he concentrates on certain key developments. These include the lives of the Prophet and of 'Umar as the basic data, *kalām* as the valid source material and a potential source of inspiration for 'progressive conservative' rationalism, and Persian poetry as the interiorization of the emotional experience of the non-Arab

Muslim community. The religious leaders, or the 'heroes' of Islam as he calls them in Carlylese terminology, represent to him these particular trends. They include al-Ghazzālī, Abū Ḥanīfa, al-Ma'mūn, and Rūmī.

Though critical of an underlying anti-Islamic cross-current in western orientalism, he is one of the first historians in modern Muslim India to pay tribute to western scholarship for its painstaking investigation of the cultural and religious resources of Islam, its search, collection, collation, and editing of manuscripts, its efforts to establish a historical and scientific perspective for the study of Islam, its objective researches into the preservation of Greek sciences by the Arabs and into the extent of the radiation of these sciences in western Europe by the Arabs, and especially for its unflinching search for the factual truth. He commends the project of the *Encyclopaedia of Islam*, and regrets that the contribution of the Indian *'ulamā'*, indeed the entire area of their scholarship, had very little to offer by comparison. He was impressed by the organization and work of the International Congress of Orientalists and even planned to attend its Rome session in 1899.[1]

The challenge of western orientalism, by which he was by turns stimulated and annoyed, can best be seen in his own version of the biography of the Prophet, which though chronologically the last, and incomplete, work of his very active career, was in his own estimate the most important of his undertakings. Western studies of the life of the Prophet he regarded as prejudiced; and he was disturbed by the impact of these studies on western-educated young Muslims who could no longer approach the primary sources in Arabic with a critical acumen of their own.[2] For their benefit he revives an element in the classical tradition itself of sceptical treatment of the given early data of the *sīra*. He then proceeds to determine the categories of what he regards as reliable data in the early *sīra* literature. These include

[1] Address to First Congress of Nadwat al-'Ulamā', 1895, in *Rasā'il* (Amritsar, 1911), pp. 1–36.

[2] Shiblī Nu'mānī and Sayyid Sulayman Nadwī, *Sīrat al-Nabī* (1953–62), i. 7–12.

'authentic' *ḥadīs* traced back in reliable *isnād* to 'Alī, Anas, or 'Abd-Allāh b. 'Amr b. 'Āṣ; documents such as the treaty of al-Ḥudaybiyya, which he argues must have been recorded and must have been available to early historians, letters sent by the Prophet to rulers and emperors abroad, which unlike some western historians he regards as authentic, and names of about 1,500 Companions of the Prophet. Like Sayyid Aḥmad Khān, he dismisses the anecdotal material in al-Wāqidī as largely apocryphal; unlike him, and despite the damaging verdict of Mālik b. Anas, he regards Ibn Isḥāq's authority as comparatively reliable. In opinions such as these Shiblī emerges, in the last analysis, a traditionalist marginally influenced by modernism. He agrees with the modernists on the criterion insisted upon by them in determining the authenticity of a *ḥadīs*: rational examination of the text of an injunction, and not of the list of narrators. But this principle of rationalist analysis is regarded by him as not modernistic but implicit in the Qur'ān itself. Among the traditions which could be rejected outright as fabrications he includes those which are contrary to reason or established principles of faith and morality or normal feeling and observation, those which are frivolous or exaggerated in the promise of reward or retribution, those which stand in contradiction to the Qur'ān or other dependable traditions or even the unanimous *ijmā'* of classical jurists, those which are not in keeping with the dignity of prophethood, those which prescribe medical treatment or foretell future events, those of apocryphal historicity, and those which are vulgar in language, expression, or content.[3]

Neither the earliest sources of the life of the Prophet nor the European deductions based upon them could be relied upon. The former suffer from an uncritical credulity of all verbally narrated episodes, while the latter, starting from the same premises, go to the other extreme of providing hypothetical motivations for actions and episodes which do not constitute authentic historical data. In this respect classical Muslim historiography from the ninth century onwards tries to steer a middle course, avoiding

[3] Ibid. pp. 44–47, 57–58.

the extremes of unquestioning credulity and wild hypothesis. He divides the European Islamists into three broad categories: general historians, unfamiliar with Arabic, who depend on secondary sources, and who despite their obvious limitation can achieve a degree of liberalism and unbiased objectivity, like Gibbon; Arabists who are not specialists of the *sīra* and yet venture into generalizations in dealing with the life of the Prophet; and Christian polemicists like Palmer, Muir, and Sprenger, who have made a thorough study of the early *sīra* literature, but whose interpretation tends to be subjective and hostile due to their emotional involvement in and self-identification with the missionary stresses in their own religion.[4]

Shiblī's own *sīra*-criticism is organized on four principles. The events of the Prophet's life mentioned in the Qur'ān have to be accepted as the core and the factual essence of the biography of the Prophet. Evidence in the six classical *ḥadīs̱* collections, especially the Bukhārī collection, should receive precedence over the corresponding episodic material in the *sīra* literature. Of the earlier sources Ibn Isḥāq, Ibn Sa'd, and Ṭabarī are the only ones who could be relied upon to some extent; others might be safely ignored. An effort has to be made to correct the errors of uncritical *sīra* literature as well as of the highly speculative hypotheses of the western historians.

If the life of the Prophet has for Shiblī a key position in the study of the doctrine, sociology, and ethics of Islam, the life of the second Caliph, 'Umar, constitutes the basis of Islamic polity, economic organization, and principles of coexistence with non-Islamic peoples. His approach to 'Umar's role in the development of Muslim legal and administrative institutions is however hagiographical; and he shows a weakness for the illustrative anecdote which he condemns in relation to the study of the life of the Prophet. The central emphasis is focused on 'Umar as the idealized symbol of Islamic justice and egalitarianism. Compared with Ṭaha Ḥusayn and other modern Muslim biographers of 'Umar, he shows a remarkable power of analysis,

[4] Ibid. pp. 95–97, 100–1.

though not an equal sense of historical perspective, in outlining the structure of the Muslim state under ʿUmar, and unlike them, or even sympathetic Shīʿī historians such as Amīr ʿAlī, he does not hesitate to emphasize material or conclusions unfavourable to ʿUmar.[5]

In Shiblī's historiographical perspective the chief area of sensitivity, and therefore of apologetic concentration, is the theory of the treatment of the non-Muslim citizen. He traces the development of the theory of 'protection' of the non-Muslims by the Muslim state to the treaty of Najrān in 629, laying down the rights and obligations of the Muslim state in relation to its non-Muslim subjects: to defend them from all external aggressors, not to interfere with their religious practices or their clergy, to guarantee the security of their lives, property, and trade interests, and to levy *jizya* (poll tax) on them but exempt them from the land tax. Any subsequent discriminatory rules or practices introduced by Muslim rulers or recommended by jurists or political thinkers are merely personal views. In any case, in historical Islam criminal law remained the same for Muslim and non-Muslim. ʿUmar's policy forbidding the alienation or purchase by a Muslim of landed property belonging to a non-Muslim was a continuation of the tradition and the spirit of the treaty of Najrān. This policy, argues Shiblī, found its legal formulation in Abū Yūsuf's ruling that the Muslim ruler cannot deprive the *zimmis* (protected Muslim subjects) of their land, and whenever this principle was violated, it was subjected to strong criticism.[6]

Against the charge made by western historians that Christians were not allowed to build new churches, Shiblī argues that according to the evidence of ʿAbd-Allāh b. ʿAbbās, this ruling was restricted at first, and therefore presumably meant to be applicable to only such purely Muslim cities as the new Muslim colonies like Kūfa where there were no non-Muslims in any case, and where Christians were not allowed to build new churches. In cities like Damascus, treaties with the Christians

[5] *al-Fārūq* (Azamgarh, 1922), *passim*.
[6] 'Ḥuqūq al-zimmiyyīn', in *Rasāʾil*, pp. 5–28.

were fully honoured guaranteeing complete religious freedom. Later Christians were allowed to construct churches in such purely Muslim cities as Cairo. Islamic jurisprudence permits a Christian to leave a grant in his will for the construction of a church but not of a mosque.[7]

Shiblī accepts as a pragmatic fact the historical truism that in no empire in history have the ruled enjoyed complete equality with the rulers. In civilizations before Islam, he asserts, the conquered people were treated like animals, and the Islamic state can at least be credited with a comparative degree of toleration and integration unsurpassed by any ancient, medieval, or modern society. Turning to legal writings prescribing discriminatory dress or inferior status, Shiblī regards them as theoretical projections of the policies of individual despots like the ʿAbbāsid al-Mutawakkil (847–61), who also persecuted the rationalist Muʿtazila; discriminatory practices ordered by ʿUmar I (or ʿUmar II) were his own personal innovation, dictated perhaps by *raison d'état*, but without any sanction or source in the Qur'ān and therefore not basically Islamic. Similarly, the case of the Medinan Jews in the Prophet's time was pertinent only to given historical situations, without any legal significance for the subsequent development of the polity of Islam. Toleration of and social relationship with non-Muslims in Islam varied from situation to situation corresponding to the amity or hostility between the Muslim state and a particular non-Muslim community. Patronage and position offered to the outstanding Jewish or Christian intellectuals or servants under the Umayyad and ʿAbbāsid caliphates far exceeded the respect or status of real equality granted by European imperial administrations to distinguished individuals of colonial races.[8]

Jizya, he argues, was originally a Sāsānid tax levied to finance military expenditure, first introduced probably by Anūshīrwān. This tax, with the entire taxation system of the Sāsānid empire, was continued by ʿUmar on his conquest of Persia.[9]

[7] Ibid. pp. 27–30.
[8] Ibid. pp. 31–39.
[9] 'al-Jizya', in *Rasā'il*, pp. 6–7.

Military service for *jihād*, which according to Shiblī is always defensive, is compulsory for every Muslim. It is therefore logical that Muslims should have been exempted from the *jizya* which was levied to finance the defensive wars, as more than their fair share of it lay in their active service, from which non-Muslims were exempt. It would have been tyrannical to impose conscription on non-Muslims for the defence of a Muslim state; but as its citizens they were guaranteed protection in the *Pax Islamica*, and it was only fair that they should contribute towards it financially. Those non-Muslims who chose of their own free will to participate in active military service were allowed to do so and were exempted from *jizya*.

The *moral* justification of the *jizya*, Shiblī concludes, is the modest financial contribution of non-combatant elements of population to the defence of the state, and to the public works from which they benefited as much as the Muslims. Conversely, the non-Muslims also benefited from the *zakāt* (tithe) which was levied exclusively on Muslims, but from which, according to ʿUmar's ruling as recorded by Abū Yūsuf, Jews and Christians were also allowed to receive contributions.[10]

Unlike Sayyid Aḥmad Khān, he is not a neo-Muʿtazilite modernist. The cast of his mind is essentially medieval, though he is prepared to make compromises with the radical responses necessitated by the challenges of Europe's scientific outlook. He is also preoccupied with the concept of 'reason', and to some extent with that of 'nature'. But for him rationalism is almost synonymous with medieval Muslim *kalām*. He takes the historically static view that all in *kalām* that was effective in the tenth to thirteenth centuries of Islam should be so even now, for the correctness or actuality of a process of thought does not alter with the passage of time. Perhaps the classical concepts of *kalām* could be restated in a more modernized terminology comprehensible in this day and age. The two essentially different categories of classical Muslim *kalām*, he says, have to be distinguished —that which was developed to resist and dissolve the challenge

[10] Ibid. pp. 7–15.

of Greek philosophy, and that which consisted of disputations between various Muslim theological schools. Shiblī concerns himself with the former, as a significant field of study which could absorb the shock of modern free-thinking.[11]

The promising growth of Ashʿarite scholasticism was arrested, not because of any inherent intellectual weakness of its own, but because of the extraneous impact of the Mongol onslaught in the thirteenth century. It has to be reconstructed and its threads picked up from the days of its free expression under al-Ma'mūn (813–32). The freedom of intellectual expression under the ʿAbbāsids, which came to a sad end under al-Mutawakkil (847–61), was *kalām's* 'greatest gift' to Muslim history, but it had its limitations even under al-Ma'mūn, for it was confined to the court and the élite, while the lower levels of intelligentsia remained intolerant, denying freedom of thought to others and themselves, consolidating a traditionalist frame of mind which led to the final triumph of the juristic schools. Abū Ḥanīfa is the only exception to the reactionary anti-libertarian trend of Islamic jurisprudence.[12]

It is, however, al-Ghazzālī who is regarded by Shiḅlī, as by Sayyid Aḥmad Khān, as the main link between medieval *kalām* and the rational emphasis of modern religious speculation. Shiblī is principally concerned to establish al-Ghazzālī's position as a scholar of *kalām* rather than as a theologian, and he therefore stresses al-Ghazzālī's repudiation of a mass of anti-rational ideas irrelevant to fundamentalist Islam. He concentrates on al-Ghazzālī's emphasis on the infallible wisdom and justice of all divine action, and his rejection of the literalism of much of the Ashʿarite exegesis. Al-Ghazzālī's synthesis of fundamentalism and mysticism in a liberal restatement of Islamic theology is also significant for modernist scholasticism and his firm stand on the principle that as long as a Muslim believed in the *shahāda* (the Muslim attestation of faith in the unity of God and in the prophethood of Muḥammad), he could not be regarded as a

[11] *ʿIlm al-Kalām* (1922), pp. 3–4, 30–31, 59–60.
[12] *Sīrat al-Nuʿmān, passim; ʿIlm al-Kālam*, pp. 160–2.

non-Muslim, however heretical his views in other minutiae of belief, encourages free speculation. Shiblī also traces to al-Ghazzālī the origins of Sayyid Aḥmad Khān's identification of *waḥy* with intuition.[13]

Kalām, according to Shiblī, is primarily the methodology of explaining the essence and significance of Islamic dogma in such a way that it could be easily grasped; in this sense he proceeds to establish that the mystic poet Jalāl al-dīn Rūmī is a scholastic. Rūmī's *kalām*, as he sums it up, is atomistic, and not a monolithic or consistent philosophical system. It is based on an eclecticism which refuses to regard any religion as absolutely false, but considers that religions are mixed in various proportions with elements of falsehood and truth. At the basis of Rūmī's gnosticism Shiblī claims to see a dualism distinguishing the material from the non-material, body from soul and reason. The non-material in its finite as well as infinite existence is not easily comprehensible by the material. The existence of the divine non-material being, God, is however inevitable and necessary. *Waḥy*, as understood by Rūmī, and indeed by al-Ghazzālī, transcends the five physical senses and is identical with intuition.[14] It is to Rūmī that Shiblī turns in quest of an angelology and an eschatology more reconcilable with orthodoxy than those of Sayyid Aḥmad Khān. Rūmī, he argues, believes in a law of nature and in the possibility of another law, unknown to man through his physical senses, which transcends the law familiar to the senses. Miracles are neither proofs of prophethood nor conducive to the acceptance of a true faith, for their impact can only be compulsive and not persuasive. The soul, like *waḥy*, operates by an ethical intuition which distinguishes good from evil. The evolution of the human soul has been basically ethical, distinguishable from the animal soul which is guided by instinct.[15]

Rūmī's evolutionism has been of special interest to Indian Islam and was earlier interpreted, possibly by analogies with

[13] *Al-Ghazzālī* (1922), pp. 121–4.
[14] Ibid. pp. 120–6, 147–9, 225.
[15] *Sawāniḥ Mawlānā Rūmī* (1938), pp. 174–5.

Hindu philosophy, as pointing vaguely to metempsychosis. Shiblī was the first to place it in a comparative context with Darwinian evolutionism. Later Iqbāl was to equate it with Bergsonian *évolution créatrice*. Other elements which Shiblī sees in common between Rūmī and nineteenth-century science are the identification of the roles of matter, energy, and reason in the universe, the law of gravity, and the death and replacement of cells in biological organisms.[16]

FACING THE WEST: AMĪR ʿALĪ

In Calcutta, which was the British imperial capital during the later nineteenth century, an independent Muslim tradition of adjustment and loyalism to the powers that be and of intellectual westernization developed, independent of the Aligarh movement, though unmistakably influenced by it since the 1870s. The chief promoter of the Calcutta tradition of Muslim modernism was ʿAbd al-Laṭīf Khān, who was later joined by Karāmat ʿAlī Jawnpūrī. Amīr ʿAlī (d. 1928) was a disciple of Karāmat ʿAlī and, like him, an orthodox Shīʿī. Inspired by Sayyid Aḥmad Khān's visit to Europe in 1869–70,[17] he proceeded to England for higher legal studies and was called to the bar at the Inner Temple. This launched him on a distinguished career and he became, in due course, the chief magistrate of Calcutta, a member of the Imperial Legislative Council of India, a judge in the High Court of Judicature in Bengal, and finally a member of the Judicial Committee of the Privy Council in London. Though he was a pillar of the British establishment in India, and lived to hold high office in London during his last years when he was in close touch with British political leaders, he became the chief polemicist of Islam in the last decades of the nineteenth and the first decades of the twentieth century. As Ḥālī has pointed out, both in his explanations and apologia of Islam to the western intelligentsia

[16] Ibid. p. 176.

[17] Ḥālī, *HJ*, i. 143; for a sketch of Amīr ʿAlī's life and career see W. C. Smith, 'Amīr ʿAlī', in *EI*², i. 442–3.

and in advancing modernistic concepts for the reorientation of the structure of Islamic social and religious thought, he followed Sayyid Aḥmad Khān.[18] On the question of Muslim separatism in Indian politics and distrust of the Indian National Congress, their views were identical. He founded in 1885 a central National Muhammadan Association with the same objectives as the Indian Patriotic Association, though the two organizations did not merge or share a common organization possibly because Amīr 'Alī's loyalism was more cautious, and he lacked the revolutionary fervour of the Aligarh movement. In his long and fruitful intellectual career Amīr 'Alī outlived Sayyid Aḥmad Khān by three decades, was helpful to the Āghā Khān in persuading Morley to concede separate electoral bodies to the Muslims,[19] and inadvertently, together with the Āghā Khān, played a fateful role in a chain of events which led to the abolition of the caliphate by the Turkish Grand National Assembly in 1924.[20]

His principal contribution remains, however, his re-statement of the history of Islam for consumption in the west, where it undoubtedly made a considerable impact. His *Spirit of Islam*, published in England, ran into nine editions between 1922 and 1961; and his *Short History of the Saracens* ran into thirteen editions between 1889 and 1961. The influence of these two works was even more profound on the western educated Muslim intelligentsia in the Indian subcontinent and in Egypt.[21]

He differs from the thinkers and historians of the Aligarh school in his unswerving adherence to Shī'ī orthodoxy, which he has however considerably liberalized in his unflinching glorification of Sunnī historical Islam. The *Spirit of Islam* brings into relief, and to some extent champions, the cultural contributions of such Shī'ī dynasties as the Fāṭimids and the Buwayhids, but in the *History of the Saracens* the emphasis is exclusively on the Sunnī caliphate. He is full of admiration for the first two Caliphs,

[18] Ḥālī, *HJ*, i. 143.

[19] Aga Khan, *Memoirs* (1954), p. 104.

[20] Text of their letter to Ismet Pasha (Inönü) in RIIA, *Survey of International Affairs 1925* (1927), app. i, pp. 571–2. For details see below, Ch. VI.

[21] Aḥmad Amīn, *Zu'amā' al-iṣlāḥ fi'l 'aṣr al-ḥadīs̱* (Cairo, 1948), pp. 139–45.

Abū Bakr and especially ʿUmar, though Indian Shīʿism especially tends to be anti-ʿUmar, and though it is an article of faith with Amīr ʿAlī that the Prophet's injunctions declaring ʿAlī to be his successor were clear and unambiguous. This leads him to distinguish between what he regards the Shīʿī concept of the 'apostolical' Imāmate and the 'pontifical' caliphate of the three orthodox Caliphs who preceded ʿAlī. The 'pontifical' and the 'apostolic' caliphate can therefore not only coexist and play diverse roles, but the latter may advise and support the former, and he confirms the Sunnī view that ʿAlī was in effect one of the chief advisers to the first two Caliphs. On ʿAlī's accession to the 'pontifical' caliphate in 656 the 'apostolic' and the 'pontifical' varieties of the caliphate were merged and unified in his person. He opposes the traditional Shīʿī criticism of haste in the selection of Abū Bakr as Muḥammad's successor and justifies it on the grounds of *raisons d'état.* For the same reasons, he asserts, ʿAlī also magnanimously waived his own claim and gave allegiance to Abū Bakr to safeguard the unity and solidarity of the Muslim community.[22] Thus on the *terra firma* of Shīʿī orthodoxy he was able to evolve not only a theory of rapprochement on Sunnī and Shīʿī Islam's most explosive point of dispute, namely the succession to the Prophet, but to extend it to the contemporary situation regarding the Ottoman caliphate until 1924. As a Shīʿī he could believe in the absent messianic Imām Muḥammad Mahdī as the 'apostolic' Imām. He could feel the sectarian pull of attachment to the shāh of Persia. But he regarded the Ottoman caliph as the 'pontiff' not merely of the Sunnīs but of the entire Muslim community.[23]

The point of Shīʿī rejection in historical Islam is drawn by Amīr ʿAlī at the Umayyads, the third Caliph ʿUthmān being a border-line case. The caliphate of the first four Caliphs (632–61) is for him, as for all Muslim revivalists, the ideal Muslim state. At the core of the Islamic civilization lies the ethical humanism

[22] Ameer Ali, *The Spirit of Islam* (*SI*) (1961), pp. 37, 103–5, 293; *A Short History of the Saracens* (*SHS*) (1961), pp. 20–54.

[23] *SI*, pp. 122–36.

of ʿAlī. This leads him to strong Muʿtazilite sympathies which are as much in the Shīʿī tradition as that of the Aligarh school. As a Shīʿī he finds it easier to reject the inhibiting externalism of the Ashʿarites.[24]

Like the radical modernists of the Aligarh school, Amīr ʿAlī believes certain injunctions of the Qur'ān as historically relevant only to the Prophet's day and age. 'To suppose, therefore, that every Islamic precept is necessarily immutable is to do an injustice to history and to the development of the human intellect.'[25] Islam itself represents the final stage in the evolution of religions; as an individual religion and as the final religion it can still develop and transcend itself in two processes of history. Islam's main contribution to history has been ethical humanism. Islamic ethical life, though integrated into the religious and moral view of the hereafter, is meant essentially for the life to be lived in the present. Its constituents are kind and dutiful human relations and physical and mental hygiene. Pan-Islamism in ethical terms is brotherly love and mutual assistance which can be enlarged to include all humanity. It is interesting that in Amīr ʿAlī's formulation of Islamic ethics there is much greater emphasis on charity and benevolence than on justice.[26]

Compared with the central importance of ethics, Islamic metaphysics or cosmology or angelology need not occupy too much attention and may be relegated to the sphere of a 'willing suspension of disbelief'. Here he relies upon the traditions of Christian apologetics to choose a different path from Sayyid Aḥmad Khān's exaggerated speculative rationalism. Probably Muḥammad, like Jesus and other teachers, believed in the existence of intermediate beings, celestial messengers from God to man. The modern disbelief in angels furnishes no reason for ridiculing the notion of our forefathers. Our disbelief is as much open to the name of superstition as their belief; only one is negative, the other positive. What we in modern times look upon as the

[24] *SHS*, pp. 45–48, 70–89; *SI*, pp. 441–87.

[25] *SI*, p. 172.

[26] Ibid. p. 178 and *passim*; *Ethics of Islam* (1893), pp. 4–26; 'The Modernity of Islam', *Islamic Culture*, i (1927), pp. 1–5.

principles of nature, they looked upon as angels, ministrants of heaven. Whether there exist intermediate beings, as Locke thinks, between God and man, just as there are intermediate beings between man and the lowest form of animal creation, is a question too deep to be fathomed by the reason of man.[27]

The question of the identification of Satan, being an ethical rather than a cosmological problem, is much more complex, and here Amīr ʿAlī echoes Sayyid Aḥmad Khān's views, though presented in a more tangible historical perspective:

> Muhammad also, like Jesus, probably believed in the existence of the Principle of Evil as a personal entity. But an analysis of his words reveals a more rationalistic element, a subjective conception clothed in language suited for the apprehension of his followers. When somebody asked him where Satan lived, he replied 'In the heart of man', whilst Christian tradition converts the Pharisee who tempted Jesus into the veritable Prince of Hell.[28]

An eminent lawyer, Amīr ʿAlī is concerned as much with the Qur'ān and the Prophet's life and *ḥadīs̱* as the data of Islamic law as material for a reconstruction of Muslim history. *Vis-à-vis* nineteenth-century Christian polemics he neither accepts nor rejects early biographers of the Prophet like Ibn Isḥāq, but chooses from them only such material as suits him to reconstruct an image of the Prophet commensurate with modern western notions of human greatness. Like most western biographers of the Prophet he recognizes the duality of Muḥammad's role as prophet and statesman. Several events in his life and administration are classed by Amīr ʿAlī as his decisions as a statesman and not as a prophet. The significance of the Prophet's life and mind cannot be judged in terms of his decision in specific contingencies, but in the inherent dynamism of his keen intellect, which can guide the Muslims in modern world situations.

> The mind of this remarkable Teacher [Muhammad] was, in its intellectualism and progressive ideals, essentially modern. Eternal 'striving' was in his teachings a necessity of human existence: 'Man cannot exist

[27] *SI*, p. 64.
[28] Ibid., quoting on this last point E. Renan, *Vie de Jésus* (Paris, 1867), p. 267.

without constant effort'; 'The effort is from me, its fulfilment comes from God.'[29]

In defending Muḥammad as a prophet and statesman against Christian polemics, Amīr 'Alī's tactics are to pass from the defensive to the offensive. This is a technique diametrically opposed to Sayyid Aḥmad Khān's religious pluralism. Again and again Amīr 'Alī compares Jesus and Muḥammad in order to establish the superiority of the latter in a historical perspective. He contrasts the acceptability, though late in life, of Muḥammad by his contemporaries with the repudiation of Jesus by his own kith and kin:

. . . the influence of Jesus himself was least among his nearest relations. His brothers never believed in him, and they even went so far as once to endeavour to obtain possession of his person, believing him to be out of his mind. Even his immediate disciples were not firm in their convictions. Perhaps this unsteadiness may have arisen from weakness of character, or it may have resulted, as Milman thinks, from the varying tone of Jesus himself; but the fact is undeniable. The intense faith and conviction on the part of the immediate followers of Mohammed is the noblest testimony to his sincerity and his utter self-absorption in his appointed task.[30]

Christianity remained an 'incomplete religion' because Christ's life was cut short violently at an early age; it was left to Muḥammad to complete his mission.

One thing is certain, that had a longer career been vouchsafed to him [Jesus], he would have placed his teachings on a more systematic basis. This fundamental defect in Christianity has been, in fact, the real cause of the assembling of councils and convocations for the establishment of articles and dogmas, which snap asunder at every slight tension of reason and free thought. The work of Jesus was left unfinished. It was reserved for another Teacher [Muḥammad] to systematize the laws of morality.[31]

Islam is therefore the continuation, the fulfilment, the completion of Christianity. Islamic vitalism corrects and balances the escapism and asceticism idealized in Christianity.[32]

[29] *SI*, pp. 81–82. 121,
[30] Ibid. p. 22.
[31] Ibid. p. 173.
[32] Ibid. pp. 202–3 and *passim*.

Christian or western polemics against historical Islam he counters by fiercer polemics against historical Christianity.

> The followers of the 'Prince of Peace' [Jesus] burnt and ravished, pillaged and murdered promiscuously, old and young, male and female, without compunction, up to recent times. And his vicegerents on earth, popes and patriarchs, bishops, priests, and presbyters, approved of their crimes, and frequently granted plenary absolution for the most heinous offences.[33]

The great tragedy of the history of human civilization is focused on the two points of Arab failure completely to subdue Christendom, which prevented the fulfilment of Muslim *mission civilisatrice*.

> The two failures of the Arabs, the one before Constantinople and the other in France, retarded the progress of the world for ages, and put back the hour-hand of time for centuries. . . . The Renaissance, civilization, the growth of intellectual liberty, would have been accelerated by seven hundred years. We should not have had to shudder over the massacre of the Albigenses or the Huguenots, or the ghastly slaughters of the Irish Catholics by the English Protestants under the Tudors and the Protectorate. We should not have had to mourn over the fate of a Bruno or a Servetus. . . . The history of the *auto-da-fe*, of the murders of the Inquisition, of the massacres of the Aztecs and the Incas; the tale of the Thirty Years' War, with its manifold miseries,—all this would have remained untold. . . . If Maslamah had succeeded in capturing Constantinople . . . the dark deeds which sully the annals of the Isaurians, the Comneni, the Palaeologi, the terrible results which attended the seizure of Byzantium by the Latins, above all the frightful outburst of unholy wars, in which Christian Europe tried to strangle the nations of Asia, would probably never have come to pass . . . the iconoclastic movement would not have proved altogether abortive, and the reformation of the Christian Church would have been accomplished centuries earlier.[34]

Complete disregard of international morality was a Roman heritage which historical Christianity could neither alter nor sublimate. On the contrary, the Christian Church fully endorsed in detail the process of predatory international immorality for over a thousand years.

[33] Ibid. p. 87.

[34] Ibid. pp. 398–9.

From the first slaughters of Charlemagne, with the full sanction of the Church, to the massacre and enslavement of the unoffending races of America, there is an unbroken series of the infringement of international duties and the claims of humanity. . . . In England, after it became Protestant, the Presbyterians, through a long succession of reigns, were imprisoned, branded, mutilated, scourged, and exposed in the pillory. In Scotland, they were hunted like criminals over the mountains; their ears were torn from the roots; they were branded with hot irons; their fingers were wrenched asunder by thumbkins; the bones of their legs were shattered in the boots. . . . Even now, Christian America burns alive a Christian negro for marrying a Christian white woman! Such has been the effect produced by Christianity.[35]

This strong attack makes the apologetic defence of historical Islam much easier for Amīr ʿAlī. In the greater part of its history, runs his thesis, with some exceptions—like the discriminations of al-Mutawakkil—which prove the rule, Islam has rejected insularity and exclusiveness; it has allowed liberty of conscience and freedom of worship to the followers of other creeds in its midst; its sects and its élite have preached toleration in religion and in politics. Every religion, in some stage of its career, has from the tendencies of its professors been aggressive. Such also has been the case with Islam. But in Christendom difference of faith is a crime, in Islam it is an accident. If there are any concepts of politically differentiated categories in Islam, they are the casuistries of theologians pandering to the ambition of 'designing chieftains'. Such are the concepts of *dār al-Islām* and *dār al-ḥarb*; but they are merely Muslim counterparts of the mutually exclusive Christian concepts of Christendom and Heathendom.[36]

This leads to the general discussion of the question of the *ẓimmīs* in Islam. Stung by Christian polemicists on this point, he accuses them of selecting in their arguments only material unfavourable to Islam. He is prepared to face such historical realities as al-Mutawakkil's discriminatory legislation against non-Muslims, but blames them on al-Mutawakkil's own wickedness and bigotry, a standpoint Amīr ʿAlī could quite genuinely take as a Shīʿī, linking al-Mutawakkil's anti-*ẓimmi* legislation with

[35] Ibid. pp. 211, 219.

[36] Ibid. pp. 211–13, 218.

his ghoulish destruction of the tomb of the Prophet's grandson Ḥusayn b. ʿAlī, his persecution of the Muʿtazilites, and his dissolute and unedifying life.[37]

On the question of slavery and its discouragement in Islam, Amīr ʿAlī's position is based on that of Sayyid Aḥmad Khān and Chirāgh ʿAlī.[38] But the polemical nature of Amīr ʿAli's argument relates the question of slavery to that of racial tolerance, where Islamic civilization can show more to its credit than medieval Christendom or the modern west. 'In Islām the slave of today is the grand vizier of tomorrow. He may marry, without discredit, his master's daughter, and become the head of the family. . . . Can Christianity point to such records as these?'[39] In this historical assessment such embarrassing episodes as the Zanj (Negro) revolt (870–83) against the ʿAbbāsids and their underlying economic and social motivation have been conveniently overlooked.

Coming to the vexed question of polygamy and the position of women in Islam, he begins with an offensive against the Christian notion of asceticism in relation to sex. That sensuousness is evil is essentially a Christian ascetic dogma, and as such can have no objective or absolute validity.[40] Asceticism explains the inhumanities and humiliations inflicted upon woman in historical Christianity. Of Christianity in its relation to womankind the less said the better. In the early ages, when the religion of the people, high and low, the ignorant and the educated, consisted only of the adoration of the mother of Jesus, the Church of Christ had placed sex under a ban. Father after Father had written upon the enormities of women, their evil tendencies, their inconceivable malignity. Tertullian represented the general feeling in a work in which he described woman as 'the devil's gateway, the unsealer of forbidden tree, the deserter of the divine law, the destroyer of God's image man'. On the other hand von Hammer has been approvingly quoted in his definition of the harem in

[37] *SI*, p. 275.
[38] Ibid. p. 262, referring to Chirāgh ʿAlī's article in *TA*, p. 118.
[39] Ibid. p. 264.
[40] Ibid. pp. 202–3.

medieval Islam as a sanctuary, prohibited to strangers not because of any lack of confidence or respect in women, but in consonance with customary law.

Amīr ʿAlī is perhaps on safer ground in tracing medieval European chivalry to Arab social and literary influences, though it is not clear to what extent, if at all, he was familiar with the researches of Julian Ribera and others. Chivalry in Islam is a recurrent theme in Amīr ʿAlī's *History of the Saracens*. He is also possibly on safer ground in emphasizing tolerance of intellectual women in classical Islam under the Umayyads and early ʿAbbāsids, compared with the superstitious intolerance of the medieval and near-modern western Inquisition. But his comparative sociology gets out of focus when he compares the worst of medieval Christian anti-feminist practices with an idealized and historically almost non-existent status of woman in Islam.

On the question of polygamy Amīr ʿAlī comes closer to a defensible historical perspective. The trend of Qur'ānic injunctions, he argues, was to restrict and finally to eliminate this vice inherited by Islam from its historical tradition. He quotes and repeats Chirāgh ʿAlī's argument equating justice with love in marriage. He then proceeds to take a more traditional view, arguing in favour of the moral permissibility of polygamy under certain circumstances and in certain given historical situations. Other disabilities of women in traditionalist Islam he analyses as historical heritages, accepted and fossilized in Islam by the jurists. Any Qur'ānic injunctions imposing disabilities on women he regards as 'temporary' and relevant only to the problems of the Arabs of that age.

He follows the Aligarh school in feeling his way towards a distinction between 'temporary' and 'permanent' injunctions of the Qur'ān, an exegetical solution to which the modernists have turned again and again, accepting the mere historicity of what they consider 'temporary', and selecting and reinterpreting the irreducible minimum that constitutes the essence of Islamic faith they consider to be 'permanent'. The Islamic code, however archaic, is resilient enough to be recast to form the basis of the constitution of a modern progressive state. This constitution can be flexible in terms of human rights and obligations. According to Amīr ʿAlī, it embraces the scope of taxation, emphasizes the equality of all citizens before the law, consecrates the principles of self-government, renders executive authority answerable to law, which itself has two components: religious sanction and moral obligation. Because of these two components Amīr ʿAlī, unlike the Aligarh school, leans heavily on the principle of *ijmāʿ* as a chief and corrective source of Muslim jurisprudence. But the *ijmāʿ* he has in mind is of the people and the élite, and not of the *ʿulamāʾ*. Thus he has already arrived at a concept which Iqbāl and his successors were to develop in full. Through *ijmāʿ*, Amīr ʿAlī continues, Muslim law provides a principle of constitutional check on the sovereign or the executive authority. He sees the origins and the basis of an ideal Islamic state in the orthodox caliphate, suspending his Shīʿī convictions, and considers this ideal state as a historical nucleus which can be evolved, extended, and liberalized to constitute a progressive modern state.[41]

Finally, he faces the problem of the decline of Islam. The explanation he offers is based on the fundamentalist diagnosis of Walī-Allāh, the influx of extraneous elements in the Muslim creed, world view, and way of life. In history this had the effect of a vicious circle. Regional and atomistic collapses of the successor states of the caliphate were accelerated by the subversion of regional cultural elements by elements alien to Islam. Then there were regionalized challenges of history: in Spain the fanaticism of the Catholic *Reconquista* and its wanton destructiveness, in North Africa the triumph of Patristicism under the Almohads, in Central Asia the disintegration of the Tīmūrid state and the rise of the Uzbeks, in Persia the eruption of the barbarous Ghilzai Afghāns in the eighteenth century, in the Ottoman empire sterile militarism which was not conducive to cultural efflorescence. And much earlier in the heartlands of *dār al-Islām* Mongol invasions, genocides, and massacres had inflicted a

[41] *SI*, pp. 251, 278–9.

systematic cultural sterilization on the most creative phase of Islamic civilization.

Khudā Bakhsh, who translated von Kremer and Mez into English, was also, like Amīr 'Alī, very close to the western studies, but his attitude was that of acceptance and adherence to the western tradition, and therefore very different from that of Amīr 'Alī.

ḤĀLĪ AND THE HISTORICAL POEM

At the request of Sayyid Aḥmad Khān, one of his close associates, Alṭāf Ḥusayn 'Ḥālī', wrote his famous poem *Musaddas Madd-o jazr-i Islām* (The Flow and Ebb of Islam), popularly known as the *Musaddas-i Ḥālī*, in 1879. This was the first Urdu poem to depart from the tradition of conventionalized classicism, and it inaugurated a cultural renaissance and a vogue for political romanticism. Until the 'Mutiny' nineteenth-century Urdu verse had few political overtones. Immediately after it there appeared a body of stirring poetry lamenting the fate of Delhi and the overthrow of Muslim culture as represented by the élite of that city. The most personal of these poems were the lyrics of Bahādur Shāh Ẓafar (*reg.* 1837–58), the last of the Mughals, who had been dragged into the Mutiny as a figurehead almost against his will by the mutineers and the rabble of Delhi. The ruins of Delhi became the symbol and the epitome of the ruin of *dār al-Islām*, helpless against external encroachment through internal decadence. In lamenting the 'ebb' of Islam in the famous *Musaddas* Ḥālī turned nostalgically to the glories of the past. As Cantwell Smith put it: 'Ḥālī differed [from Sayyid Aḥmad Khān] most significantly in his proud reconstruction of the Islamic past, in his appeal to the Muslims' own glorious history. This is exceedingly important, for it forms the basis for the whole next period in religious development'.[42] With the publication of the *Musaddas*, revivalism and the political romanticism it generated became the dominant trend in Urdu poetry with the exception

[42] Smith, *Modern Islām in India*, p. 38.

of the *ghazal*.[43] The poem was recited aloud at political and educational conferences and on social occasions, and it was featured in bold calligraphy on the front page of daily and weekly journals. Even Ḥālī had to protest against its extravagant use.[44] In short, it engendered a surge of political propaganda.

The *Musaddas* underlines the lethargy of contemporary Islam by first turning to pagan Arabia, equally lethargic and insular, but also savage and barbarous. It was transformed within a generation into a cradle of universal culture with the advent of the Prophet, who impressed on the intransigent Arab mind the creed of the unity of God but took every precaution against his own deification. Islam's political expansion accorded with the logic of the history of civilization: it happened to fill the vacuum created by the decadence and imminent disintegration of earlier cultures, Roman, Persian, and Indian. The vital role of Islam in history was spiritual and cultural rather than political. It revived Greek science, borrowed elements from the cultures it came in contact with, assimilating these borrowings into its own cultural identity.[45] The Arab diaspora spread to distant lands; Arab geographers traversed all the known continents. The ruins of Seville, Granada, and Cordoba bear witness to their civilizing role. Spain and the Muslim east developed the sciences Europe was to inherit.[46] The glory of the civilization of Islam remained unimpaired as long as its followers retained their faith in purity.

But when extraneous impurities polluted Islam, prosperity and honour were lost and science fell into disuse. This moral and spiritual disintegration in Islam has been nowhere more palpable than in India. Decadent, inactive, a disgrace to their land, the Muslims of India 'have betrayed the noble heritage of the Arabs'. Held in contempt by their rulers, looked down upon by

[43] The form of lyrical poetry in the Muslim East.

[44] *Makātīb*, ed. M. Ismā'īl Pānīpatī, pp. 49–52.

[45] *Musaddas* (1935), pp. 15–19, 24–32.

[46] The cult of Spain introduced by Ḥālī soon developed into one of the dominant trends in revivalistic political romanticism and in Muslim historiography in India. See Aziz Ahmad, 'Islam d'Espagne et d'Inde musulmane moderne', in *Études d'orientalisme dédiées à la mémoire de Lévi-Provençal* (Paris, 1962), ii. 461–70; Smith, pp. 38, 61–62.

their non-Muslim compatriots, they have earned no position for themselves in administration or commerce or industry. They doggedly refuse to follow the example of the west which is dominating the world by unflagging effort and advancement. The Muslims of India are still content in their poverty and plight, trading on the names of their ancestors, or doing menial jobs or begging or just starving. Honest work in professions or crafts they regard as beneath their dignity; trade and agriculture they find too complicated; and service under the British is of course, according to their myopic theologians, repugnant to religious law.[47]

When a culture declines, its élite is the first to become degenerate. Muslims who are still well to do neither conserve their resources nor help the poor. The *'ulamā'* are beggars in disguise, peddling their hollow scholarship and their poverty, specializing in rudeness and intolerance, excommunicating liberal Muslims rather than trying to convert non-Muslims. A religion which was once the fountainhead of ethics has become a rigid jumble of ritual and prayer in the hands of those who regard their own traditional interpretations as more authoritative than the simple word of God or of His Prophet. The physicians cling to the obsolescent Greek pharmacopœia and ignore all the vital discoveries of modern medical science. The poets wallow in emotional filth, living as parasites on a bankrupt society. In short, the plight of Muslim society in India is an endless tale of woe. It could be and should have been quite otherwise. Under British rule they have freedom of conscience and profession, security of life and property, opportunities to travel and see the world, to enter into the free and competitive professions of industry and commerce. Leaders (like Sayyid Aḥmad Khān) have emerged to tide them over the transition to a rejuvenated existence. But if Muslim society does not mend its ways, there is only one foreseeable end—absolute disaster.[48]

Later Ḥālī added a supplement to counteract the pessimism of his poem. Muslim society had no doubt become ossified; it had

[47] *Musaddas*, pp. 42–43, 46–47, 51. [48] Ibid. pp. 58–83.

receded from the glory that was Islam; it had lost its historical magnificence. But even in its decline there was a style and dignity. It could still lay claim to a few individuals who could transform its destiny. There were signs of a new current of life in still and stagnant waters. There was some consciousness of decadence after all. It looked back at the grandeur of its past and hung its head in shame. But the highway of history passed over varied terrain, over high ground and low. The Muslim community had only to strive harder and more persistently, to regain the heights of the past, which were attainable by an uphill ascent. Our ancestors were not a superior breed. The political empire of Islam was irrevocably lost but its intellectual heritage could still be retrieved through knowledge, which can change man's life and physical environment. The quest of knowledge in Islamic history, the spirit and tradition of the great schools of Baghdad, Damascus, and Cairo, still remained the hope and the ideal of Islam today. The poem ended with an invocation to God to guide the Muslim community, to teach it to prepare itself for a better and happier future for the sake of its Prophet who came as a blessing to all mankind and who preached equality between all human beings.[49]

In Ḥālī the revivalistic note is to some extent subordinated to one of creative dynamism. In Shiblī's poems revivalism is self-sufficient and backward looking to the point of nostalgia. Most of his short 'historical' poems are anecdotal, illustrating instances of justice and egalitarianism in historical Islam. As in his more serious historiographical work, the Caliph 'Umar emerges as the ideal just ruler; but the value of justice is emphasized as the principal contribution of Islamic culture.[50] With Shiblī also begins the powerful topical poem full of rage and anguish at the aggression of western empires in Morocco, Persia, and the Ottoman dominions in the first decade of the twentieth century, and at the 'let-down' of British diplomacy in failing to defend Muslim interests abroad.

[49] Ibid. pp. 89–121, 128–9.
[50] Shiblī Nu'mānī, *Kulliyyāt* (Urdu) (Azamgarh, 1921), *passim*.

The political poem became a form of vitriolic journalism in the verse of Ẓafar ʿAlī Khān, and was one of the chief attractions of his paper *Zamīndār*. It suffered from interminable shiftings of personal ground and undeserved personal invective.

In less personal and more balanced political verse, literary or journalistic, the theme of numerous poets between 1900 and 1918 is the pan-Islamic anguish at the proposed partition of Persia, the extension and consolidation of French control in North Africa, and especially Italy's occupation of Tripoli and the Balkan war of 1912–13.[51] Between 1911 and 1919 Enver Pasha emerges in Urdu verse as a hero and the symbol of the cult of Turkey. During the first world war this theme was driven underground; it became oblique, ironical, and surreptitious; nevertheless it re-emerged with more intensive fury in 1919.

Compared with this political romanticism, which was the popular vogue, the emotions of the leaders of the Khilāfat movement, Muḥammad ʿAlī and Ḥasrat Mohānī, both of whom had spent several years in British prisons, were expressed with a subdued dignity.[52] Out of the bric-à-brac of the conventional material of the *ghazal*, an experience of personal suffering, a political maxim, a formulated ideal comes to the surface and is crystallized in poetic diction. Political suffering is transformed through the imagery of resurgence that follows all repression into an optimism which has its roots in conviction rather than emotion.

Among political satirists Akbar Allāhābādī (1846–1921) occupied a unique position in his long career. A merciless satirist, he was gifted with an unusual talent in the manipulation of rhyme, word-play, *double entendre*, nuance, and innuendo, and equipped with an irrepressible sense of humour. All this he employed in the service of an amused but stubborn conservatism. Though he was a judge of a Small Causes Court in the British Indian

[51] Represented in several anthologies such as Ilyās Baranī (Elyas Burney), ed., *Maʿārif-i millat* (1924), 6 vols.; *Jazbāt-i ḥurriyyat* (Lahore, 1921); Sha'n al-Ḥaqq Ḥaqqī, *Nashīd-i ḥurriyyat* (Karachi, 1957).

[52] Muḥ. ʿAlī, *Kalām-i Jawhar* (Delhi, 1938); Faẓl al-Ḥasan Ḥasrat Mohānī, *Kulliyyāt* (Hyderabad, 1943).

administration and was presumably a loyal civil servant, everything European or Europeanized, every institution modern or modernized was the target of his mockery. Despite this, at heart he felt a sense of the eventual doom of the traditional *mores* of the culture he idolized. Because of his satire, it is difficult to say how far he was actually committed to the uncompromising conservatism he professed. He ridiculed Sayyid Aḥmad Khān and the Aligarh College but paid a glowing tribute on his death. He gave his own children a thoroughly western education. In his serious poems there is a tone of moderation, providing a balance between conserving the values of the past and making inevitable adjustments to the needs of the future in a relentlessly changing world.[53]

Finally, in the poems of Iqbāl the political poem rose to heights and achieved a dynamic impact the like of which was unprecedented in the history of Islam. For it was the crystallization of Iqbāl's essentially poetic genius in terms of political philosophy that provided Muslim India with the criteria of self-identification and national self-definition which created the nation and state of Pakistan.

[53] Akbar Allāhābādī, *Kulliyyāt* (Karachi, 1952).

CHAPTER FIVE

THE TRADITIONALIST REVIVAL

THE GREAT SCHOOLS

THERE were three principal centres of theological education in nineteenth-century Muslim India. Most pre-eminent of these was the school of Walī-Allāh in Delhi, where his son Shāh ʿAbd al-ʿAzīz and his grandson Shāh Muḥammad Isḥāq continued his tradition with a consistently increasing shift in emphasis from speculative fundamentalism towards eclectic traditionalism. The oldest of these educational centres, and the one which was almost exclusively preoccupied with scholarship rather than society or politics, was the Farangī Maḥal at Lucknow. Finally, there was the seminary of Khayrabad. In Delhi the emphasis was principally on the teaching of Qur'ānic *tafsīr* and *ḥadīs̱*. The Farangī Maḥal had conserved the sixteenth-century Transoxanian emphasis on rationalism and jurisprudence, counterbalanced by a penchant for mysticism. Khayrabad specialized in the studies of medieval philosophy and logic.[1]

The school of Walī-Allāh suffered organizationally from the migration of Muḥammad Isḥāq to Mecca after the failure of the Mujāhidīn movement.[2] Its momentum and its mission survived in the minds and work of individual divines or scholars who attached themselves to other institutions, or retired into seclusion concentrating on the creation of a new generation of scholars to develop elements of the Walī-Allāhī tradition in a new environment. One of these scholars was Mamlūk al-ʿAlī, who joined the staff of the British-aided Delhi College and had the distinction of teaching, among others, Sayyid Aḥmad Khān and his great traditionalist opposite numbers, Muḥammad Qāsim Nānotawī and Rashīd Aḥmad Gangohī, who later founded the seminary at

[1] Maḥbūb Riẓwī, *Tā'rīkh-i Deoband* (*TD*) (1952), p. 104.
[2] See above, p. 20.

Deoband and were both disciples of another divine of the Walī-Allāhī school, Imdād-Allāh, who had for a time followed Muḥammad Isḥāq in his self-imposed exile to the Hijāz. He as well as his two disciples took some part in the Uprising of 1857, but since nothing very definite could be proved, no drastic action was taken against them.[3]

In the phase of the reconstruction of Muslim society which followed the 'Mutiny', Muḥammad Qāsim Nānotawī and a group of *'ulamā'* decided to establish a seminary at Deoband, a small town near Delhi, to conserve traditional theological learning in general and certain elements of the teachings of the school of Walī-Allāh in particular. Classes were opened in 1867, a few years earlier than those of Sayyid Aḥmad Khān's MAO College at Aligarh. As 'Ubayd-Allāh Sindhī pointed out, the two institutions were inspired by two facets of the theological heritage of Walī-Allāh.[4] The founders of Deoband emphasized the elements of orthodoxy in Walī-Allāh's thought, those of Aligarh the element of religious speculation. In dogma the *'ulamā'* of Deoband followed the Ash'arite and Māturīdī schools. In *fiqh* they were strict Ḥanafites.[5]

The objectives of the Deoband seminary, as envisaged by Nānotawī and his life-long associate Rashīd Aḥmad Gangohī, were to re-establish contact between the *'ālim* and the average Muslim, and to reorientate the Muslim community to its 'original' cultural and religious identity. A traditionalist course of studies was planned to the exclusion of modern sciences, and it was believed that the 'perfection' of the Muslim community lay in the conservation of its traditional heritage in an age in which the modern physical or rational sciences (*ma'qūlāt*) could easily be learned in a number of government institutions, but the Muslim traditional sciences (*manqūlāt*) were undergoing an unprecedented and precipitous decline. Medieval rational sciences generally accepted in classical Muslim educational curricula were included as a 'bridge' between medieval Islamic and modern

[3] Muḥ. Miyān, *'Ulamā'-i Hind*, i, *passim*.

[4] *Shāh Walī-Allāh*, p. 88.

[5] Madanī, *Naqsh-i ḥayāt*, i. 119.

western rationalism; so that a student, if he so wished, could join a modern school or university after completing his theological education at Deoband. Thus theoretically at least Deoband regarded itself at the outset as an institution complementary and preliminary to modern westernized schools and not as an antithesis. But this theory could hardly be translated into practice, except in very rare cases, because of the duration of the courses at Deoband. Modern sciences were excluded from its syllabus on the plea that the scope of studies would become too unwieldy, and possibly irreconcilable with simultaneous instruction in theological studies. Rashīd Aḥmad Gangohī was opposed to the inclusion even of the medieval rationalist sciences.[6]

As a conservative theological seminary Deoband aimed at and succeeded in attaining great distinction, unrivalled, except for al-Azhar, by any other theological school in the modern world of Islam. It comprehensively synthesized the traditions of the schools of Delhi, Lucknow, and Khayrabad. Its syllabus covered Arabic and Persian grammar, prosody and literature, history of Islam, logic, Greco-Arab philosophy, *kalām*, dialectics, disputation, medieval geometry and astronomy, Greco-Arab medicine, jurisprudence, the *ḥadīṣ* and *tafsīr*. The courses spread over ten years in the earlier phase and were later reduced to six. The entire syllabus consisted of 106 texts, and the students were classed by the textbooks they studied rather than the years of their study.[7]

Judicial rulings on the problems referred to by members of the Muslim public developed in 1893 into a Department of *iftā'* (juristic rulings). It covered a wide range of legalities, minutiae of ritual, social, or political problems as well as decisions of *panchāyats* and official courts that came under the purview of Muslim personal or family law. Between 1911 and 1951 nearly 150,000 *fatāwī* were pronounced by the department in Deoband.[8]

Muḥammad Qāsim Nānotawī (d. 1879), the chief promoter of

[6] *Makātīb-i Rashīdī* (Delhi), p. 27; Manāẓir Aḥsan Gīlānī, *Sawāniḥ-i Qāsimī* (1953), ii. 292–3.

[7] *TD*, pp. 104–7; Gīlānī, ii. 286.

[8] *TD*, pp. 130–2; Gīlānī, i. 386–7.

Deoband, seems, according to the consensus of the earlier sources of his life and work, more an intelligent and attractive personality than a profound theological scholar. He was possibly registered at the Delhi College, but since there is no trace of any awareness of modern sciences or a modern methodology in his later academic life and work, it seems likely that he studied under Mamlūk al-ʿAlī privately and not at that college. As a traditionalist *ʿālim* he stands opposed not only to the speculative trend of the Aligarh modernists but also to the Ahl-i Ḥadīs̱ who minimized or rejected the authority of the great schools. Nānotawī's traditionalist refutation or rather confutation of the fifteen principles of *tafsīr* laid down by Sayyid Aḥmad Khān is an unoriginal affirmation of the orthodox Ḥanafī juristic and theological view on these points, and represents the epitome of Deoband's reaction to Aligarh modernism.[9]

The views of Nānotawī's close associate, Rashīd Aḥmad Gangohī, who rejected any association with the Aligarh reformer, were closer to Walī-Allāhī fundamentalism in their main emphasis and more hostile to Sayyid Aḥmad Khān's speculative 'naturalism'. He conceded that Sayyid Aḥmad Khān might be a well-wisher of Muslims but regarded his religious ideas as a 'deadly poison' for Islam. The total rejection of any association with Sayyid Aḥmad Khān included a rejection of his political separatism in India, and the first juristic injunction pronounced by a Deoband *ʿālim* in favour of Muslim co-operation with the Indian National Congress and the Hindus, provided it did not lead to any infringement of the canon law or to the humiliation of the Muslim community.[10]

On such social questions as remarriage of widows, women's legal rights of inheritance, and the rejection of financially ruinous ceremonies borrowed from Hinduism, the Deoband group preserved the fundamentalist heritage of the *Mujāhidīn* movement.

[9] Muḥ. Yaʿqūb, *Sawāniḥ*, reprinted in Gīlānī, i. 28–29. For Nānotawī's refutation of the fifteen points, see above, p. 43, n. 30. See also Muḥ. Miyān, *'Ulamā'-i Ḥaqq* (1946), i. 82 ff.

[10] Miyān, *'Ulamā'-i Ḥaqq*, pp. 98–100; Hafeez Malik, *Moslem Nationalism in India and Pakistan* (1963), p, 196.

In the rejection of *bidaʿ* and insistence on conformity to the *sunna* their views did not differ from those of Sayyid Aḥmad Khān in his pre-modernist phase. According to Nānotawī, *bidʿa* could be defined as an alteration to, an addition to, or a deduction from a given *sunna*. Alteration in a given dogma or ritual was a major *bidʿa*. Changes in theological principles or minutiae could be defined respectively as major or minor *bidaʿ*.[11]

Deoband's anti-fundamentalism consisted of practices disapproved by Walī-Allāh and the Wahhābīs, such as visits to saints' tombs and belief in their power of intercession. More seriously it manifested itself in Nānotawī's negation of Walī-Allāh's efforts to create an interjuristic discipline of Muslim theology and law and his rigid adherence to the school of Abū Ḥanīfa.

Nanotawī, who was an impressive public speaker, took an active part in public discussions of religious controversies about the anti-Islamic polemics of Christian as well as Hindu Ārya Samāj missionaries, and in 1876 he participated in a 'religious fair' in which his chief adversary was the Reverend Tārā Chand, a Hindu convert to Christianity. He sent challenges of public disputation to Swāmī Dayānand Saraswatī, the founder of the Ārya Samāj movement.[2] Despite its deep-rooted nationalist sympathies, Deoband entered the arena of religious controversies once again when movements of Shuddhi and Sanghaṭan were organized by the Ārya Samāj for the mass conversion of Muslims in 1926.

On mystical experience in general the Deobandī position had been close to that of the theologians of Farangī Maḥal in their veneration of orthodox Ṣūfīs and opposition to the Wahhābīs. Unlike the latter, the Deobandīs believed in the physical survival of prophets and saints after their death and in the immortality of their bodies as well as their souls. On the question of the finality of Muḥammad's prophethood the Deobandīs took a

[11] Gīlānī, ii. 44–47.

[12] *Guft-o gū-yi maẕhabī* (*c.* 1930) is a commentary on Nānotawī's disputation with Hindu and Christian missionaries held in 1871.

strongly orthodox view, possibly in reaction to the prophetic claims of Mirzā Ghulām Aḥmad of Qādiyān, founder of the Aḥmadī sect. The finality of Muḥammad's prophethood was triple in nature—in rank, in chronology, and in space.

Maḥmūd al-Ḥasan (1850–1921) is by far the most outstanding figure in the generation that followed Nānotawī and Gangohī. Under his direction Deoband achieved an international reputation and attracted students from other parts of the Islamic world, and the gulf between Deoband and Aligarh narrowed after 1910 to the extent of exchanging scholars with each other.[13] But in 1920 Maḥmūd al-Ḥasan shared the anger of Muḥammad 'Alī and other leaders of the Caliphate movement at the dependence of Aligarh's finances on government grants and consequently the subservience of that institution's administrators. This led to the foundation of the Jāmi'a-i Milliyya-i Islāmiyya (Muslim National University) as an institution breaking with Aligarh's loyalist tradition. Maḥmūd al-Ḥasan's second complaint against Aligarh was the old orthodox one, the cultural 'Christianization' of its students and their 'heretical scepticism'.[14]

In contrast to the Aligarh movement the attitude of Maḥmūd al-Ḥasan on the question of *jihād* was classical and unapologetic, 'as rationally necessary for the welfare and betterment of human society'.[15] He has been credited with planning a call and programme (*da'wat*) for Muslim India before the first world war when the political movement of the Indian National Congress had not yet become revolutionary. He opened a chain of theological schools for this purpose in the North-West Frontier area and sent his *agents provocateurs*, notably 'Ubayd-Allāh Sindhī, to Afghanistan.[16]

Deoband meanwhile rose to the stature of one of the most outstanding theological seminaries in the Muslim world. It received a visit from Rashīd Riḍā, and forged links with the *'ulamā'*

[13] Presidential Address at inauguration of Muslim National University at Aligarh, 29 Oct. 1920; Madanī, ii. 257.

[14] Madanī, ii. 257.

[15] Ibid. p. 221.

[16] Ibid. pp. 135–6; Ghulām Rasūl Mihr, *Sarguzasht-i mujāhidīn* (Lahore, 1956), pp. 552–3.

of al-Azhar. In 1947 50 out of its 1,350 students were foreigners from South Africa, Malaya, Central Asia, Afghanistan, and Iran. 'Abd al-Razzāq, who rose to be the Chief Qāẓī of Afghanistan, was a student at Deoband.[17] Within the subcontinent it produced most of the great *'ulamā'* of the second quarter of the twentieth century: Ashraf 'Alī Thānawī, who popularized traditional Islam among the less educated, apart from his authorship of monumental theological works; Ḥusayn Aḥmad Madanī, who succeeded Maḥmūd al-Ḥasan as the Director of the Deoband Seminary, and his colleague and political opponent, Shabbīr Aḥmad 'Us̱mānī, who was appointed Pakistan's *Shaykh al-Islām.* Other Deoband scholars include 'Ubayd-Allāh Sindhī and Ḥifẓ al-Raḥmān Sihwārwī, who developed theories of Islamic socialism; the eminent physician Ḥakīm Ajmal Khān, S̱anā-Allāh Amritsarī, who later joined the Ahl-i Ḥadīs̱ movement; and Iḥtishām al-Ḥaqq Thānawī, Pakistan's influential conservative traditionalist.

Nadwat al-'Ulamā', which developed into another great seminary of Islamic India in recent times, was founded at Lucknow in 1894 by Shiblī Nu'mānī and a group of other *'ulamā'* who had responded more sensitively and positively to the stimulus and challenge of western sciences. It was conceived as a middle-of-the-road institution between the extremes of Aligarh's 'secularism' and Deoband's rigid conservatism. The central problem which had inspired its creation was set forth by Shiblī in his address to its First Congress, as essentially the determination of the role of the *'ulamā'* and the nature of their obligations to the Muslim community in a historical situation which was fundamentally different from that experienced by Islam in its long history. In the non-Islamic British state in India the *'ulamā'* no longer constituted the judiciary except in matters of personal law. The functions of religion and politics had been separated. Unprepared to readjust their role and their learning to this challenging state of affairs, the *'ulamā'* of Muslim India had sunk into apathy and fossilized dogma, concerning themselves

[17] *TD*, pp. 90–102.

exclusively with insignificant minutiae of ritual and in fruitless disputations. Instead they might have given the Muslim community in India a moral lead. They might have continued the reformist mission of Walī-Allāh, preaching against superstition and extravagance. They might have tried to propagate a broad-minded view of Islam among the masses. Atheism which was spreading in the wake of a secular government was neither the responsibility of the British government nor within its control. It was eroding Christianity in Europe as it was eroding Islam in India. It was clearly the responsibility of religious leaders to counterbalance these scientific trends of agnosticism, specticism, and atheism, and they should strive to offer an enlightened interpretation of religion. With this objective in view, the *ʿulamā'* of India should combine and organize themselves. They have, indeed, every right to hold individual or sectarian opinions, but these differences need not go beyond the specific points of detail. Jurists had their differences in the early centuries of Islam; but these did not divide them into hostile camps. Relegating points of doctrinal difference to the background, the *ʿulamā'* of modern India could still have a common platform: to reorganize Arabic and Persian studies in the government schools, and to exert pressure on the government for a revision if not a reversal of its legal policy, reviving the Anglo-Muhammadan law of the early days of the East India Company and suspending the operation of British common law. The *ʿulamā'* should control and efficiently administer *waqfs*. They might continue to indulge in their favourite pastime of preaching conformity, but this should take the form of rationally convincing persuasion and not rigidly formalistic fanaticism. Their principal intellectual responsibility was, however, to develop a new *ʿilm al-kalām*, a modern system of theological dialectics to meet the challenges of atheism, just as the medieval scholars al-Rāzī, al-Ghazzālī, and Averroës integrated Greek thought into a framework which was as rationalistic as it was basically Islamic.[18]

[18] Shiblī Nuʿmānī, Address to First Congress of Nadwat al-ʿUlamā' held on 12 Apr. 1895, reprinted in *Rasā'il* (Amritsar, 1911), pp. 1–16.

Aligarh's response to the foundation of the Nadwat al-'Ulamā' was sympathetic. Shiblī had been a link between them. Muḥsin al-Mulk voiced the official view of Aligarh that the modernists themselves were conscious of the dangers of the study of modern science, which, without the counterbalancing discipline of a rationalized study of theology, might lead the younger generation of Muslims to sceptical pessimism and to heresy or atheism.[19] The Aligarh leaders agreed with the organizers of the Nadwa also on the feasibility of national rather than individual enterprise in education, and on the necessity of arranging congresses of '*ulamā*' of all Muslim sects, holding all shades of opinion, to discuss with full freedom of expression the challenges they faced in common in relation to the new problems of their community. They endorsed the view that Islam has no material philosophy or astronomy or mathematics of its own which could not be superseded; that it is a spiritual and an ethical discipline which can easily accommodate and coexist with modern physical and social sciences. Sponsors of the Nadwa were encouraged in their projects of bringing together the Indian '*ulamā*' and the students of the new theological schools to study modernist trends in other parts of the world of Islam, especially the *al-Manār* group in Egypt, to divert their scholarly endeavours from the minutiae of ritualistic dogma to the broader vision of their own heritage made available by scholarly editions of Islamic classics published in Europe and the Levant, which would imply a complete revision of the structure of the syllabus for theological studies in India.[20]

Muḥsin al-Mulk, however, warned the sponsors of the Nadwat al-'Ulamā' against Shiblī's historical obsession with medieval rationalism as a response to the challenges of the modern world. Medieval knowledge was rooted in metaphysics and was no doubt closer to the essence of religion with which it could be harmonized. If there was a conflict between religion and medieval

[19] Speech, supporting resolution of sympathy on objectives of Nadwat al-'Ulamā' in 19th session of Muhammedan Educational Conference at Aligarh, 29 Dec. 1894 (Agra, 1895), pp. 4–7.

[20] Ibid. pp. 7–8, 15–16, 40–42.

philosophy, the latter had to retreat, and if it refused to do so, its adherents could be suppressed or persecuted. In modern times the situation was radically different. Science can submit to no confines or limitations; it is not merely speculative, it is pragmatic, demonstrable and experimental. No Inquisition can inhibit its growth. It has confuted the traditional concepts of religion to such an extent that only two alternatives remain: either to allow religion to die a natural death, or to reinterpret it in the light of the new knowledge.[21]

The Nadwat al-'Ulamā' was, however, not always responsive to the overtures of Aligarh. A letter sent by Sayyid Aḥmad Khān welcoming its inauguration was suppressed. Shiblī, who was the main link between Aligarh and the Nadwa, and who actively took charge of its administration in 1904, turned against Aligarh in 1908 under pan-Islamic influences. The Nadwat al-'Ulamā', which was a unique experiment of middle-of-the-road theological liberalism, produced a few scholars of considerable stature like Sayyid Sulaymān Nadwī, but in its drift away from Aligarh modernism towards conservative orthodoxy, in time its scholars and their work became almost indistinguishable from those of Deoband. One of its outgrowths, the research institute called Dār al-Muṣannifīn of Azamgarh, however, became a publishing institution of considerable significance, keeping Islamic orthodoxy in India in touch with at least the fringe and the frontier of modern western thought and methodology.

By 1920 the scholars of the Nadwa had adopted an attitude directly repudiatory of the exegetical rationalism of Sayyid Aḥmad Khān and the Aligarh modernists. This trend is reflected in the articles published in the Nadwa journal *Ma'ārif*. 'Abd al-Salām Nadwī took up the non-orthodox position that it was wrong to stretch the verses of the Qur'ān to bring their interpretation in line with the theories of modern western knowledge and to call Islam a 'religion of nature' in that sense. This is to confuse the issues. Religion and science operate in distinctly separate spheres. Religion is concerned only with the faith and

[21] *TA*, i. 304–18.

action of man. Science is not primarily concerned with these but with the nature and property of things. A person professing religion may have to face a tension between materialism and spirituality. But this would not really be a conflict between religion and science. It would rather be a conflict in which he is psychologically involved as an individual. Islam is a 'religion of nature' in a different sense, as being closer to human nature by its juxtaposition of spiritual and physical life, and is in this sense a 'natural' synthesis of both.[22]

The Farangī Maḥal in Lucknow, the oldest theological seminary in modern Muslim India, chose to continue its pre-modernist, essentially educational mission, unperturbed by intellectual controversies between the modernists and the traditionalists. It combined a medieval rationalistic heritage with a proclivity towards Ṣūfism, which explains much of its detachment from controversy. One of its founders, Mullā Niẓām al-dīn, compiled the famous *Niẓāmiyya* syllabus which most traditionalist schools followed. It included the study of Arabic and Persian grammar, medieval mathematics and philosophy, *fiqh*, *kalām*, exegetical science and tradition, though there was much greater emphasis on the *ma'qūlāt* than on the *manqūlāt* sciences.

NEO-TRADITIONALISM: THE AHL-I ḤADIṢ

Contacts with the Hijāz, which had been facilitated by western navigation in the Indian Ocean by the beginning of the seventeenth century, had transplanted to India the discipline of the specialized study of *ḥadīṣ*. An Indian school established in Mecca under the direction of Sayyid 'Alī Muttaqī and his disciple 'Abd al-Wahhāb Muttaqī formed the first link between the Hijāz and India for the promotion of this discipline.[23] The messianistic movements of the later sixteenth-century Muslim India, which could be termed collectively the Alfī ('millennary') movements, tending towards heterodoxies marking the end of a

[22] 'Dīn-i fiṭrat yā dīn-i ḥanīf', *Ma'ārif* (Azamgarh), vi/1 (1920), pp. 51–56.
[23] See above, p. 2.

millennium after the Prophet's advent, and including such diversified manifestations as the Mahdawī movement at Jaunpur, the Rawshanniyya sect among the tribesmen of the North-Western Frontier, and the Divine Faith (*Dīn-i Ilāhī*) a syncretistic heresy devised by the liberal Mughal emperor Akbar the Great, had weakened the image of the Prophet in Indian Islam.[24] Emphasis on the specialized study of *ḥadīs̱* by the eminent divine ʿAbd al-Ḥaqq Muḥaddis̱ of Delhi was a reversal of these trends.[25]

In the early eighteenth century Walī-Allāh brought back from his studies in the Muslim holy cities not merely a renewed emphasis on the conservative study of *ḥadīs̱*, but the principle of its right of primacy over the rulings of juristic schools.[26] This particular trend in Walī-Allāhī fundamentalism, though rigidly balanced in his own writings and qualified by his emphasis on analysis and *ijtihād*, formed the starting-point of a movement for an exclusive and comparatively uncritical preoccupation with the traditional corpus of the *ḥadīs̱* by a group of nineteenth-century *ʿulamā*', the most prominent of them being Ṣiddīq Ḥasan Khān and Naẕīr Ḥusayn, who regarded it as the principal source of law and the ideal guide to social behaviour and individual piety.

The creed of these *ʿulamā*', the Ahl-i Ḥadīs̱, has been stated by Ṣiddīq Ḥasan Khān as that of a group which does not follow, either in broad principles or in minutiae of canon law, any of the four juristic schools, and which in theological dogma subscribes to the views of neither the Ashʿarites nor the Māturīdīs nor the Ḥanbalites, but binds itself to the clear injunctions of the Qur'ān and the word and practice (*ḥadīs̱* and *sunna*) of the Prophet. In this respect he admits the likeness of the Ahl-i Ḥadīs̱ to the externalist Ẕāhirites, with the difference that unlike the latter they accept the Ṣūfī doctrine of mystical illumination while rejecting the speculative excesses of Ṣūfism.[27]

[24] H. Blochmann, Introd. to his Eng. trans. of Abu'l Faẕl ʿAllāmī's *Ā'īn-i Akbarī*, i, xi. ff.

[25] Khalīq Aḥmad Niẕāmī, *Ḥayāt-i ʿAbd al-Ḥaqq Muḥaddis̱ Dihlawī* (Delhi, 1953), pp. 242–7.

[26] *Ḥujjat*, i. 33; ii. 1–2.

[27] *Kitāb al-muʿtaqad al-muntaqad* (1887), p. 4.

The Ahl-i Ḥadīs̱ accepted the entire corpus of the Prophet's *ḥadīs̱* in the classical collections as genuine and repudiated the speculative scepticism of the Aligarh modernists, 'who lack the capacity of determining the correct *ḥadīs̱* by comparing it scientifically with the incorrect'. Only the classical specialists in *ḥadīs̱*, such as Bukhārī and Muslim, were equipped with the resources, the evidence, and the methodology for discriminating between the genuine and attributed *dicta* of the Prophet.[28] The science of *ḥadīs̱* is for the moderns a repetitive and not a critical science. Nevertheless it is the most distinguished of all human sciences.[29]

Knowledge can be of two kinds, beneficial or futile. The former had been commended in the Qur'ān, but the latter condemned as the preoccupation of those who allow themselves to be misled. The same distinctive criteria, beneficial and futile, are applicable to religious studies. Futility in religious studies lies in the direction of exegetical disputations and in rationalist speculation on dialectical criteria attempting to analyse or define the divine Self, as by the Mu'tazilites. The knowledge of the ancients is superior to that of the moderns because they were closer to the times of the Prophet, who is the exclusive source of all religious authority. The intellectual exercise of the modernists who indulge in minutiae of far-fetched dialectics trying to supersede the ancients is futile. *Bid'a*, classical or modern, is the antithesis of *sunna*, the practice of the Prophet, and must be rejected under all circumstances. The Ahl-i Ḥadīs̱ regard the classically condoned 'commendable innovation' (*bid'a ḥasana*) as equally repugnant as it has no precedent in the life and thought of the Prophet.[30]

The credo of the Ahl-i Ḥadīs̱ was belief in God, His books, His prophets, and His angels as enjoined in the Qur'ān. The belief in God was an indivisible totality embracing all His attributes mentioned in the Qur'ān and the *ḥadīs̱* 'without modification, selection, suspension, symbolization or intellectualization'.

28 Ibid. pp. 6–14.

29 Ṣiddīq Ḥasan Khān, *'Āqibat al-muttaqīn* (1904), p. 16.

30 *al-Mu'taqad al-muntaqad*, pp. 5–10, 161–4.

This concept of the deity would reject the rationalist Muʿtazilite and the traditionalist Ashʿarite positions alike.[31]

Divine grace manifests itself to humanity by three signs: Islam, *īmān* (faith), and *iḥsān* (beneficence). A Muslim can progress from the formal profession of Islam to the deeper religious essence of *īmān* only if his life in word, deed, and intuition is guided by the word of God and the Prophet's *ḥadīs̱*, the two sources of conformity for the rectitude of thought and action, leading to the sincerity of intent (*ikhlāṣ*) which the *ʿulamāʾ* call *iḥsān* and the mystics *sulūk* (mystical aspiration). The good life of a Muslim has three components, faith, piety, and virtuous action. In these he can be guided only by an unswerving obedience to God and beneficent treatment of his creatures. A man comes to a good or bad end according to the preponderance of his good or bad deeds. A sinful Muslim cannot be placed outside the pale of Islam; his faith is nevertheless defective.[32]

The life of a pious Muslim is a life of 'conformity', a term which in the *lexique technique* of the Ahl-i Ḥadīs̱ does not mean *taqlīd*, which they repudiate as vehemently as do the Aligarh modernists or the fundamentalist Wahhābīs, but a conformist obedience (*ittibāʿ*) to norms of the life of the Prophet to the point of absolute self-indentification with it.[33] Juristic traditionalism is a growth of accretions accumulated three centuries after the advent of the Prophet, and is in certain cases false to the extent of polytheism.[34] Piety consists in sincerity, truthfulness, and honesty of intent, in following the Qur'ān and the *sunna*, in exemplary life which might be a beacon to others, in quest of knowledge and scholarship (especially in the science of *ḥadīs̱*), in associating with and deference for the *ʿulamāʾ*, in impeccable conformity to the minutiae of all prescribed ritual, including the *jihād*, and in conformity to an exemplary pattern of peaceful domestic life.[35]

[31] *ʿĀqibat al-muttaqīn*, p. 4.
[32] *Ḥaṣṣ al-insān* (1889), p. 11.
[33] *ʿĀqibat al muttaqīn*, pp. 3–13.
[34] *al-Muʿtaqad al-muntaqad*, p. 16.
[35] *ʿĀqibat al-muttaqīn*, pp. 10–20, 25–103, 158 and *passim*.

Man is regarded responsible between the given possibilities of good and evil, and yet the Ahl-i Ḥadīs̱ not only deny him the exercise of free will, but indulge in recurrent polemics against classical Qadarite anti-determinism[36] which had been revived in a modernistic form in contemporary Muslim India.

The religious thought of the Ahl-i Ḥadīs̱ reveals a profound sensitiveness to pain and suffering in this world and a pious apprehension of retribution in the world to come. Ethical activism and the emphasis on piety is almost overshadowed by an all-embracing pessimism which derives heavily from the Meccan *sūras* of the Qur'ān and certain *ḥadīs̱* sources. There is an undercurrent of deterministic involvement with the fear of the forthcoming end of the world, the Day of Judgement, and the passionate necessity for repentance.[37] Ṣiddīq Ḥasan Khān's formulation of pietistic ethics is founded essentially on the spiritual involvement with life after death, an apprehension of the approaching end of the world, and with the religious and moral duties of the Muslims to gain admittance into paradise. Since man's creation and the assignment of his role in this world was according to a pre-ordained plan, man has been given a religious and ethical code recommending certain practices which assist, and prohibiting others which prevent, the living of a holy life; and if in his weakness he errs, he can obtain divine remission by penitence.

In history, as in politics, the pietistic quietism of the Ahl-i Ḥadīs̱ had a horror of involvement in anarchy which interferes with the good life of the individual as of the community. 'You should break your bows and arrows in times of trouble'. A perfect Muslim should never participate in *fitna* (chaos and anarchy), whether political or religious. *Fitna* operates in a movement of tyranny and excess aimed at the undesirable, and might lead to unbelief, sin, disgrace, breakdown of morality and social turmoil. *Fitna* can take two forms: it can be internal in an individual or external in society.[38] The history of Islam is plagued by

[36] *al-Mu'taqad al-muntaqad*, pp. 170–8 and *passim*.

[37] *Mahw al-hawba bi-īs̱ār* (Benares, 1890); *Khalq al-insān* (Agra, 1889), pp. 3–11.

[38] Ṣiddīq Ḥasan Khān, *Iqtirāb al-sā'a* (1904), pp. 5–9.

anarchic evils which herald the approach of the Day of Judgement. These began, in fact, immediately after the death of the Prophet (632). Among these anarchic upheavals are such historical landmarks as the murder of the third orthodox Caliph ʿUthmān (656), the civil wars during the rule of ʿAlī (656–61), the apostasy and uprising of the Khārijites, the abdication of Ḥasan b. ʿAlī in favour of the Umayyad Muʿāwiya in 661, which marked the end of the real caliphate and the beginning of monarchy in Islam, the massacre of Ḥusayn ibn ʿAlī and his handful of followers at Karbala by the Umayyads in 680, and later the desecration and destruction of the *kaʿba* during their campaigns against ʿAbd-Allāh ibn Zubayr (683). Even the overthrow of the Umayyads and the foundation of the ʿAbbāsid power was rooted in plans and actions of anarchic upheaval. Under the ʿAbbāsids and after them the history of Islam remained a chain of nightmares, dotted with the rise and depredations of the Carmathians, the onslaught of the abomination of abominations, the Mongols, who included among their 'progeny' the Mughal emperors of India, the rise of the Shīʿīs, 'who are polytheists according to *ḥadīs̱*' and whose excesses led to the decline and fall of Lucknow, the rise of messianistic anti-Christs who claimed to be prophets or Mahdīs and founded apostatic sects. To this category belong the Shīʿī extremists (*ghulāt*), the Fāṭimids, the Ḥulūlīs, who believe in divine incarnation, the Alfī heretic Mahdī of Jaunpur in sixteenth-century India, modern false messiahs like the Mahdī of the Sudan or Mirzā Ghulām Aḥmad of Qādiyān, and last but not least the 'modern prophet of nature-worshippers', Sayyid Aḥmad Khān. In short the entire history of Islam appeared to Ṣiddīq Ḥasan Khān and the Ahl-i Ḥadīs̱ as a senseless, continuous chaos, mischief, an anarchy spread over 1,300 years, a precipitous falling away from the perfections of the days when the Prophet lived on this earth, the golden age of humanity, to the final and inevitable annihilation of the Day of Judgement.[39] Neo-traditionalist orthodoxy thus travelled to the extreme opposite of the revivalistic glorification of historical Islam by Shiblī,

[39] Ibid. pp. 2–4, 16–38.

Amīr 'Alī, and Ḥālī. Modern movements in Islam appeared to Ṣiddīq Ḥasan Khān as the heresies of a mushroom crop of anti-Christs and among the signs of the close approach of Doomsday. These signs were the 'reversal of the laws' of religion and conformity laid down by the Prophet, and such manifestations as a state of affairs 'when women would be supreme and fools shall be lords' as in present times.[40]

With all their horror of *fitna*, chaos and uprising, with all their passionate attachment to quietism, the pacifism of the Ahl-i Ḥadīs̱ was not entirely non-violent. They accepted *jihād* in certain circumstances, not only as a fact of life but as an act of piety. Unlike the modernists they offer no apologetics to explain it as a defensive institution. The purity of purpose in *jihād* lies only in the principle that it should be waged 'for the sake of God' and not in quest of booty. It cannot be waged against a Muslim ruler. It is beneficent only when it is intended to propagate Islam, a view which is again exactly the opposite of that of the modernists. It can only be waged in absolute obedience to the reigning caliph. *Jihād* on the high seas, presumably because it may lead to the control of the sea routes to the Hijāz by the Muslims, is twice as meritorious as that on land.[41]

Much of the life and practice of the leaders of the Ahl-i Ḥadīs̱ fell short of their idealistic theories. Ṣiddiq Ḥasan Khān regarded association with rulers, Muslim or non-Muslim, as morally perilous,[42] yet he married the ruling princess of Bhopal, where his position was made uncomfortable by his enemies who accused him of being Wahhābī at a time when Wahhābism was considered suspect to the extent of being treasonable by the British Indian government. His colleague Naẕīr Ḥusayn had been involved in the 'Mutiny'. His explanation and defence of Wahhābism was not very different from that of Sayyid Aḥmad Khān in defining the term 'Wahhābī' in popular Indian theological parlance as the antithesis of *bid'atī*, an innovator.[43]

[40] Ibid. p. 40; *Ṣalāḥ-i ẕāt al-bayn* (1891), pp. 4–8, 16, 26–34.
[41] *'Āqibat al-muttaqīn*, pp. 109–12.
[42] Ibid. pp. 172–5, 199.
[43] *Tarjumān-i Wahhābiyyat* (1897), pp. 3–4, 14–25, 32, 49.

The main polemical attack on the Ahl-i Ḥadīs̱ was launched by a fundamentalist splinter-group which called itself Ahl al-Qur'ān. It relied entirely on the chapter and verse of the scripture. The Ahl-i Ḥadīs̱ had made themselves vulnerable in dogma in their excessive championship of *ḥadīs̱* by trying to make a distinction between the word of God and the word of the Prophet; by describing the first as 'open revelation' (*waḥy-i jalī*) and the latter (*ḥadīs̱*) as 'concealed' (i.e. implicit) revelation, the second elaborating the first.[44] The Ahl-i Ḥadīs̱ had thus exposed themselves to the charge not only of revelational dualism, but of promoting a dogma which in logical analysis would present the Prophetic intellect itself as schizophrenic. The position taken up by 'Abd-Allāh Chakrālawī, leader of the Ahl al-Qur'ān, movement was that the Qur'ān itself was the most perfect source of tradition (*aḥsan ḥadīs̱*) and could be exclusively followed. The Prophet could receive only one form of *waḥy*, and that was the Qur'ān. Therefore there could not possibly be two divergent categories of his observations or injunctions as a Prophet. Any other remarks or actions were relevant only to his human situation. The Qur'ān comprehensively covered all the basic injunctions for Muslims, and by implication left them free in other matters to exercise their own judgement. It was the only record of divine wisdom (*ḥikma*), the only source of the Prophet's teaching. It superseded and made redundant the entire corpus of *ḥadīs̱*.[45]

Counter-polemics were written by an Ahl-i Ḥadīs̱ scholar Muḥammad Ḥusayn Baṭālawī, and the controversy between him and Chakrālawī reached such a pitch of virulence that the government of India had to intervene to protect Chakrālawī's life.[46] It left a durable impression on the dogmatics of the later theologians of the Ahl-i Ḥadīs̱ movement, and shift in emphasis from *ḥadīs̱* to the Qur'ān is discernible in their writings.

S̱anā-Allāh Amritsarī begins attacking Aligarh modernists

[44] 'Abd-Allāh Chakrālawī, *Ishā'at al-Qur'ān* (Lahore, 1902), p. 36.
[45] Ibid. pp. 35–49.
[46] Ibid. pp. 84–85; Muḥ. Ḥusayn Baṭālawī, *Ishā'at al-sunna* (1902).

and the Ahl al-Qur'ān with an affirmation of the generally accepted principle that a thorough knowledge of classical Arabic is absolutely essential before any exegesis is attempted. He accuses Sayyid Aḥmad Khān of misunderstanding and therefore misrepresenting the eschatology and the angelology of the Qur'ān, of attributing meanings to the Qur'ānic verses which would have been quite incomprehensible to the Arabs of the Prophet's day and age, according to whose measure of understanding its language and idiom were devised. Qur'ānic exegesis has to be literal to be accurate. It cannot be so if it tends towards allegorical or symbolical explanation.[47]

The *ḥadīs̱*, argues Amritsarī, is recognized as an indisputable source of law in the Qur'ān itself, as an explanation of the divine word, and in its own right. The relationship of a *ḥadīs̱* to the Qur'ān could be of three kinds. It could be in harmony with and explanatory to a Qur'ānic text, in which case it was totally binding. Or it might lay down an injunction not found in the Qur'ān, in which case it was complementary. Or else it might contradict a Qur'ānic injunction, in which case the interpretations of various classical jurists and compilers of *ḥadīs̱* must be studied, and instead of rejecting such a *ḥadīs̱* totally, it should be interpreted in such manner that its 'apparent contradiction' with the Qur'ānic law is either removed or resolved by interpretation. In short, Amritsarī reserves for his group the right of extravagant speculative juggling with *ḥadīs̱*, denying to the modernists the right of similar speculation in Qur'ānic exegesis. He, however, concedes that the possibilities of exegetical interpretation, though they are necessarily confined by linguistic and traditionalist disciplines are, theoretically at least, infinitely extensive. In the case of 'vague verses' (*āyāt mutashābihāt*) of the Qur'ān, every age and law can try to find explanations of them, as the classical exegetes generally disagree on their precise meaning. This was the largest concession in principle the neo-traditionalists ever made to the modernists.[48]

The Ahl-i Ḥadīs̱ movement survives to the present day,

[47] *Āyāt-i mutashābihāt* (1904), pp. 4–9. [48] Ibid. pp. 10–26.

though it has not produced much in the way of remarkable thinking. One of its leaders in Pakistan has been Dā'ūd Ghaznawī, who was member of the Punjab Legislative Assembly in the 1950s.[49]

[49] Ibrāhīm Mīr Siyālkoṭī, *Tā'rīkh-i Ahl-i ḥadīs̱* (1953), pp. 447–8.

CHAPTER SIX

CALIPHATE AND PAN-ISLAMISM

THE FIRST PHASE (1870–1910)

THE involvement of all cross-currents of Indo-Muslim religious and political thought, conservative, moderate, and modernist, in the pan-Islamic movement and with the image of the Ottoman caliphate, between 1870 and 1924 was a response to the psychological pull of extra-Indian Islam. Its psychological significance lay partly in relation to a feeling of insecurity in the midst of Hindu majority and in a feeling of humiliation in relation to the successful advance of the western empires at the expense of *dār al-Islām*. It revealed itself in a special interest in historical Islam's successful encounter with Europe: Moorish Spain and the Ottoman empire. There was an undercurrent of historical heritage in this attitude towards the Ottomans. But it was not until the treaty of Küchük Kaynarja,[1] signed in 1774, after the enforced separation of the Crimea from the Ottoman empire, that the Ottoman sultan's claim to be the caliph of all the Muslims was advanced by the Turks and accepted by the Russians. 'The High Contracting Parties thus tacitly agreed to accept as applicable the Western distinction between "temporal" and "spiritual" power.'[2] Although Shāh Walī-Allāh, who believed strongly in the necessity of universal caliphate, considered it in accordance with the classical theory as the exclusive privilege of the Quraysh, Indo-Muslim orthodoxy began to take an interest in the Ottoman claim to the caliphate during the 1840s. His grandson, Shāh Muḥammad Isḥāq, migrated to the Hijāz in 1841 and undertook to support Ottoman political policies. With him begins the phase

[1] Turkish text in Ahmed Cevdet, *Waqā'i' Devlet-i 'Āliye* (Istanbul, 1855), i. 56; see also GB. Foreign Office, *Treaties . . . between Turkey and Foreign Powers* (1855).

[2] RIIA, *Survey 1925*, i. 36.

in which the *'ulamā'* of the Walī-Allāhī school and later the orthodox schools of Deoband and Nadwat al-'Ulamā' almost implicitly gave the Ottoman claim to the universal Islamic caliphate a religious recognition in India.[3]

During the century which began with the treaty of Küchük Kaynarja and ended with the accession of 'Abd al-Ḥamīd II in 1876, the Ottoman claim ceased to be merely titular and became an active factor in international politics. During the Uprising of 1857 the British obtained a proclamation from the Ottoman caliph advising the Indian Muslims to remain loyal to his British allies. British policy in India was to encourage a pro-Turkish attitude in Muslim India from the Crimean War to 1878. Already by 1876 the Indian Muslims were trying to influence the British government in the direction of a pro-Turkish policy.[4] Indo-Muslim agitation during the Russo-Turkish war of 1877 was reflected in the Urdu press, and huge sums were contributed by Indian Muslims to be sent to Turkey.

With the accession of 'Abd al-Ḥamīd II his agents penetrated India, as other Muslim lands, to enlist pan-Islamic sympathy for his caliphal claims. With the shift in British policy regarding Turkey tension began to develop in Indo-Muslim politics between those loyal to the British and those who were pan-Islamists.

> Whatever may have been the defects of the old Ottoman alliance [comments Wilfrid Scawen Blunt during his visit to India in 1884] there is no question that it was popular in Muhammedan India, that it symbolized the friendship of England for the outside world of Islam, and that it left to Russia the invidious part of Islam's chief enemy. But the doubtful arrangements of the Berlin Treaty, the discredited acquisition of Cyprus and the abandonment of Tunis—when these things came slowly to be understood—operated a change in men's minds, and prepared them for still stronger reprobations, when, for the first time, England showed herself distinctly the aggressor in Egypt.[5]

[3] Sayyid Maḥmūd, *Khilāfat awr Islām* (1922), p. 80.

[4] Garcin de Tassy, *La langue et la littérature hindoustanie en 1870–6* (Paris, 1871–7), pp. 108–9.

[5] *Diaries* (1932), p. 96.

Sayyid Aḥmad Khān had been pro-Turkish as long as this was British policy. He had popularized the fez in India. In 1870 he complimented Sultan ʿAbd al-ʿAzīz as one who graced and 'defends the throne of the Caliph'.[6] In articles in the *Tahẕīb al-akhlāq* he had congratulated the Ottoman sultans on the reforms introduced during the *Tanẓīmāt* and later. But the change in Britain's foreign policy and the growing anti-Turkish trend in the measures taken by Rosebery and Salisbury were soon reflected in his writings. He had witnessed the tragedy of anti-British insurgence in 1857, and his lifelong mission had been to salvage the wreck of his community on the raft of loyalism. He could not cut loose from this sheet anchor. His stand regarding Turkey during the 1880s and 1890s is represented by such statements as: 'We are devoted and loyal subjects of the British government', 'We are not the subjects of Sultan ʿAbd al-Ḥamīd II; . . . he neither had, nor can have any spiritual jurisdiction over us as *khalīfa*. His title of caliph is effective only in his own land and only over the Muslims under his sway.'[7] He argued that the real caliphate was limited only to the first four orthodox Caliphs; the Umayyads and the ʿAbbāsids were merely nominally caliphs, but under them the caliphate became a monarchy. In that sense the Ottomans could call themselves caliphs, but only in their own territory.

He argued that, in the context of India especially, politics and religion must not be confounded. He regarded Turcophilia in Muslim India as natural and understandable and analysed some of it as a reaction to Gladstone's anti-Turkish vituperations. On the other hand he considered any direct contact of the Ottoman agents with the Indian Muslims as unconstitutional and a breach of protocol.[8] The Indian Muslims were legally bound to obey the writ not of an external Muslim caliph but of the British Indian government, even if it were oppressive.[9]

Shiblī Nuʿmānī, who later turned towards pan-Islamism,

[6] Graham, pp. 114–15.

[7] *Ākhirī Maẓāmīn*, pp. 32–33; *The Truth About Khilafat* (1916).

[8] *Ākhirī Maẓāmīn*, pp. 51–53, 59–69. [9] Ibid. pp. 111–13.

supported Sayyid Aḥmad Khān's views during the 1890s on two specific points: on the traditional theory that the real caliphate was confined only to the first four orthodox Caliphs, and on the issue that it was wrong of ʿAbd al-Ḥamīd II to suppress freedom of expression and discussion on this point.[10]

The separatist line taken by Sayyid Aḥmad Khān in relation to Hindu-Muslim politics was accepted by the Muslim consensus in India with extensive concessions to his loyalist attitude, but his loyalism was rejected when it came into conflict with pan-Islamic sympathies. A large section of the Urdu press of the 1890s reflects this trend. Muslim India's sympathies with pan-Islamism and the Ottoman caliphate were largely an indigenous development, though later it came to be associated with the legendary name and personality of Jamāl al-dīn al-Afghānī.[11] His work expresses views which are the antithesis of those of Sayyid Aḥmad Khān in the political and often in the religious field. Of Persian origin, he had taken some part in Afghan dynastic civil strife before 1859, when he is reported to have visited India for the first time. A learned divine, a mystic, apostle of modern pan-Islamism, reformist, revolutionary, and *agent provocateur par excellence*, he sowed the seeds of political and intellectual awakening in most Muslim lands, Persia, the Ottoman empire, Egypt, Muslim India, and Muslim Russia. In some of these countries, especially Egypt and Syria, he founded a tradition of middle-of-the-road reformism through his disciples. In India his immediate impact does not seem to have had a comparable effect on his notable contemporaries; but a generation later, in the first decades of the twentieth century, as a symbol and a legend his mission exercised a powerful influence on the pan-Islamic movement.

His polemical attacks on Sayyid Aḥmad Khān's political and religious thought began in 1879 when he visited Hyderabad and

[10] *Maqālat* (Azamgarh, 1930–4), i. 182–7 and *Safarnāma* (Agra, 1894), p. 79.

[11] For a study of Jamāl al-dīn al-Afghānī see Iraj Afshar and Asghar Mahdawi, *Documents inédits concernant Jamal al-din al-Afghani* (Tehran, 1963); Qāẓī ʿAbd al-Ghāffar, *Āṣār-i Jamāl al-dīn Afghānī* (Delhi, 1940); Murtaẓā Mudarrisī Chahārdihī, *Sayyid Jamāl al-dīn al-Afghānī* (Tehran 1334 AH); E. Kedourie, 'Nouvelle lumière sur Afghani et ʿAbduh', *Orient*, xxx and xxi (1964).

Calcutta, expelled by the Khedive Tawfīq from Eygpt. Later, with some modification, the substance of these Persian articles published in India was reprinted in the *'Urwa al-wuthqā*, an anti-imperialist and especially anti-British journal that he published in collaboration with his Egyptian disciple and colleague, Shaykh Muḥammad 'Abduh.[12] Opposed though he was to the extremism of Sayyid Aḥmad Khān's speculations, his reformism followed largely the same principles. The basic difference lay in the final aim and end of a reformism, which for Sayyid Aḥmad Khān meant a final adjustment with the west, but for al-Afghānī an eventual and inevitable confrontation with western imperialism. The crux of the controversy lay in their diametrically opposed political standpoints. Self-protection was regarded by al-Afghānī as a total and indivisible problem facing the entire world of Islam, in which the final interests of the Indian Muslims were inseparable from those of the rest of the Muslim world. He regarded the entire history of Islam as a single continuity, and the political tragedy of the Muslim world around him was that it was being conquered in detail without any concerted resistance.

The same lack of a monolithic political unity was, according to al-Afghānī, the basic cause of the decline of Islam as a cohesive system of religious thought. The division of the world of Islam into petty states had also divided the theologians and the common people of one Muslim land from the other. Reinterpretation of Islamic jurisprudence, reorientation of Muslim institutions, and a readjustment of Islam to the modern world of science and technology were possible only in a pan-Islamic society, under the symbolic jurisdiction of a single universal caliph, who could have the acknowledged authority to constitute regional centres to reinterpret Islam in various Muslim lands.[13]

Al-Afghānī's views on the caliphate and pan-Islamism were inspired by an idealism which was entirely unconnected with the

[12] Reprinted in Beirut in 1933; see also Aziz Ahmad, 'Sayyid Ahmad Khān, Jamāl al-dīn al-Afghānī and Muslim India', *Studia Islamica*, xiii (1960), pp. 55–78.

[13] *al-'Urwa* (Cairo reprint, 1957), pp. 13–22, 67–73.

Machiavellian propaganda of ʿAbd al-Ḥamīd II, whom he mistrusted, and at various times he considered the Mahdī of the Sudan or the Sharīf of Mecca or the Egyptian khedive, ʿAbbās Ḥilmī, as possible alternatives. But in the end he seems to have come to the conclusion that the inherited title, the strategic position, and the organizing genius of the Ottoman sultan could not be ignored. During the last years of his life he accepted ʿAbd al-Ḥamīd II's invitation to settle in Istanbul and to work for him. There he remained an influential figure for a short time; then, like so many other idealists, he fell into disgrace through court intrigues, and died in 1897.

In relation to Muslim India the exact nature and extent of al-Afghānī's influence has to be carefully determined. His Persian articles attacking Sayyid Aḥmad Khān, written during his visit to India in 1879, were published in an obscure journal, *Muʿallim-i shafīq*, in Hyderabad, and do not seem to have caused any stir at the time. But he made some impact during the 1880s when articles from the *ʿUrwa al-wuthqā*, which was officially banned in India but which certainly reached several subscribers and admirers there, were translated and published in *Dār al-salṭanat* (Calcutta) and *Mushīr-i Qayṣar* (Lucknow).[14]

As for his contacts in India, interesting material seems to be available in his unpublished papers in Iran.[15] Apart from these, one has to rely principally on the evidence of Blunt and on occasional references in the archives of the political department of the government of British India. The people he contacted, such as Rasūl Yār Khān, Sayyid ʿAlī Shūstarī, Muḥammad Saʿīd, and ʿAlī Ḥaydar, mentioned by Blunt[16] and Taghizade, were non-entities who exerted no religious or political influence in Muslim India. In Hyderabad Sayyid ʿAlī Bilgrāmī, an influential dignitary and the translator of Le Bon, regarded al-Afghānī as too much of a socialist and a firebrand to carry through a reformation of Islam; while his brother, Sayyid Ḥusayn Bilgrāmī (ʿImād

[14] Afshar & Mahdawi, pp. 22, 26–27, 30–37, 62, 68.

[15] Ibid.

[16] *Secret History of the English Occupation of Egypt* (*SH*) (1907), ii. 100, 105–6, 141.

al-Mulk), a close sympathizer of Sayyid Aḥmad Khān, who rose to be the prime minister of Hyderabad state, seems to have helped the British Resident to keep an eye on al-Afghānī's movements and to have worked as an informant against him.[17] It is possible that ʿImād al-Mulk was the person attacked in the most virulent of al-Afghānī's articles during his stay in Hyderabad in 1879–90.[18]

Among Sayyid Aḥmad Khān's associates, Shiblī Nuʿmānī was the only one who came in contact with Shaykh Muḥammad ʿAbduh in Cairo in 1893, but he did not meet al-Afghānī during his visits to Constantinople.[19] It was not until the beginning of the twentieth century that al-Afghānī became the symbol of the pan-Islamic movement. Al-Afghānī's theory of pan-Islamism was developed in 1912–13 by Abu'l-Kalām Āzād, who had had direct contacts with the *al-Manār* group, in a series of articles in *al-Hilāl* and *al-Balāgh*, the two journals he edited in Calcutta, and in a series of addresses after the first world war, and much of Āzād's attack on the Aligarh movement was also a heritage of al-Afghānī.[20]

Iqbāl seems to have made some study of al-Afghānī's writings, and his influence on his middle-of-the-road neo-modernism could hardly be exaggerated:

> The man . . . who fully realized the importance and immensity of this task [i.e. of rethinking the whole system of Islam without completely breaking with the past], and whose deep insight into the inner meaning of the history of Muslim thought and life, combined with a broad vision engendered by his wide experience of men and manners, would have made him a living link between the past and the future, was Jamal-ud-Din Afghani. If his indefatigable but divided energy could have devoted itself entirely to Islam as a system of human belief and conduct, the world of Islam, intellectually speaking, would have been on a much more solid ground today.[21]

[17] Ibid. ii. 150.
[18] 'Sharḥ-i ḥāl-i Aghūriyān', *Muʿallim-i shafīq* (1879).
[19] Shiblī, *Safarnāma*, pp. 217–18.
[20] *Mas'ala-i Khilāfat* (1963).
[21] *The Reconstruction of Religious Thought in Islam* (1934), p. 92.

In his reflective eschatological narrative poem, the *Jāwīd Nāma*, Iqbāl portrayed al-Afghānī as the mouthpiece of his own definition of the ideal Islamic state, the Kingdom of God on earth.

One of the most curious features of the pan-Islamic movement is the pragmatic support of Shīʿī intellectuals for the Ottoman caliphate, in India as elsewhere. Its philosophical basis, as we have seen, is the distinction worked out by Amīr ʿAlī between the 'immaculate spiritual *imāmate*' of the Shīʿī *imāms*, and the 'pontifical' or temporal caliphate of a monarchical head of the entire Muslim community, both of whom he regards as mutually compatible.

As early as 1879 Badr al-dīn Ṭayyibjī, the Shīʿī Bohra leader, wrote a letter in the *Bombay Gazette* refuting British press comments on Turkey's 'Bulgarian atrocities' and petitioned Queen Victoria to support Turkey against Russia.[22] Chirāgh ʿAlī chose Turkey as a model rather than Shīʿite Persia in his suggestions for political and religious reforms because of Turkey's primacy among Muslim states. In 1882, in opposition to Sayyid Aḥmad Khān's views, he defended the Ottoman administration, emphasizing its liberalism in employing non-Muslim officials, and collected and quoted western views supporting Turkey on the Armenian question. He was opposed to the views of Blunt on the transfer of caliphate to a Qurayshite Arab.[23] This movement among Shīʿī the intellectuals in India was not without its parallels abroad. Shāmil's Sunnī and Shīʿī disciples fought jointly against the Russians, while in Astrakhan Sunnīs attended prayers in Shīʿī mosques, and the Muslim Congress at Kazan recommended the same theological syllabus for both the sects. Similar movements for uniting Sunnīs and Shīʿīs were visible in the early twentieth century in the social and religious life of Iraq.[24] In India this attitude did not interfere with the Shīʿī attachment to

[22] H. Tyabji, *Badruddin Tyabji* (Bombay, 1952); Blunt, *SH*, ii. 101, 107.

[23] Cheragh Ali, *Proposed . . . Reforms*, xix–xxxi, 41–49, 82–88, 93–95.

[24] I. Goldziher, *Muhammad and Islam* (New Haven, 1917), pp. 335–6; H. A. R. Gibb, ed., *Whither Islam?* (1932), p. 360; H. Taghizade, 'Le Panislamisme et le Panturkisme', *R. du Monde musulman*, xxii (1913), pp. 179–220.

Persia, which is especially discernible in the writings of Amīr ʿAlī.[25]

THE SECOND PHASE (1911–1924)

International and Indian political developments between 1911 and 1914 exposed Muslim politics in India to severe stresses which brought it even closer to the pan-Islamic movement. The partition of Bengal was annulled in 1911. This reversal of an administrative arrangement made earlier by Curzon for the economic betterment of the Muslims of the area convinced the Muslim leadership of the instability of British patronage, and led it to the conclusion that a policy of loyalism did not pay dividends as rich as that of aggressive resistance adopted by the Indian National Congress. In 1911 the loyalist Muslim League proclaimed self-government for India as its final objective, and overtures were made for an alliance with the Indian National Congress, which was sealed in the 'Lucknow pact' of 1916 between the two parties on the basis of a draft prepared by Muḥammad ʿAlī Jinnāḥ.

Even greater was the pan-Islamic emotional stress caused by the threat to the independence of the surviving Muslim states. There was frustration over the extension of the French protectorate over Morocco with the connivance of Britain, and British inaction in face of the Italian occupation of the Ottoman province of Libya. Anglo-Russian secret deals to divide Persia and possibly Turkey came to be strongly suspected. During the Balkan war of 1913 a medical mission was sent under the leadership of Mukhtār Aḥmad Anṣārī. Direct contacts were established between the Turkish leaders Enver and Jamāl and the Indian Muslim élite; and political sentiment in Islamic India favoured the Young Turks in their struggle against the Ottoman sultan. In the popular Indo-Muslim imagination Enver Pasha became a legendary hero to whom glowing tributes were paid in press and poetry. The romantic mythology around Enver continued to grow

[25] Ameer Ali, *The Rights of Persia* (London, 1919), pp. 7–9, 18–19; cf. Taghizade.

during the first world war, and glorified his resistance at the head of the Basmachis against the Bolshevik forces in Central Asia.

Muḥammad ʿAlī, a brilliant Aligarh journalist, wrote a fiery article, 'The Choice of the Turks', in his newspaper the *Comrade*, when Turkey entered the conflict on the side of the Central Powers in 1914, and he was sent to jail, where he remained until 1919. During the war Abu'l-Kalām Āzād was also interned.

Muḥammad ʿAlī's article was a rejoinder to one with the same title published by *The Times*.

> To the extent [he wrote] that the Turk has wantonly destroyed the capital of goodwill that stood to his credit in the days of Palmerston, of the 'Great Elchi' and of Disraeli, he stands guilty and condemned. But how many Mussalmans are convinced that not an iota of responsibility lies at the door of England, of cynical Salisbury, of sleepy Lowther, and a whole host of present day Ministers, both of the silent and the babbling varieties, for the deplorable estrangement of today.

He argued that Turkey's entry meant that the war should be viewed essentially and primarily as a Greco-Turkish war for the recovery of the Turkish *wilāyet* of Salonika, ignominiously surrendered during the Balkan war by the Turkish ministers Kāmil and Nāẓim under British diplomatic pressure. In 1911, before the Turks lost it to the Greeks, Salonika was not a Greek city; half of its population consisted of Sephardic Jews, descendants of sixteenth-century refugees who entered the Ottoman empire after the *Reconquista* in Spain, which

> was no longer ruled by the Moors, but was under the Christian sway of Ferdinand and his successors who persecuted and exiled Moslem and Jew alike with perfect impartiality. . . . Indian Mussalmans hate the idea of a British-Ottoman collision, whether military or diplomatic. But Greece is not Great Britain. . . . Neither honour nor interest require her intervention in any conflict between Greece and Turkey.

It would be morally right if Turkey took advantage of French and Russian involvement in the war to redress her grievances against these two powers, for Russia had instigated every revolt against Turkey in Europe and Asia Minor, and France had aggressively occupied Tunisia in 1881. The Turks or the Egyptians would be morally justified if they urged the British evacuation of Egypt in view of British pledges to that effect given from 1882 to 1893. But the Turks should fight their own battles, and not Germany's. As far as possible they should not fight the British. 'If by some evil chance they engage in hostilities against our Government, we shall ask them to pray for us also, for they can only imagine the mental anguish and the heart-pangs that will be ours.'[26]

Finally, Muḥammad ʿAlī faced the inescapable dilemma of the question of the loyalty of Muslim India during the Turco-British conflict. He sought guidance on this point in Sayyid Aḥmad Khān's solution: 'Our attitude towards the Government established in this country must be guided only by one consideration—the attitude of that Government towards ourselves.'[27]

The government of India's decision to intern Muḥammad ʿAlī for the duration of the war for this article, which was not altogether seditious, turned out to be short-sighted. After five years he emerged as the most dynamic and influential leader of Muslim India. He founded the Khilāfat Conference in 1919, and carried the élite and masses of the Muslims with him into the Indian National Congress, which for three years, and until his own disillusionment with it, became for the first and the last time as representative of Muslim as it was of Hindu opinion.

The *ʿulamā'* of Deoband were the first group in Muslim India to evolve a policy of contacts with the Turks during the first world war, and to enlist the support of the frontier tribesmen with the object of the eventual overthrow of the British rule in India. Maḥmūd al-Ḥasan of Deoband left for the Hijāz during the war, where he established contacts with Ghālib Pasha, the governor, and with the Turkish ministers Jamāl and Enver, who gave a pledge that Turkey and her allies would support India's demand for self-rule at the peace conference after the victory of the central powers. The document based on this pledge was

[26] *Comrade*, 26 Sept. 1914, reprinted in his *Select Speeches and Writings*, ed. Afẓal Iqbāl (1963), i. 179–217, 191, 197–201.

[27] Ibid. p. 213.

smuggled into India, photographed and distributed, and was traced and found by the British Intelligence.[28]

In the Hijāz Sharīf Ḥusayn who, at British instigation, rose in revolt against the Turks, obtained a *fatwā* from the *'ulamā'* of Mecca accusing the Turks of apostasy for having deposed 'Abd al-Ḥamīd II. Paradoxically the *fatwā* denied the Ottomans the right and title of the caliphate as they were not Qurayshites. By implication the Meccan *fatwā* thus cleared the way for Sharīf Ḥusayn, a Qurayshite, to advance his own claim to the universal caliphate. Maḥmūd al-Ḥasan, refusing to sign the *fatwā*, stated that the charge of apostasy against the entire Turkish nation was contrary to the injunctions of Islam; and that the Qur'ān nowhere enjoined that the caliphate should be the exclusive privilege of any single tribe or race;[29] he was arrested by Sharīf Ḥusayn's men and was handed over to the British, who interned him in Malta from 1917 to 1920.

Maḥmūd al-Ḥasan had also sent his emissaries to Afghanistan to try to enlist the government and the tribesmen in a struggle against the British in India. Unrest was promoted in the North-Western Frontier areas to the extent that the British had to send five large-scale military expeditions to Waziristan. German and Turkish agents were in contact in Afghanistan with an Indian 'government in exile' which had a Hindu agitator, Rājā Mahindra Pratāp, as its 'prime minister' and included among others 'Ubayd-Allāh Sindhī, a disciple and emissary of Maḥmūd al-Ḥasan.[30]

One of the principal results of the preoccupation of the *'ulamā'* of Deoband was the passionate adherence of the Indian Muslim political élite to the concept of the caliphate as a free institution and of the caliph as a free agent. During the allied occupation of Istanbul after the war, political sentiment in Muslim India centred on the abstract conception of the Ottoman caliphate without any profession of personal loyalty to Mehmet VI

[28] Muḥ. Miyān, *'Ulamā'-i Ḥaqq*, i. 131–42.

[29] Madanī, *Naqsh-i ḥayāt*, ii. 282.

[30] RIIA, *Survey 1925*, i. 551; 'Ubayd-Allāh Sindhī, *Kābul men sāt sāl* (1955), pp. 24–26, 52–64.

(Waḥīd al-dīn), who was virtually a prisoner in the hands of the allies. Indian Muslim sympathies were entirely and exclusively with Muṣṭafā Kamāl, his movement and his army. The attitude of uncompromising hostility to Sharīf Ḥusayn's claim to the caliphate was an intensification of the same attitude, as he was regarded as a British puppet.[31]

After the war the *'ulamā'* of Deoband, Farangī Maḥal, and Nadwat al-'Ulamā' founded a political organization, the Jam'iyyat al-'Ulamā'-i Hind, which held its first session in 1919. It was committed to a political alliance with the Indian National Congress and a religio-political preoccupation with the Ottoman caliphate. The same year, on his release from prison, Muḥammad 'Alī founded the Khilāfat Conference, which drove the moderate and erstwhile loyalist Muslim League into the political wilderness. The Khilāfat movement, which soon gathered the explosive momentum of a mass agitation in Muslim India, had two political components. Its principal objective was to stop the British government, by persuasion and by revolutionary agitation, from imposing the treaty of Sèvres on Turkey, which if implemented would have left Turkey not merely shorn of her non-Turkish provinces, including the Hijāz, but would have mutilated the Turkish homelands. Its second component was a political alignment with the Indian National Congress under the leadership of M. K. Gāndhī. Just then Indian nationalism was bitterly incensed against the imposition of the Rowlatt Act, a repressive law which sought to perpetuate wartime restrictions on civil liberties. Gāndhī had developed at that stage his shrewd political technique of passive resistance and non-violent non-co-operation, which he preached from the platform of the Indian National Congress and the Khilāfat Conference alike.

In its international role the Khilāfat Conference was less successful. A deputation led by Muḥammad 'Alī visited London in 1920 and laid before Lloyd George and H. A. L. Fisher the demands that the Ottoman caliph should be allowed to retain

[31] Abu'l Ḥasanāt 'Alī Nadwī, 'Mas'la-i Khilāfat', *Ma'ārif*, v/3 (1920), pp. 168–9.

custody of the three holy cities of Mecca, Medina and Jerusalem, that he should retain sovereignty over the Arabian peninsula, Syria, and Iraq, and that Turkey should retain her pre-war frontiers.[32]

A *fatwā* was issued in 1920, in consonance with the classical theory that Indian Muslims might migrate to Muslim Afghanistan, as India under the British was the *dār al-ḥarb*, i.e. enemy territory. It was issued with the consensus of the *ʿulamā*ʾ, but its chief theoretician was Abu'l-Kalām Āzād, who argued that 'migration from India before the world war was desirable, now it is mandatory'. He advised only such Muslims to stay behind in India as were actively engaged in the struggle for the survival and integrity of the caliphate, and even they should not give up their enthusiasm for emigration. The *hijra* should be organized collectively, fixing priorities for early and late émigrés.[33] In its enthusiasm the *hijra* movement overlooked all economic realities. Afghanistan, itself a poor country, was hardly capable of absorbing vast masses of self-invited refugees from India. The movement involved 18,000 Muslims, most of them of poorer classes, in great suffering as they were turned away from the Afghan border, and thousands died on the road of sickness and hunger. Muḥammad ʿAlī Jinnāḥ, who was generally sympathetic to the Khilāfat movement, though he did not actively participate in it, was among the few Muslim leaders who were opposed to the *hijra* movement.[34]

Abu'l-Kalām Āzād was also the principal theoretician of the Khilāfat movement. His views were based on those of al-Afghānī, though his approach was more dialectic. All collective societies, he argues, have to struggle between two opposing forces, the cohesive and the divisive. In the case of Islamic society the cohesive forces lead to a monolithic *jamāʿa* (organization), and the

[32] RIIA, *Survey 1925*, i. 49; Ra'īs Aḥmad Jaʿfarī, *Sīrat-i Muḥammad ʿAlī* (Delhi, 1932), pp. 280–306; C. H. Philips and others, eds., *The Evolution of India and Pakistan, 1858 to 1947; Select Documents* (London, 1962), p. 219.

[33] 'Hijrat kā fatwā', *Ahl-i ḥadīs̱* (Amritsar), 30 July 1920.

[34] RIIA, *Survey 1925*, pp. 554–5; R. L. F. Williams, *The State of Pakistan* (1962), p. 19.

divisive forces to ignorance and chaos (*jāhiliyya*). The powers of centralized direction of the Muslim *jamā'a* were concentrated in the hands of the Prophet and then in those of the four orthodox Caliphs. The Umayyads, the 'Abbāsids, and the Ottomans who followed them represent a different kind of centralization, not of a religious but of a monarchical universal caliphate. Through them the caliphate has remained the legal authority and the cognizable political centre of the Islamic world. The foundations of pan-Islamic society rest on five sociological pillars: its adherence to a single caliph; its rallying to his call; its obedience to him; emigration from a *dār al-ḥarb*, including a former Muslim territory occupied by non-Muslims, to an Islamic land for the reorganization of resistance; and *jihād*, which could take several forms. Every Muslim country with a considerable Muslim element should have its own *imām* or religious leader owing allegiance and loyalty to the sovereignty of the universal caliph. For India, Āzād suggested that Maḥmūd al-Ḥasan should hold that position. The loyalty of the Muslim community to the caliph must be political and not religious, as in Islam political leadership is the exclusive privilege of God and His Prophet. But this political loyalty has to be absolute unless the caliph acts contrarily to the injunctions of the Qur'ān or the teachings of the Prophet.[35]

Turkey, however, fought its battles under Muṣṭafā Kamāl (Atatürk) for its survival, revival, and metamorphosis, and tackled the problem of the caliphate in its own way. On 13 November 1922 the Turkish Grand National Assembly elected 'Abd al-Majīd as caliph but not as sultan; and for a little over a year a curious situation developed in the history of Islam with a caliph who was a symbolic 'pontiff', resident in a republic, without even the aura of nominal suzerainty and without any political authority.

The two principal Indian Muslim organizations concerned with the problem of the caliphate accepted the Turkish National

[35] *Khuṭbāt* (1944), pp. 207–8 and *Mas'ala-i Khilāfat*, pp. 19–25.

Assembly's decision after some spirited discussion.[36] On 24 November 1923, a fateful letter was sent by the Āghā Khān and Amīr ʿAlī to Ismet Pasha, Prime Minister of Turkey, in which both these leaders, who were Shīʿis, championed what they considered to be Sunnī Islam's concern over the caliph being shorn of even the semblance of sovereignty and requested the enhancement of his position and power.[37] It was viewed by the Turkish government with serious concern and alarm, and 'it was actually insinuated at Angora', comments Toynbee, '—though not officially—that they had acted at the instigation of the British Government.'[38] The letter influenced and possibly precipitated the decision of the Turkish National Assembly taken on 3 March 1924 to abolish the caliphate and to exile ʿAbd al-Majīd. This marked the end of a centuries-old institution and of an era in the history of Islam.

Two days later Sharīf Ḥusayn of Mecca proclaimed himself caliph. His claim was recognized in the Arab lands under British mandate, Iraq, Jordan, and Palestine. It was rejected by Eygpt and Muslim India. The Indian Muslim leadership regarded him as an imperial stooge who was not a free agent, and who had been a traitor to the Turks and therefore to pan-Islamic solidarity. To cover its error of judgement the British government, like the Indian Khilāfat Conference, seems to have encouraged the invasion and occupation of the Hijāz by Ibn Saʿūd, the Wahhābī ruler of Najd.[39] Sharīf Ḥusayn was overthrown seven months after proclaiming himself caliph.

The abolition of the caliphate by the Turks had deprived the Khilāfat Conference of its *raison d'être*. By that time its alliance with the Indian National Congress was also breaking up because of the re-emergence of Hindu and Muslim separatism, communal riots, missionary activities directed by each community against the other, and the polarization of the Congress itself into

[36] *Oriente Moderno*, 1922: ii. 705; iii/7, 409; iv/2, 84–85; RIIA *Survey 1925*, pp. 53, 84–85.

[37] Text in RIIA *Survey 1925*, pp. 571–2.

[38] Ibid., p. 59.

[39] *Oriente Moderno*, iv/10, 645–6.

a conservative Hindu and a liberal pro-Muslim wing, a schism which weakened the authority if not the prestige of Gāndhī and led to the re-alienation of the Muslims from the Congress.

The new international political platform on which the Khilāfat Conference struggled for survival for a few more years was the question of liberating the Hijāz from non-Muslim control. With Ibn Saʿūd's success, a new controversy developed. As a Wahhābī he had scant respect for the holy Muslim shrines. In 1925 his siege and bombardment of Medina divided the 'secular' section of the Khilāfat movement, led by Muḥammad ʿAlī, from its 'theological' section, led by his spiritual preceptor, ʿAbd al-Bārī of the Farangī Maḥal.[40] In 1926 congresses were held in Cairo and the Hijāz to discuss the question of the caliphate. Neither the Khilāfat Conference nor the Jamʿiyyat-i ʿUlamā'-i Hind participated in the Cairene Congress. But Indian delegations, invited by Ibn Saʿūd in the Hijāz, did participate in this Congress, which did not discuss the question of the caliphate at all but led to the development of Ibn Saʿūd's realistic policy of curbing the zeal of his iconoclastic followers, so as not to offend the sentiments of the traditionalist Muslims from abroad on the question of the shrines.[41]

The first sigh of relief at the abolition of the caliphate was breathed by the historian Khudā Bakhsh, who regarded the event as the 'final fruition of purely Islamic ideas long struggling into supremacy. It ends a fiction and ushers in modern as opposed to mediaeval ideas; it lays open the path for the development of nationalism and removes the embargo on liberalism.'[42]

The principle of the caliphate in relation to Muslim politics in the modern world was finally nullified in Indian Islam by the poet-philosopher Muḥammad Iqbāl. He argued that the responsibility for the political administration of an Islamic state or states was vested in the Muslim community and not in a single individual. If the community selects an individual as the head

[40] ʿAbd al-Majīd Daryābādī, *Muḥammad ʿAlī* (1954–6), i. 58.
[41] Ibid. pp. 253 ff.
[42] Quoted by M. L. Ferrar, in Gibb, *Whither Islam?*, p. 225.

of the state, he is invested with an authority which is more presidential than sovereign. If at a stage in history the exigencies of the situation demand a novel approach to a problem, such as the one facing the world of Islam in the twentieth century when the concept of a universal caliphate was not a practical proposition, the consensus of Muslim opinion could be considered a sovereign authority which could propose or adopt alternative solutions. The Turkish National Assembly was therefore within its rights in seeking an alternative, i.e. a republican solution. He agreed with Ziya Gökalp that though a universal caliphate continued to remain an ideal, it was difficult to establish in the present political situation of the world, and in the meantime each Muslim state should first try to put its own house in order. Though Iqbāl recognized the legality of the Turkish National Assembly's action in abolishing the caliphate, as sanctioned by the consensus of the Turkish people, he found Turkish secularism and the separation of religion from politics an un-Islamic error of decision. Iqbāl clearly distinguished between caliphate and pan-Islamism as two separate and independent issues. The first was outdated, the second necessarily remained valid. Here he returned to Sa'īd Ḥalīm Pasha's view that Islam was 'a harmony of idealism and positivism' and 'a unity of eternal verities of freedom, equality and solidarity has no fatherland'. There could be no Turkish, Persian, Arab, or Indian Islam. In terms of modern politics this meant that in the existing world situation Islam could best survive neither by narrow nationalism nor in the naïve dream of re-establishing a universal state, but in a multi-national free association, in something like a League of Nations of Islam.[43] It was within the concept of this multi-national neo-pan-Islamism that Iqbāl evolved the theory of Pakistan.

[43] *Reconstruction*, pp. 153–9; Gibb, *Whither Islam?*, p. 364.

CHAPTER SEVEN

IQBĀL: SPECULATIVE NEO-MODERNISM

CHOICE OF VALUES

MUḤAMMAD Iqbāl (1875–1938), poet, philosopher, and political thinker, dominates Islamic religious and political thought in the twentieth century as did Sayyid Aḥmad Khān in the nineteenth. Iqbāl's intellectual personality was shaped first by classical Islamic learning and later by western education at Lahore, where he studied under T. W. Arnold. From 1905 to 1908 he studied at Cambridge, completing his doctorate on the development of metaphysics in Persia at Munich.

Iqbāl's early work was written before 1905 in Urdu, and includes some simple and touching poems for children, nature poems, and political verse which is tinged with Indian nationalism. Between 1905 and 1908, during his stay in Europe, he turned from Indian nationalism to pan-Islamism. The third phase of his early Urdu verse lasted from 1908 to 1924, when the *Bāng-i Darā* was published. His work of this period is mainly romantically political, concerned with the plight of Islam in the modern world.

In the 1920s his poetry became more reflective. He then began to be concerned with the nature and development of the individual self (*khudī*), in its own right and in relation to society. His philosophy of self and 'selflessness' in relation to society is expounded in two long narrative poems in Persian, *Asrār-i Khudī* and *Rumūz-i Bīkhudī*.

In 1923 he published a collection of Persian poems, the *Payām-i Mashriq*, covering a wide range of themes, mystical, romantic, topical, and philosophical, influenced to some extent by the German romanticism of the *Sturm und Drang* period. In 1927 he published *Zabūr-i 'Ajam*, another collection of Persian poems, mainly *ghazals* with a political or philosophical flavour. Iqbāl's narrative poem, perhaps the most profound of his poetical works, the *Jawīd Nama*, was inspired by Dante's *Divina Commedia*.[1]

In the 1930s he turned once more to Urdu and published his second collection of Urdu poems, the *Bāl-i Jibrīl*, which contains some of his finest verse. His third Urdu collection, *Ẓarb-i Kalīm*, consists of more topical political poems. A volume of Persian and Urdu verse, *Armaghān-i Ḥijāz*, appeared posthumously.

Much of Iqbāl's philosophical thought occurs in the form of flashes of insight in his Urdu verse[2] as well as in his narrative poems in Persian. Some distinct values, such as movement, power, evolutionism ethically interpreted, and freedom, emerge in his work.

With the '*Khiẓar-i Rāh*',[3] written shortly after the first world war, a revolutionary trend makes its appearance in Iqbāl's verse, with still greater emphasis on the value of movement and social development. In the *Asrār-i Khudī* he rejects the static world-view of Greek thought in general and of Plato in particular.[4] He regards Islam's role in the development of the Greek philosophical heritage as essentially dynamic—a view which many Islamists would contest. In Islamic philosophy and mysticism he dislikes quietistic trends borrowed from Neo-Platonism or Christianity, as well as those which developed internally, according to him in the historical period of the decline of Islam. He regards the teachings of the Qur'ān as tending towards an essentially dynamic world view. *Ijtihād* as a source of law, he argues, underlies this principle.

The movement of the individual self is directly related to the principle of movement in the universe, from chaos towards a

[1] A. Bausani, 'Dante and Iqbāl', in *Crescent and Green; a Miscellany of Writings on Pakistan* (London, 1955).

[2] A selection of his Urdu poems has been translated into English by V. Kiernan, *Poems from Iqbal* (London, 1955). Another translated selection is Iqbāl, *Poesie* (Parma, 1956), rendered into Italian by A. Bausani.

[3] In *Bāng-i Darā* (1944), pp. 288–302.

[4] *Asrār-i Khudī* (Lahore, n.d.), pp. 34–36 (Nicholson, pp. 56–59).

pattern of order.[5] Universe as well as life are involved in a process of continuous becoming; and man, who stands at the peak of evolution, can maintain, in himself and in the society to which he belongs, the momentum of this primeval movement by ever-new conquest of the forces of nature. If he stands still these very forces would destroy him.[6] Action is the organization of a man's potentiality for movement directed towards the conquest of nature.[7] In this constant struggle with life and nature man cannot save himself by convincing himself of determinism. Destiny exists no doubt, but not as something predetermined. Destiny as assigned by God is identical with pure, non-serial time, and has, like it, a wide range of alternative possibilities.

The principle of movement in man is distinguishable from the same principle in nature by the value of ethical purposiveness. Nature is wasteful, unscrupulous, brutal, and amoral in its movement forward. Man is, at least potentially, human. His movement and progress, individually and socially, have to be conditioned by moral norms.

Man is not merely free to choose and act; he has also the potentiality to create, with the given raw material of life and nature. God has described himself as the 'best of creators' (*aḥsan al-khāliqīn*). This implies that there can be other creators as well. Man has the capacity of becoming such a creator, if his creativity is purposeful in the direction of evolving moral values as he proceeds from one creative activity to another.[8]

Movement in history is necessarily a movement forward. Iqbāl rejects Nietszche's theory of historical recurrence,[9] though in general he is considerably influenced by certain dynamic elements of the German philosopher's thought. According to Iqbāl, history is modelled on the progressive pattern of life itself; and in life the process or recurrence has no place or

[5] Ibid. p. 50 (Nicholson, p. 82); *Bāl-i Jibrīl* (1942), pp. 29, 44 f.
[6] *Rumūz-i Bīkhudī* (Lahore, n.d.), pp. 165–6 (Arberry, pp. 56–57).
[7] *Asrār*, pp. 26–29, 54 (Nicholson, pp. 43–47, 89–90).
[8] *Dībācha-i Asrār-i Khudī* (Lahore, 1908), p. 3; *Ḥikmat-i Iqbāl*, ed. G. D. Rashīd (Hyderabad, 1945), p. 12; *Bāl*, pp. 55–81.
[9] *Reconstruction*, pp. 115–16.

meaning.[10] History is also the collective memory of a people, sustaining it and providing it with the continuum of a sense of identity. The conservation of specific values or traditions of a culture is a historical activity which should not be confused with revivalism.[11] The Muslim community should not keep its eyes fixed on the glory that was Baghdad. It should look discerningly towards the unexplored future.[12] Movement in history, as in life, strives towards a future which it works hard to mould.[13] In this process it conserves the values which have given basic shape to a culture.[14] These values have to be absorbed ever anew in the onward march of a culture. In periods of political demoralization history may even take a step backwards and rely on conservative conformity rather than fresh speculation.[15]

Another value indispensable for man's conquest of nature is power. In overpowering the forces of nature and harnessing them for his own use, man is actively aided by God.

In Iqbāl's verse there is occasionally a preoccupation with power for its own sake. The eagle predominates in his imagery. His admiration of Satan's accumulation and exercise of dynamic power borders at times on the verge of dualism.[16] Man requires something of Satan's devotion, inquisitiveness, and anguish.[17]

In Iqbāl's romantic involvement with power the occasional suspension of a moral criterion stands in contrast with his insistence on a moral purposiveness in the principle of movement. Under the influence of Nietzsche he endorses the distinction between *Herrenmoral* and *Heerdenmoral*.[18] His ethical lapses in paying tribute to Napoleon and Mussolini correspond with his

[10] 'Sāqī Nāma', in *Bāl*, p. 170.

[11] *Payām-i Mashriq* (1942), p. 264; *Rumūz*, pp. 172–3 (Arberry, pp. 61–62).

[12] *Bāl*, p. 101.

[13] 'Zamāna', ibid. pp. 175–6; 'Nawā-i waqt', in *Payām*, p. 102.

[14] *Asrār*, pp. 65–69 (Nicholson, pp. 108–15).

[15] Ibid. p. 23 (Nicholson, p. 36); *Rumūz*, pp. 143–5 (Arberry, pp. 40–42).

[16] *Jāwīd Nāma*, pp. 157–8; *Payām*, pp. 97–98; *Bāl*, pp. 192–4; *Armaghān-i Ḥijāz* (1938), pp. 213–28.

[17] *Armaghān*, pp. 177–83; *Jāwīd Nāma*, pp. 160–1; also 'Taqdīr', in *Bāl*, adapted from Ibn al-'Arabī.

[18] *Asrār*, pp. 29–33 (Nicholson, pp. 48–55).

cosmological admiration of Satan,[19] but fortunately this trend is ambivalent. It is counterbalanced in other poems by a denunciation of fascist aggression and the abuse of power.[20]

On the other hand Iqbāl's view of evolution is dominated by an ethical sense of causation and purpose. Bergsonian evolutionism permeates his *Sāqī Nāma*[21] and other verses. Organic matter is distinguished from inorganic in direct statement and in imagery. *Élan vital* ascends the evolutionary spiral by progressing from the indetermination of lowly animal life to the status of man, and may evolve further to become the superman of the future or the 'Perfect Man' of history, who in Iqbāl's mind is connected with 'Abd al-Karīm al-Jīlī's and Muḥyi al-dīn Ibn al-'Arabī's doctrine of the 'reality of Muḥammad' (*al-ḥaqīqat al-Muḥammadiyya*).

Iqbāl agrees with Bergson that life has chosen two different paths of evolution, instinct in animals and reason in man. The superman of the future may choose, as the Perfect Man of history actually chose, a third path, that of intuition, which is the essence of instinct and the essence of reason. For intuition Iqbāl uses a number of terms derived from theology and mysticism: *'ishq* (love), *yaqīn* (certainty, true faith), and *īmān* (faith).

The actual evolution of the superman outside the rank of the prophets may take some considerable time. But Iqbāl's verse often refers to an unspecified 'man of faith' (*mu'min*) who already exists somewhere on the road of moral evolution from man to superman. He is a person with a highly developed personality, or self. He is also described by the romantic, mystical term *qalandar* (a kind of itinerant monk who abandons everything and wanders in the world), as one of the features of his character is disciplined, but not ascetic *faqr* (a life of poverty with resignation and content).[22] The *qalandar* or *faqīr* cannot accept any charity, either spiritual or material.[23]

[19] *Bāl*, pp. 201–3; *Ẓarb-i Kalīm* (1937), p. 151.
[20] *Ẓarb*, pp. 23, 147.
[21] *Bāl*, pp. 166–74; also letter to R. A. Nicholson, Urdu tr. in *Makātīb* (1944), pp. 457–74.
[22] *Bāl*, pp. 64, 213; *Ẓarb*, p. 47; *Armaghān*, p. 262.
[23] *Asrār*, pp. 24–26 (Nicholson, pp. 38–42); *Ẓarb*, pp. 25, 88, 178.

To explain the wisdom of the 'man of faith' Iqbāl distinguishes between two kinds of reason, dialectical and intuitional.[24] Dialectical reason feeds upon itself; intuitional reason, which is the wisdom of the 'man of faith', has angelic insight. With the 'anguish of Adam's heart' it can assess the universe. It is not far removed from *'ishq* or from intuition itself. Intuitional reason guides the creative faculty of the 'man of faith' and posits, in terms of serial time, immortal thought and art.[25] In the act of creation the 'man of faith' absorbs time and space unto himself.[26]

Freedom is a value as necessary for the ordinary man as for the 'man of faith', as essential for the individual as for society. Man is the creature of God; he owes obedience to no one else. Servitude is the death of the mind; it breaks up human society into parasitic individualities.[27] Art produced in the state of servitude has the flavour of death.[28] Servitude is even more fatal for religion. It divides religious ritual from faith. Religion becomes a commodity and is bought and sold. The slave has the name of God on his lips; in his heart is terror of his master. Pantheistic trends and doctrines of annihilation (*fanā'*) in mysticism are traceable to the periods of society's political servitude.[29] Faith is the force which braces man or society to struggle against the state of slavery. Faith awakens one to look into the depths of freedom in oneself. It reveals to the enslaved the secrets of the dignity and splendour of individual and political freedom.

Iqbāl's attitude to the west is largely conditioned by his championship of the freedom of Islamic society in particular. The greater part of his revolutionary verse was written between 1918 and 1938, a period when with a few exceptions the entire world of Islam had come under the sway of western empires. He

[24] *Pas chi bāyad kard ay aqwām-i Sharq?* (1947), pp. 12–18; *Bāl*, p. 31.
[25] 'Masjid-i Qurtuba', in *Bāl*, pp. 127–30.
[26] Ibid. pp. 110–11, 131–8; *Ẓarb*, pp. 39, 41, 47; *Pas chi bāyad kard*, pp. 23–27; *Zabūr-i 'Ajam* (1944), pp. 170–1.
[27] *Payām*, p. 157; *Asrār*, pp. 82–83; *Bāl*, p. 80; *Pas chi bāyad kard*, pp. 32–35.
[28] 'Bandagī Nāma', in *Zabūr*, pp. 251–7, 262–4; *Bāl*, pp. 40, 49; *Ẓarb*, pp. 99, 117, 123, 128; *Jāwīd Nāma*, p. 45.
[29] *Rumūz*, pp. 125–8 (Arberry, pp. 26–28); *Ẓarb*, p. 36; *Armaghān*, p. 97.

is severely critical of racialism in the west, which he regards as the cornerstone of imperialism.[30] He does not ignore the element of racialism in Islamic political thought and denounces Ibn Khaldūn's views on *'aṣabiyya* (group solidarity) as reflecting a period of decadence. Democracy in the west tends to be plutocratic as it has no religious moorings. The profit motive in private enterprise leads to cut-throat competition and is anti-humanistic.[31]

The theme of the contrast of east (Islamic Orient) and west occurs frequently in Iqbāl's poetry. He is critical of both. The east has an imagination 'which soars from the roof-tops to the stars', without the realization that the test of man's self and the field of his action is this material world and no other. The east has withdrawn from the struggle of existence, watching the march of history and science as a bystander. The heights to which oriental imagination soars are actually being reached by western technology. The west is active and dynamic, but also selfish, crafty, and unscrupulous. It lacks love and faith. It is throttled by the coils of reason which bite it like a serpent. It has harnessed the rays of the sun, but it has failed to illuminate the night of human misery.[32]

In short, the east is bad enough; but the west is worse. The tragedy of the east is that it is being attracted merely by the external glitter of the west, and not by its scientific creativity.[33]

RELIGIOUS SPECULATION

Iqbāl's thought is more systematically formulated in his *Reconstruction of Religious Thought in Islam.* Unlike that of any previous modernist, the central discipline of his scholarship was western. His interpretation, or rather dramatization, of the Islamic heritage in his thought was influenced and reoriented by the

[30] 'Ṭ'ulū'-i Islām', in *Bāng*, pp. 303–15.
[31] 'Gulshan-i rāz-i jadīd', in *Zabūr*, p. 233; *Pas chi bāyad kard*, pp. 46–47, 56–63.
[32] *Payām*, pp. 225–33; *Ẓarb*, p. 67.
[33] *Ẓarb*, pp. 28, 79; *Zabūr*, p. 71, 118; *Bāl*, pp. 38–39, 145; *Armaghān*, p. 63.

dynamism of Nietzsche and Fichte and by the vitalism of Bergson. Often he superimposed Bergson on al-Jīlī or Nietzsche on Rūmī. In the fusion of two different streams of civilization, modern western and medieval Islamic, of two currents of thought, philosophic and mystic, and two strands of value-recognition, ethical and dynamic, what he achieved was not a synthesis but his own thought-process and thought-structure, which is an individual expression embracing a vast range of isolated positions of western and Islamic schemes of thought. The atomistic elements which he selected from the theological, mystical, or rationalist thought in Islam, or from the philosophical or political thought of the modern west, he re-defined, reinterpreted (making his own discoveries of parallelism or contrast) and tried to assimilate with varying success in the totality of his own thought-structure.

Intuition, he argues, is a higher form of intellect and is not opposed to it. Religion, which derives its sanction through intuition, is therefore cognizable by philosophical intellect, as these two sources of knowledge are complementary rather than opposed. The totality of reality, referred to in the Qur'ān (83: 20) as the 'Preserved Tablet', is perceptible to intuition as a whole, but to intellect only as a 'series of definite specifications which cannot be understood except by a reciprocal reference'.[34] With the tremendous advance of science, human intellect is outgrowing its primary categories of definition (time, space, and causality), and is moving towards intuition, which is the *modus operandi* of religion.[35]

In this light intellect can examine the Qur'ānic determination of man's relations with God and the universe. Created by a divine plan, the universe is capable of extension, change, evolution; and it can be harnessed or conquered by man, who is situated at the peak of evolution and has the status of God's vicegerent on earth.[36] 'And in this process of progressive change God

[34] *Reconstruction*, p. 6.
[35] Ibid. p. 3.
[36] Ibid. pp. 10–12, quoting *Qur'ān*, 44: 38, 3: 188, 35: 1, 29: 19 &c.

becomes a co-worker with him, provided man takes the initiative.'[37] The Qur'ān (2: 28–31) mentions the endowment of man with the faculty of naming things, that is to say forming concepts of them. The nature of human knowledge is conceptual. It can operate on the intellectual and mystical planes alike. Mysticism is therefore as valid a discipline for the cognition of reality as rationalism, though its processes of operation are entirely different. Its cognitive experience is immediate, total, transcendental, incommunicable, and beyond the normal physical experience of time and space.[38]

The principal vitalist theme in the Qur'ān is, according to Iqbāl, its emphasis on the ontological reality of change and movement. In its references to nature's passage through time the Qur'ān presents the clue to the ultimate nature of reality. Iqbāl explains 'the Qur'ānic concept of time' in terms of the Bergsonian distinction between pure duration and spatial or serial time.[39] Existence is life in time. The existent self has two sides, appreciative and efficient. The efficient side of the self operates in relation to the world of space and therefore in spatial time. The appreciative side of the self penetrates into the inner centre of experience and is a totality which embraces all pluralities into a single and indivisible unity:

> There is change and movement, but this change and movement are indivisible; their elements inter-penetrate and are wholly non-serial in character. It appears that the time of the appreciative-self is a single 'now', which the efficient-self, in its traffic with the world of space, pulverizes into a series of 'nows'.[40]

Exegetically Iqbāl quotes the Qur'ān, 54: 50 in his support:

> Surely We have created everything
> in measure.
> Our commandment is but one word,
> as the twinkling of an eye.

[37] *Reconstruction*, pp. 11–12.
[38] Ibid. pp. 2, 13, 18–24.
[39] *Asrār*, pp. 80–82 (Nicholson, pp. 134–8).
[40] *Reconstruction*, p. 46, quoting Qur'ān, 10: 6, 31: 28 &c.

This Iqbāl regards as pertinent to the appreciative side of the Divine Self, while another reference (25:60) in the Qur'ān, as in early scriptures, to the creation of the universe in six days, relates figuratively to the efficient side of the self, which operates in relation to serial time.[41] This helps Iqbāl to approach the problem of free will:

> Destiny is time regarded as prior to the disclosure of its realizable possibilities; . . . it is the inward reach of a thing, its realizable possibilities which lie within the depths of its nature, and serially actualize themselves without any feeling of external compulsion.[42]

On the analogy of our conscious experience we can define the universe as a free creative movement. It is not a thing but an act. On the same analogy Iqbāl rejects the extremism of Bergsonian vitalism:

> Reality is not a blind vital impulse wholly unilluminated by idea. Its nature is through and through teleological. . . . The ultimate Reality is a rationally directed creative life. . . . Intuition reveals life as a centralizing ego . . . the ultimate nature of Reality is spiritual and must be conceived as an ego.[43]

The infinity of the Ultimate Ego consists in 'the infinite wealth of His own undetermined creative possibilities'.[44] This Iqbāl emphasizes, together with five other divine attributes mentioned in the Qur'ān: creativeness, knowledge, omnipotence, and eternity. The creative method chosen by divine energy is atomistic, according to the Ashʿarites, a traditional view to which Iqbāl subscribes, as he regards atomism in Islam as an intellectual revolt against the Aristotelian concept of an immutable universe.[45]

From the Ultimate Self created selfs proceed and function as ego-entities. Rising in the scale of evolution the ego-entities achieve perfection in man. The knowledge of these ego-entities is discursive, and, unlike divine knowledge, circumscribed by

[41] Ibid. pp. 49–50, 76–77.
[42] Ibid. p. 47; *Asrār*, pp. 12–15 (Nicholson, pp. 16–22).
[43] *Reconstruction*, pp. 51, 58.
[44] Ibid. p. 73.
[45] Ibid. pp. 64–68.

space and time. But it is not predetermined. In the case of the human self, the Qur'ānic, as distinct from the Biblical, account of the Fall of Adam symbolizes it. The legend indicates

> man's rise from a primitive state of instinctive appetite to the conscious possession of a free self, capable of doubt and disobedience. The Fall does not mean any moral depravity: it is man's transition from simple consciousness to the first flash of self-consciousness, a kind of waking from the dream of nature with a throb of personal causality in one's own being. . . . Man's first act of disobedience was also his first act of free choice.[46]

The legend of the Fall also underlines the emergence of a social order in which multiplicating individualities seek their own possibilities and strive to assert their will on others. This internecine conflict of individualities is the *Weltschmerz* of human society. Because of its finite nature, man's self has good as well as bad elements. This mutual conflict, according to Iqbāl, is the meaning underlying the Qur'ānic verse 33:72:

> We offered the trust to the heavens and the earth
> and the mountains, but they refused to carry it
> and were afraid of it; and man carried it. Surely
> he is sinful, very foolish.

Therefore the revelation received intuitionally by the prophets is a re-establishment of moral contact between God and man for the organization of human society, and in order to define and control the rights and obligations of human ego-entities in that society. The act of ritual prayer is a form of reflection; it is also a process of assimilation by inner experience of the norms of knowledge and ethics. Prayer is therefore a contact between man and God which the moral needs of human society have motivated; its object is better achieved when it is congregational.[47]

The individual self, which encounters problems of good and evil in society, and problems of free will and determination in life, is in reality free and immortal. In its emphasis on the individuality and uniqueness of man, the Qur'ān rejects the New

[46] Ibid. pp. 78–82.

[47] Ibid. p. 87.

Testament thesis of redemption. According to the Qur'ān, God has invested man with a threefold uniqueness: he is the chosen of God; with all his faults he is the vicegerent and representative of God on earth; he is the trustee of a free personality which he accepted at his own risk.[48]

Divine activity is directive as well as creative. Analogically the entire reality of human selfhood lies in the directive attitude. Man's experience is a series of acts held together by the unity of a directive purpose. Streams of causality flow from nature into human experience and vice versa. In this process the human self acquires what configuration psychology calls 'insight' or an appreciation of the spatial and causal relation of things and a principle of choice between the complex of things.

> Thus the element of guidance and directive control in the ego's activity clearly shows that the ego [self] is a free personal causality. He shares in the life and freedom of the Ultimate Ego, who, by permitting the emergence of a finite ego, capable of private initiative, has limited this freedom of His own free will.[49]

In this conclusion Iqbāl has telescoped a modernist presentation of the doctrine of free will with the Naqshbandī mystical thesis of phenomenological monism (*waḥdat al-shuhūd*) developed by Shaykh Aḥmad Sirhindī in India in the seventeenth century.

The free will available to man is, however, not absolute. Qur'ānic references to 'destiny' are frequent, but they refer to the destiny of man as partly ethical and partly biological. Life is an ethical and biological opportunity for the self, and death is the first test of its 'synthetic activity'. Personal immortality for a human self or soul is not there by right; it is to be achieved by personal effort.[50]

A community is born of the plurality and interaction of human selves. In a community the human self can evolve to perfection which is prophethood. Through prophetic instruction the community receives fulfilment. In this context Iqbāl superimposes 'Abd al-Karīm al-Jīlī's doctrine of the Perfect Man on Bergson's

[48] Ibid. p. 90.
[49] Ibid. pp. 102–3.
[50] Ibid. p. 113; *Rumūz*, pp. 8–10 (Arberry, pp. 8–9).

theory of creative evolution. Iqbāl defines the role of the Prophet of Islam as the Perfect Man.

> A prophet may be defined as a type of mystic consciousness in which 'unitary experience' tends to overflow its boundaries, and seeks opportunities of redirecting or refashioning the forces of collective life. . . . Now during the minority of mankind psychic energy develops what I call prophetic consciousness—a mode of economizing individual thought and choice by providing ready-made judgements, choices, and ways of action. With the birth of reason and critical faculty, however, life, in its own interest, inhibits the formation and growth of non-rational modes of consciousness through which psychic energy flowed at an earlier stage of human evolution. . . . The Prophet of Islam seems to stand between the ancient and the modern world. In so far as the source of his revelation is concerned he belongs to the ancient world; in so far as the spirit of his revelation is concerned he belongs to the modern world. In him life discovers other sources of knowledge suitable to its new direction. The birth of Islam . . . is the birth of inductive intellect. In Islam prophecy reaches its perfection in discovering the need of its own abolition. . . . The abolition of priesthood and hereditary kingship in Islam, the constant appeal to reason and experience in the Qur'an, and the emphasis that it lays on Nature and History as sources of human knowledge, are all different aspects of the same idea of finality.[51]

Therefore in its intellectual revolt against the static world-view of Greek philosophy and sciences and in evolving a dynamic conception of the universe, all trends of Muslim thought, rationalist, traditionalist, and mystic, converge. Intellectual Islam has paved the way for modern western civilization.[52]

Ijtihād is the principle of legal advance in Islam. What has 'gone wrong with Islamic history' is the loss of this dynamic element of its civilization, under the pressure of certain given historical situations, such as the final political triumph of the conservative '*ulamā*' under al-Mutawakkil over the Mu'tazila, who in their turn could have been less extravagant in their rationalizations; the rise and growth of ascetic Ṣūfism with its rejection of involvement with the realities of this world; and finally the destruction of Baghdad by the Mongols in 1258.

[51] *Reconstruction*, pp. 119–20. [52] Ibid. p. 122.

These historical situations stabilized in traditional Muslim theology the doctrine that the *bāb al-ijtihād* was closed. Ibn Taymiyya, and in his wake some *'ulamā'*, including the founders of the pre-modernist fundamentalist movements, Muḥammad b. 'Abd al-Wahhāb, Shāh Wali-Allāh, and others protested against this theological dogma and reasserted the right of *ijtihād*. Modernists in Egypt and Turkey have closely followed in the footsteps of these fundamentalists in exercising this right.[53]

In Turkey the idea of dynamic speculation in the evolution and adjustment of institutions has long been at work. Ḥalīm S̱ābit's theory of Muslim law is based on modern sociological concepts. In this context Iqbāl made the fateful prophecy which has largely come true in the predominant religious and political thought of Islamic India and Pakistan today:

> We too one day, like the Turks, will have to re-evaluate our intellectual inheritance. And if we cannot make any original contribution to the general thought of Islam, we may, by healthy conservative criticism, serve at least as a check on the rapid movement of liberalism in the world of Islam.[54]

Muslim law is not an unalterable code. Under the impact of *ijtihād* it can be changed to meet the requirements of a modern society. It is not sacrosanct and is not an essential element of Islamic faith. Apart from the Qur'ān there was no written law of Islam until the rise of the 'Abbāsids. From the middle of the first to the beginning of the third Islamic centuries there were no less than nineteen schools of legal opinion in Islam, whose diversities of juristic views reflect the response to the necessities of a growing civilization. The fossilization of Islamic law in subsequent schools of jurisprudence is an artificial situation which can be eroded by a return through *ijtihād* to the other three sources of Islamic legislation: the Qur'ān, which has to be studied and interpreted in the light and requirements of this day and age; the *ḥadīs̱*, which need not be used indiscriminately as a source of law; and the *ijmā'*.[55]

Ijmā' had been categorically rejected, in the classical sense of

[53] Ibid. pp. 145–6. [54] Ibid. [55] Ibid. pp. 157–67.

being the exclusive privilege of the *'ulamā'*, by the early modernists, Sayyid Aḥmad Khān and Chirāgh 'Alī. Iqbāl accepts it 'as the most important legal notion in Islam'. But it is *ijmā'* in a revolutionary sense, as a consensus arrived at through a parliamentary system of government in an Islamic state. 'The pressure of new world forces and the political experience of European nations are impressing on the mind of modern Islam the value and possibilities of the idea of Ijma.'[56] The growth of democracy in Islamic states was an encouraging sign.

> The transfer of the power of Ijtihad from individual representatives of [classical] schools [of law] to a Muslim legislative assembly which, in view of the growth of opposing sects, is the one possible form Ijma can take in modern times, will secure contributions to legal discussions from laymen who happen to possess a keen insight into affairs.[57]

This he considers to be the only way to blast a way out of the cul-de-sac of traditionalist Islam towards new avenues.

Iqbāl's special contribution to the development of Muslim legal thought in Muslim India and Pakistan has been the re-establishment of the principle he advocated, i.e. the enlargement of the scope and authority of *ijmā'*. His view was quickly accepted by the westernized Muslim intelligentsia in the subcontinent, and came to be equated with public opinion and with parliamentary institutions. This view has its parallels in other Muslim lands, especially Turkey and Egypt. But the 'moderating conservatism' which forms the other half of his system of religious and political thought saw a difficulty in the unrestrained transfer of the right of constituting *ijmā'* to the masses of people or to an élite unschooled in religious law. This was a problem which the creators of Pakistan had to face since its inception. On this point Iqbāl faces, and submits to, the inevitability of providing some representation for the *'ulamā'* in legislative institutions. This was precisely the solution accepted by the ruling élite of Pakistan, though with a number of checks and balances. And yet this problem has been Pakistan's chief dilemma in constitution-making and legislation.

[56] Ibid. pp. 164–5. [57] Ibid. p. 165.

CHAPTER EIGHT

THE GENESIS OF PAKISTAN

IQBĀL'S THEORY OF PAKISTAN

THE most intelligent analysis of Iqbāl's mind in its pilgrimage to the shrines of so many ideals in search of a solution for Muslim India is the one offered by Sir Hamilton Gibb:

> Perhaps the right way to look at Iqbal is to see in him one who reflected and put into vivid words the diverse currents of ideas that were agitating the minds of the Indian Muslims. His sensitive poetic temperament mirrored all that impinged upon it—the backward-looking romanticism of the liberals, the socialist leaning of the young intellectuals, the longing of the militant Muslim Leaguers for a strong leader to restore the political power of Islam.[1]

In the pan-Islamic phase of his writings, which began in 1908 and continued until his death in 1938, Iqbāl dissociated politics from nationalism and tried to correlate it with religion and culture. This also implied the rejection of the modern western concept of the duality of church and state.

> If you begin with the conception of religion as complete other-worldliness, then what has happened to Christianity in Europe is perfectly natural. The universal ethics of Jesus is displaced by nationalist systems of ethics and policy. The conclusion to which Europe is consequently driven is that religion is a private affair of the individual, and has nothing to do with what is called man's temporal life. Islam does not bifurcate the unity of man into an irreconcilable duality of spirit and matter. In Islam God and the universe, spirit and matter, church and state are organic to each other.[2]

The real significance of the Prophet's *hijra* from Mecca to Medina in 622 lay in the repudiation of the concept of local

[1] *Modern Trends in Islam* (1945), p. 61.

[2] Presidential Address at Annual Session of Muslim League at Allahabad, 1930 (Philips, p. 239).

patriotism.[3] The concept of political society in Islam does not accept geographical regionalism or a common race as valid criteria for defining an ethnic group. The earth belongs to God, and as such is the common habitation of all men. Potentially Muslim people can live in any part of it. In their universal political life in the midst of humanity in general there can be only two criteria of political grouping in so far as Islam is concerned—Muslims and non-Muslims. All non-Muslims constitute a single community, he argues on the basis of a *ḥadīṣ* which is probably apocryphal, and are antithetical to the community of Islam.[4] This does not justify a striving for a Muslim imperialism at the expense of others. In fact the success of historical Islam in carving out empires was detrimental to Islam's cultural growth because of irrelevant borrowings from external cultures. Nor does it mean that Muslims are in any sense a superior or a chosen people. In fact the Muslim community is potentially and not actually the *khayr al-umam* (best among the communities), not by the mere virtue of following the Prophet of Islam, whose prophethood was meant to promulgate freedom, equality, and brotherhood among *all* mankind, but by the community's own maximum effort to apply the ethical values of the Prophet's teachings to harnessing the forces of nature.[5]

How is this community of Islam in diaspora all over the world to be held together? Its central focus can be found in the basic Islamic concept of the unity of God (*tawḥīd*); its externalization as a social force is reflected in the brotherhood of Islam, which is based on the Qur'ān and the *sunna*. Its external symbol, or as Iqbāl calls it, its 'cognizable centre' (*markaz-i maḥsūs*) is the *ka'ba* which, he says, is nothing more than the cynosure of the mind and the eye: the circumambulation is not merely going round and round a relic: 'but between us [Muslims] and the *ka'ba* there is a symbolic association of which even Gabriel is unaware'. This was a poetic way of restating the Walī-Allāhī

[3] 'Jughrāfiyā'-ī ḥudūd awr musalmān', in *Maẓāmīn* (1943), pp. 180–96.

[4] Letter to R. A. Nicholson (Urdu tr. in *Makātīb* (1944), p. 471; see also *Asrār*, pp. 69–72 (Nicholson, pp. 116–20).

[5] *Rumūz*, pp. 119–28 (Arberry, pp. 21–28, 56–59).

emphasis that by attracting Muslims from all parts of the world for *ḥajj* (pilgrimage) and bringing them together, the *kaʿba* symbolizes the unity of Islamic society.[6]

The state to which the universal Islamic society can belong is so far an unrealized ideal Muslim state. A great deal of effort is devoted throughout the works of Iqbāl to the attempt to define this ideal state in terms of modern ideologies. Of these he rejects modern western democracy as essentially plutocratic and based on racial inequality and the exploitation of the weak. He does not regard Islam and socialism as necessarily mutually exclusive or antagonistic: he regards the Islamic concept of equality and Muslim rejection of racialism as similar to that in socialist theory, and the socialist elimination of monarchical institutions as parallel to Muslim iconoclasm. In explaining the institution of *zakāt* as a voluntary super-tax, Iqbāl sees the possibility of eliminating the accumulation of wealth in the hands of the few.[7]

Having stressed all these common values, Iqbāl finally rejects communism as the ideal form of world government in comparison with Islam. His argument is based on a speculative explanation of the Muslim *kalima* (the attestation of faith): 'There is no God but God'. He argues that in the dialectics of existence the law of a negative thesis and a positive antithesis operates, in order to arrive at the synthesis of truth. 'No' (*lā*), the negative particle in the Muslim attestation of faith is destructive; the conditional 'but' (*illā*), the positive one, is affirmative and constructive. The nature of life and the universe is a movement from *lā* to *illā*, from negation to positivism, from denial to affirmation. Welded together in an order of experienced truth, *la* and *illa* constitute the means of stocktaking the universe and of its subjugation. The particle *lā* in isolation denotes revolution, destruction of false gods, but not value-creating construction. Communism has got bogged down in the stage of *lā*, in negativeness, in destruction of old injustices as well as of old values, but

[6] Ibid. pp. 104–8 (Arberry, pp. 11–21); *Armaghān*, p. 148; cf. Walī-Allāh, *Ḥujjat*, ii. 180.

[7] *Payām*, pp. 236–8, 244, 255–8; *Armaghān*, pp. 148–52; *Ẓarb*, pp. 138–9.

has failed to emerge so far into the creative stage of *illā*. 'The religion of that God-ignoring prophet [Karl Marx] is based on the equality of all stomachs.' Communism has, therefore, much in common with western imperialism: 'Both are dynamic and restless. Both ignore God and betray man. One does this by revolution, the other by exploitation. Between these two mill-stones humanity is ground to dust.'[8]

The ideal state is therefore to be sought not in any other contemporary system but in Islam itself. Thus one arrives at the concept of the Qur'ānic state which is an ideal so far unrealized in Islamic history, and which must not be confused with the caliphate of the four orthodox Caliphs, as is done by most Muslim revivalists. The Qur'ānic state is still unrealized and dormant in the mind and conscience of man. This Qur'ānic state cannot be built upon any regional or racial or group loyalty. It would not accept personal rule, and would equate the concept of the caliphate with the service of humanity. In this ideal state man's vicegerency of God would fulfil itself and honour its trust, by acknowledging that the ownership of all land (i.e. the means of production) vests in God, and by accepting that man's duty is to produce wealth for the benefit of all humanity.[9]

While this ideal state was Iqbāl's dream of the future, his immediate concern was the fate of the Muslims in the slowly emerging pattern of self-government in India. Here he once again modified his theory of 'cognizable centre' to apply to the specific problem of Muslim India: a Muslim majority in the north-west and a Muslim diaspora in the rest of the subcontinent. Whereas the *ka'ba* remained the symbolic 'cognizable centre' of the entire Muslim world, a regional centre in a politically defined regional state was necessary for the survival of Muslims in the subcontinent. The Muslim-majority areas thus constituted a politically realizable 'cognizable centre' in relation to the diaspora. This marked a retreat from Iqbāl's original position, his idealistic denunciation of regionalism. He had now come to the conclusion that while a universal Muslim caliphate

[8] *Pas chi bāyad kard*, pp. 19–22; *Jāwīd Nāma*, p. 69. [9] Ibid. pp. 74–83.

was impracticable in the modern world, the only tangible form the political expression of pan-Islamism could take was that of multi-nationalism, realizing itself in regional national states.[10]

Iqbāl first put forward a proposal for the creation of a separate state in India in 1930, in his presidential address to the annual session of the Muslim League. He began by asserting that

> Islam, regarded as an ethical ideal plus a certain kind of polity—by which expression I mean a social structure, regulated by a legal system and animated by a specific ethical ideal—has been the chief formative factor in the life-history of the Muslims of India. It has furnished the basic emotions and loyalties which gradually unify scattered individuals and groups, and finally transform them into a well-defined people possessing a moral consciousness of their own. . . . Is it possible to retain Islam as an ethical ideal and to reject it as a polity in favour of national polities in which the religious attitude is not permitted to play any part? This question becomes of special importance in India where the Muslims happen to be in a minority.

Iqbāl's answer to this question was:

> The religious order of Islam is organically related to the social order which it has created. The rejection of the one will eventually involve the rejection of the other. Therefore the construction of a polity on Indian national lines, if it means a displacement of the Islamic principles of solidarity, is simply unthinkable to a Muslim.[11]

In comparing the concept of Islamic solidarity as a social unity with the modern western concept of a nation, Iqbāl had taken his cue from Ernest Renan, who had pointed out that the concept of nationalism was, after all, something new and a product of modern western history. It was unknown in the same sense in ancient history. But what constitutes modern nationalism? Is it the concept of a common race? But ethnographic considerations do not seem to have formed modern nations: 'la France est celtique, ibérique, germanique. L'Allemagne est germanique, celtique, et slave'.[12] A similar race mixture is

[10] *Reconstruction*, p. 151.
[11] *Struggle for Independence*, pp. 12–15.
[12] *Qu'est-ce qu'une nation?* (Paris, 1882), p. 15.

observable in every European country. Then does a common language constitute a nation? Language, says Renan, tends to unite people, but does not force them into a common nationality. In the case of Britain and the United States of America, or Spain and Latin America, a common language has been unable to sustain the principle of nationhood, while Switzerland, which has three languages, constituted itself into a nation.[13] Unlike Iqbāl, Renan held that religion alone cannot constitute a nation; they agreed that neither could geography, though both religion and geography played important roles in the formation of nationhoods. Renan's definition of a nation is that it is

une âme, un principe spirituel. L'une est dans le passé, l'autre dans le présent. L'une est la possession en commun d'un riche legs de souvenirs; l'autre est le consentement actuel, le désir de vivre ensemble, la volonté de continuer à faire valoir l'héritage qu'on a reçu indivis. . . . Avoir de gloires communes dans le passé, une volonté commune dans le présent; avoir fait de grandes choses ensemble, vouloir en faire encore, voilà la condition essentiel pour être un peuple. . . . Une nation est donc une grand solidarité, constitué par le sentiment de sacrifice qu'on a fait et de ceux qu'on a disposé à faire encore. Elle suppose un passé; elle se résume pourtant dans le présent par un fait tangible; le consentement, le désir clairement exprimé de continuer la vie commune.[14]

Iqbāl thoroughly assimilated Renan's argument in his own political thought, applying it to the Indian situation. Judged by this standard the Hindu-Muslim political complex cannot be defined as constituting a single nationhood. In the past the two communities were divided against one another. There was no clear indication of any will to merge their identities in the future. On the other hand by this standard Muslim India constituted a nation by itself. On this point Iqbāl quoted Renan:

L'homme n'est esclave ni de sa race, ni de sa langue, ni de sa religion, ni du course des fleuves, ni de la direction des chaînes de montagnes. Une grande agrégation d'hommes, saine d'esprit et chaude de cœur, crée une conscience morale qui s'appelle une nation.[15]

[13] Ibid. pp. 19–20, 22–25.
[14] Ibid. pp. 26–27.
[15] Ibid. p. 29, quoted and tr. by Iqbāl in his Pres. Add. (*Struggle*, p. 15).

According to Iqbāl, the emotional and psychological homogeneity which inspires the will to create a nation does not exist in the subcontinent. It might have been achieved if the administrative and social eclecticism of Akbar or the mystic syncretism of Kabīr had succeeded in catching the imagination of the vast masses of India. Instead, these experiments shrivelled into syncretisms because of their rejection by the great religious groupings and by the caste structure of Hindu society. The fact of diversity within the Indian nation has therefore to be recognized. Ignoring it can only lead to inner tensions. Its recognition may well lead to co-operation between its two major communities. Hindu solidarity has its cultural affinities with the Buddhist world in East and South-East Asia; while Muslim solidarity has its religio-political ties with the Middle East. India is Asia in miniature.[16]

This was a significant pronouncement, unapologetically forecasting the 'two-nation theory' which had been vaguely suggested by Sayyid Aḥmad Khān and Mawlānā Muḥammad 'Alī earlier and was finally developed by Jinnāḥ. Vague suggestions of the desirability of a separate Indian Muslim state had been made sporadically and casually, but they remained largely isolated. Iqbāl was the first explicitly to formulate the theory of the necessity of the creation of such a state:

> The principle of European democracy cannot be applied to India without recognizing the facts of communal groups. . . . The Muslim demand for the creation of a Muslim India is, therefore, perfectly justified. . . . I would like to see the Punjab, North-Western Frontier Province, Sind and Baluchistan amalgamated into a single state. Self-Government within the British Empire, or without the British Empire, the formation of a consolidated North-West Indian Muslim state appears to me to be the final destiny of the Muslims at least of North-West India.[17]

Iqbāl makes a distinction between Islam as conceived as the legal basis of the state and theocracy which connotes fanaticism.

[16] *Struggle*, pp. 15–16.

[17] Ibid. pp. 16–17.

A separate Muslim state within the subcontinent would not be a theocracy. It would provide, on the other hand, an opportunity for Islam 'to rid itself of the stamp that Arabian imperialism was forced to give it, to mobilize its law, its education, its culture, and to bring them into closer contact with its original spirit and with the spirit of modern times'. This mixture of modernism and fundamentalism which he has in mind makes hardly any provision for a secular state for Muslims, like Turkey. 'One lesson', he continues, 'I have learnt from the history of the Muslims. At critical moments in their history it is Islam that has saved Muslims and not vice-versa.'[18]

During 1936–7 Iqbāl and Jinnāḥ came into very close contact politically. In a series of letters to Jinnāḥ, Iqbāl pressed the view that the creation of a separate Muslim state was the only feasible solution for the Muslims and for peace in India. The Muslims of north-west India and Bengal should ignore Muslim-minority provinces in the interest of Indian Muslims as a whole. The real problem facing Muslim leadership was that of Muslim poverty: 'the Muslim League will have to finally decide whether it will remain a body representing the upper classes of Indian Muslims or Muslim masses.'

> Happily there is a solution in the enforcement of the law of Islam and its further development in the light of modern ideas. . . . If this system of law is properly understood and applied, at least the right to subsistence is secured to everybody . . . For Islam the acceptance of social democracy in some suitable form and consistent with the legal principles of Islam is not a revolution but a return to the original purity of Islam.[19]

In his introduction to this series of Iqbāl's letters Jinnāḥ acknowledged that Iqbāl's views finally led him to the same conclusions, i.e. the demand for a separate Muslim state which found due expression in the 'Pakistan' resolution passed by the Muslim League in its annual session in 1940.[20]

[18] Ibid. pp. 18 and 27.

[19] Reprinted ibid. app. v, pp. 33–36.

[20] Ibid. p. 21.

MUḤAMMAD ʿALĪ JINNĀḤ AND THE TWO-NATION THEORY

Steeped in the liberalism of Dādābhāī Naorojī and Gopāl Krishna Gokhale, Muḥammad ʿAlī Jinnāḥ began his career in the liberal wing of the Indian National Congress. In 1913 he was persuaded by Mawlānā Muḥammad ʿAlī and Wazīr Ḥasan to join the Muslim League at a time when that organization came very close to the views of the Congress, and on the assurance that it would continue to do so.[21] In 1916 he drafted the famous formula of a Congress–League pact which envisaged the election of Muslims to the provincial and central legislative councils through separate electoral bodies, weightage for Muslims in the central and several provincial councils, though not in the Punjab and Bengal, and the provision that any resolution affecting a community could be passed only if three-quarters of the total members of that community in a provincial or the central council supported it.[22] This formula was accepted also by the orthodox Hindu leaders of the right wing of the Congress, including the revivalist and anti-Muslim Tilak. Jinnāḥ thus emerged at that early date as one of the chief architects of Hindu-Muslim political unity, which lasted until 1923–4.

In the days of the civil disobedience and non-co-operation movements of the Indian National Congress during the early 1920s, Jinnāḥ remained aloof and did not actively participate in what he considered unconstitutional revolutionary activities.[23] Though a Khoja Shīʿī, he was sympathetic to the Khilāfat movement, but did not take an active part in it.

The next landmark in Jinnāḥ's political career was his formulation of 'Fourteen Points', summing up the reaction of the All-Muslim Conference to the report of the committee appointed by the Indian National Congress under the chairmanship of Motīlāl Nehrū in 1928 to recommend the principles of a constitution for

[21] Sarojini Naidu's introd. to *Mohamed Ali Jinnah, an Ambassador of Unity* (Madras); Bolitho, *Jinnah: Creator of Pakistan* (London, 1954), pp. 57–58.
[22] Report of 31st Indian National Congress, 1916, pp. 77–81 (Philips, pp. 171–3).
[23] Jawaharlal Nehru, *An Autobiography* (London, 1958), pp. 67–68.

India. The recommendations of the Nehrū report were largely secular in character, and provided neither safeguards nor weightage nor separate electoral bodies for Muslims, though they advocated full provincial status for the Muslim areas of the North-Western Frontier and Sind.[24] Jinnāḥs Fourteen Points, which remained the main plank of Muslim politics in India during the next decade, demanded a federal system with complete autonomy and residuary powers vested in the provinces; separate electoral bodies and weightage for the Muslims; and safeguards for the protection and promotion of Muslim education, language, religion, personal laws and *waqfs*.[25]

During the Round Table Conferences held in London in 1930 and 1931 Jinnāḥ's 'disillusion about the prospects of the Muslims receiving a fair deal from the Congress became visibly stronger as the proceedings went on'.[26] The tragic spectacle of the failure of the Congress in general and of Gāndhī in particular to solve the communal problem led to his final breach with Indian nationalism. He retired from politics for two years, but returned to the Indian political scene in 1934 at the entreaty of the Muslim League leader, Liyāqat 'Alī Khān. Between 1934 and 1937 he revived the Muslim League. As hostility between the Congress and the League deepened between 1937 and 1939, the period when Congress governments ruled several provinces, the Muslim League emerged as the representative organization of the Muslims and Jinnāḥ as their principal leader.

The first open reference to Hindus and Muslims as two separate nations was made during a session of the Sind provincial Muslim League in October 1938. The 'Two-Nation theory' was elaborated by Jinnāḥ in 1940 in an article in *Time and Tide*. He began his argument by quoting from the report of the Joint Select Committee on Indian Constitutional Reforms set up by the British Government:

[24] All Parties Conference, *Report of the Committee appointed to determine the principles of the Constitution of India, 1928*. (Philips, pp. 228 ff.)

[25] *Indian Quarterly Register*, i. (1929), pp. 365–6 (Philips, pp. 235–7).

[26] Williams, *State of Pakistan* (London, 1962), p. 20.

> India is inhabited by many races . . . often as distinct from one another in origin, tradition and manner of life as are nations of Europe. Two-thirds of its inhabitants profess Hinduism in one form or other as their religion, over seventy millions are followers of Islam; and the difference between the two is not only of religion in the stricter sense but also of law and culture.

'Hinduism and Islam', continued Jinnāḥ, 'represent two distinct and separate civilizations and, moreover, are as distinct from one another in origin, tradition and manner of life as are nations of Europe.'

From this premiss Jinnāḥ proceeded to argue further: 'If, therefore, it is accepted that there are in India a major and a minor nation, it follows that parliamentary system based on the majority principle must inevitably mean the rule of the major nation.[27]

Jinnāḥ was aware that this position would be exposed to the charge of a theocratic or ultra-conservative view of politics from the modern western standpoint. He therefore continued:

> The British people . . . sometimes forget the religious wars of their own history, and today consider religion as a private and personal matter between man and God. This can never be the case in Hinduism and Islam, for both these religions are definite social codes which govern not so much man's relation with his God as man's relation with his neighbour. They govern not only his law and culture but every aspect of his social life and such religions, essentially exclusive, completely preclude the merging of identity and unity of thought on which Western democracy is based and inevitably bring about vertical rather than the horizontal divisions democracy envisages.[28]

Since India was composed of two nations, Hindu and Muslim, a vast number of the latter being concentrated in certain contiguous areas, the scheme of a central federal government as envisaged in the Government of India Act of 1935 could only be detrimental to the interests of the Muslims of those areas, and was therefore unacceptable to the Muslim League. The

[27] Reprinted in Jamil-ud-Din Ahmed, ed., *Speeches and Writings of Mr Jinnah* (1952), i, 116–17.

[28] Ibid.

problem in India was not inter-communal; it was international and had to be so treated. So long as this fact was not recognized, any constitution imposed on unwilling ethnic components would lead to disaster. 'The only course open to us all is to allow the major nations separate homelands by dividing India into autonomous national states.' Jinnāḥ saw a future chance of peaceful coexistence only in the division of the subcontinent, for 'the rivalry and the natural desire and efforts on the part of one to dominate the social order and establish political supremacy over the other in the government of the country will disappear'.[29]

Against the argument of the geographical unity of India, Jinnāḥ quoted a number of historical precedents. Compact geographical areas much smaller than the Indian subcontinent stood divided into a number of states, for example the Balkan and Iberian peninsulas. Likewise the Portuguese stood divided in the Iberian peninsula.[30]

> India never was one, never was a nation, never was a country governed by one single power even with the sword. It is a Sub-Continent of different nationalities and peoples. It was never governed in history by one single power. Even today when constitutionally and legally Britain is ruling over India, one-third [of it] is not British. This administrative oneness is entirely the making of the British. . . . Its sanction is the British bayonet, and not the sanction of the peoples.[31]

This argument led to the inexorable logic of history: 'Musalmans are a nation according to any definition of a nation, and they must have their homelands, their territory and their state.' Since the Indian Muslims constituted a nation by themselves, it was for them alone to determine their future.[32]

CROSS-CURRENTS IN THE PAKISTAN MOVEMENT

Vague gropings towards the concept of a separate Muslim

[29] Pres. Address to Lahore (1940) session of Muslim League, ibid. i. 145, 159–60 (Philips, pp. 353–4).

[30] Ibid. p. 161.

[31] Speech at meeting of Muslim League Council, Delhi, 9 Nov. 1942 (Ahmed), *Speeches and Writings of Mr Jinnah*, i. 425).

[32] Ibid. pp. 162 and 442.

homeland for Muslims in India are considerably older historically than the theories of Iqbāl and Jinnāḥ.[33]

Between Jamāl al-dīn al-Afghānī, probably quite eponymously credited as having first conceived the idea of a central-Asian-and-north-west-Indian state in the 1880s, and Iqbāl, who worked out a political philosophy for it in 1930, the feeling of territorial separatism was generally, though not quite coherently, taking shape in the minds of Indian Muslims. In his evidence given before the North-West Frontier Inquiry Committee set up by the Government of India in 1924, Sardār Muḥammad Gul Khān, an insignificant tribal chief, mentioned the desirability of a homeland for the Muslims stretching from the western frontier to the valley of the Jumna.[34] In 1928 the suggestion for a separate Muslim state 'within the body-politic of India' was put forward for the consideration of the Nehru Committee and rejected mainly due to the opposition of Shrīnivās Shāstrī and other conservative Hindu leaders who regarded it as a potential threat to the effectiveness of a central Indian government.[35] Politically much more conscious of the growing Muslim aspiration for territorial separatism was the stand of Mawlānā Muḥammad ʿAlī during the Round Table Conference of 1930. He opposed the principle of weightage for the non-Muslims in the Muslim-majority provinces of Punjab and Bengal, and to keep the Muslims there in effective control he proposed that these provinces should be given residuary powers.

> India was about to have what she never had before . . . 'majority rule'. That would be intolerable. . . . I could see no ray of hope if the Muslims were everywhere in a minority: but luckily there are Muslim majorities in certain provinces . . . that gives us our safeguard.[36]

After Iqbāl's formulation of the theory of a separate state, a few students at Cambridge, the most prominent among whom was Chawdharī Raḥmat ʿAlī, coined a name for the new state

[33] S. S. Pirzada, *Evolution of Pakistan* (Lahore, 1963).
[34] NWFP Inquiry Committee, 1924, *Report*, pp. 122–3.
[35] Iqbal, Pres. Add., p. 17.
[36] R. Coupland, *The Indian Problem* (Oxford, 1942–3), iii. 73.

which became very popular. The name 'Pakistan' was mnemonically formed from the names of Muslim-majority provinces of the north-west areas, *P*unjab, *A*fghania (North-West Frontier Province), *K*ashmir, *S*ind, and Baluchis*tan*.[37] To the popular mind it suggested the creation of a land of the 'pure', implying that the rest of the subcontinent was 'impure'. It can be safely said that this name was the only contribution of the Cambridge group to the Pakistan movement, and even on this point Jinnāḥ clarified the position to Gāndhī in 1944, saying that 'it does not bear the original meaning [i.e. the land of the pure]'; and that it was used because it had become synonymous in the Muslim mind with Muslim League's Lahore resolution of 1940 demanding the creation of a separate Muslim state.[38] The Cambridge movement was critical of Iqbāl's provision for a possible confederation with Hindu India.[39] In its other demands the movement was an illustration of obscurantist political eccentricity which, because of its confusion with the genuine Pakistan movement, exposed it to a great deal of embarrassment. The Cambridge movement denounced 'minorityism' and argued that Muslim nationalism should acquire more states not only in the Muslim-majority areas, where the principle of self-determination favoured such a stand, but also in the Indian states ruled by Muslim princes though consisting of Hindu majorities, and in land-locked areas like Ajmer, sacred to Muslim saints. These 'individual Muslim nations' within the subcontinent were to be co-ordinated under the 'Pak Commonwealth of Nations', converting India into *Dīnia* (Faith-land) and uniting ultimately with an undefined pan-Islamic 'Pakasia'.[40] Chawdharī Raḥmat 'Alī and his associates had no contact with Muslim masses or the political life of Muslim India. Their views embarrassed the

[37] Chowdhari Rahmat Ali, *The Millat of Islam and the Menace of Indianism* (Cambridge, 1941), i. 4 and *Now or Never* (Cambridge, 1933).

[38] Quoted in P. C. Joshi, *They Must Meet Again* (Bombay, 1945), p. 19; Jinnah, *Speeches and Writings*, i. 509.

[39] Coupland, ii. 199.

[40] Chowdhari Rahmat Ali, *The Millat and the Mission* (Cambridge, 1942), pp. 1–18.

Muslim political leadership and inspired some virulent criticism in the Hindu press between 1933 and 1947.

In 1937 the Indian National Congress, after its overwhelming success in the elections, formed governments in almost all those provinces where Hindus constituted a majority. The Muslim League did not do so well in Muslim-majority areas. The Congress declined to form coalitions with the League, though the two organizations had co-operated during the elections. The League regarded this as a breach of faith, while the Congress argued in favour of a one-party government on the plea that only a purely Congress government could present the British governor with schemes of social and political reforms and carry them out. During their period of office between 1937 and 1939 the Congress governments, especially that of the Central Provinces, initiated and adopted religious, cultural, and economic policies which the Muslims considered detrimental to their survival as a religious and cultural entity. In response to this challenge the Muslim League emerged as the chief and the strongest party in opposition to the Congress, and within two years became almost the sole representative of the Muslim élite, enjoying the fullest support of the Muslim masses.[41]

In October 1938 the Sind Provincial Muslim League meeting in Karachi referred to India not as a country but as a subcontinent, and advocated separate political self-determination for Hindus and Muslims.[42] It also recommended devising a constitution under which the Muslims might attain full independence. Several schemes of Muslim autonomy within the Indian federation and of independent Muslim states were drafted by various Muslims, including Dr A. Laṭīf, who advocated the division of the proposed Indian federation into eleven Hindu and

[41] Ahmed, *Speeches and Writings of Mr Jinnah*, i. 121; see also Committee appointed by the Council of the All-India Muslim League to Inquire into Muslim Grievances in Congress Provinces, *Report* (the Pirpur Report), (Delhi, 1938); Committee appointed by the Council of the All-India Muslim League to examine the Wardha Scheme, *Report*, [Kamal Yar Jung Committee Report] (Calcutta, 1942).

[42] *Resolutions of All-India Muslim League from Oct. 1937 to Dec. 1938*, Annexure, pp. 65–68; I. H. Qureshi, *The Struggle for Pakistan* (1965), p. 126.

four Muslim cultural zones; Sayyid Ẓafr al-Ḥasan and Afzal Ḥusayn Qādirī, who envisaged the carving out of three Muslim states: North-West, Bengal, and the Hyderabad state; Shāh Nawāz Khān Mamdot, who proposed the division of India into five zones; Sir ʿAbd-Allāh Hārūn, who suggested a separate Muslim federation of north-west areas and Kashmir but left the problem of Bengal and Hyderabad state untouched; and Sir Sikandar Ḥayāt Khān, who proposed a two-tier federation consisting of seven zones, a scheme which was really a modification of the Government of India Act of 1935.[43] Almost all these schemes either made extravagant Muslim claims or failed to satisfy Muslim aspirations not only for separation but also for complete independence.

On 26 March 1940 the Muslim League in its annual session held at Lahore resolved that geographically contiguous units should be demarcated into regions

> which should be so constituted, with such territorial readjustments as may be necessary, that the areas in which the Muslims are numerically in a majority, as in the north-western and eastern zones of India, should be grouped to constitute 'independent states' in which the constituent units shall be autonomous and sovereign.[44]

Despite the reference to plural states, the commentary of the Muslim League leaders made it clear that the resolution actually envisaged the creation of a single Muslim state constituting the north-western and eastern (Bengal) Muslim-majority zones.[45]

It is surprising how quickly the conception of Pakistan impressed itself on some outstanding individuals as a tangible solution. It soon made a powerful impact on Muslim politics and on all subsequent negotiations between the British, the

[43] S. A. Latif, *The Cultural Future of India* (Bombay, 1938) and *A Federation of Cultural Zones for India* (Sikandarabad, 1938) Sir Abdullah Harun, introd. to Latif's *Muslim Problem in India* (Bombay, 1939); Sikander Hayat Khan, *Outlines of a Scheme of Indian Federation* (Lahore, 1939).

[44] *Resolutions of AIML Dec. 1938–Mar, 1940*, pp. 47–48.

[45] Khalid bin Sayeed, *Pakistan: the Formative Phase* (Karachi, 1960), pp. 124–6.

Indian National Congress, and the Muslim League. B. R. Ambedkar, the leader of the Hindu depressed castes who was afterwards to draft the constitution of independent India, was the first non-Muslim of intellectual stature to write a brilliant analysis of the demand for Pakistan, and he arrived at conclusions which were anti-Muslim but pro-Pakistan. In March 1942, when the Japanese armies were pressing against the eastern frontier of India after their occupation of Burma, the British War Cabinet sent Sir Stafford Cripps with proposals to accelerate Indian independence if the major political parties gave full support in the war effort. The 'Cripps proposals' conceded the principle of self-determination contained in the demand for Pakistan, conceding

> the right of any Province of British India that is not prepared to accept the new Constitution to retain its present constitutional position, provision being made for its subsequent accession if it so decides. With such non-acceding Provinces, should they so desire, His Majesty's Government will be prepared to agree upon a new Constitution, giving them the same full status as the Indian Union, and arrived at by a procedure analogous to that here laid down.[46]

Though the 'Cripps proposals' were rejected by the Congress because, among other reasons, they conceded the principle of Pakistan, the Muslim League also rejected them on the ground that their commitment to a separate Muslim homeland was not sufficiently clear and direct. Within a month a broad-minded conservative leader of the Indian National Congress, C. Rājāgopālachārya, recommended to the Congress Working Committee some concession to the Muslim demand for a separate state if it could be envisaged within an Indian federation. The resolution was overwhelmingly rejected and a counter-resolution was passed to take cognizance of the principle of self-determination by conceding that the Congress could not think in terms of compelling the people of any territorial unit to remain in the Indian Union against its 'declared and established will', but while recognizing the principle, the Committee felt that conditions

[46] Philips, p. 372.

should be created which could help in developing a common and co-operative national life.[47]

Rājāgopālāchārya's formula had stipulated a Congress–League interim government during a transitional period with the common objective of obtaining complete independence, the formation of a commission after the war to demarcate the frontiers of Hindu and Muslim zones (in the latter the secession to take effect after a plebiscite of all inhabitants preferably on the basis of adult franchise); and the independence of the seceding Muslim state, to be linked to India in a confederal pattern of common defence, commerce, and communications. In September 1944 this formed one of the bases for discussions between Gāndhī and Jinnāḥ, which were unsuccessful.[48]

After the end of the war, a British Cabinet Mission arrived in India in March 1946 and proposed a three-zone federation, Zone A consisting of the bulk of Indian provinces with Hindu majorities situated in the middle and the greater part of the subcontinent: Zone B consisting of the north-western provinces with considerable Muslim majorities; Zone C consisting of Bengal and Assam with a slight Muslim majority. This ingenious scheme was designed to give Congress the subcontinental unity it stood for; it gave to the Muslims the substance of autonomous, though not independent, Pakistan plus weightage in the centre. The Congress accepted it after some hesitation and so did the Muslim League. But soon afterwards in a statement Jawāharlāl Nehrū asserted the right to modify the plan after independence, which seemed to Muslim League as striking at the very basis of the Cabinet Mission's solution. The position Nehrū had taken was fraught with those very dangers which wrecked a similar formula in the later case of Cyprus. There was also sympathy in the Congress high command for the Assam Congress leaders' demand that their province should be included in the predominantly Hindu Zone A. The Muslim League withdrew its acceptance of the plan and, because of the manœuvres of the Congress

[47] Ibid. p. 373.

[48] Text ibid. pp. 356–60.

leaders on these points of revision, the Congress lost the opportunity of retaining a united India.[49]

On 3 June 1947 the Congress and the Muslim League accepted Lord Mountbatten's plan for partitioning India into two sovereign states, India and Pakistan.

[49] Azad, *India Wins Freedom*, p. 155.

CHAPTER NINE

ABU'L-KALĀM ĀZĀD: EXEGETICAL ECLECTICISM

ABU'L-Kalām Āzād (1888–1958) complements certain aspects of Iqbāl's religious thought. In certain others, such as his approach to exegesis of the Qur'ān and understanding of the relationship between God and man, his approach is very different. Iqbāl approaches the Qur'ān equipped with dialectical methodology and an attitude of metaphysical speculation. Āzād proceeds from the revealed word of God to the explanation of the phenomena of the universe and the physical and moral laws that bind humanity. In religious law Āzād is almost exclusively preoccupied with its primary source, the Qur'ān, quoting the *ḥadīs̱* only when it suits him to fortify his own exegetical argument; while Iqbāl is concerned with all the four sources, and especially the last two, *ijtihād* and *ijmā'*, which he regarded as the principal human, as distinguished from revelational or *ḥadīs̱*, instruments of legal evolution. *Ijtihād* as well as *ijmā'* in the interpretations of Iqbāl bear the stamp of the twentieth century. Āzād, on the other hand, replaces the legal concept of *ijtihād* by that of *ta'sīs* (reconsolidation), arguing that in modern times what is needed is not free or new legal speculation, but a consolidation of what he interprets as Islam's fundamental verities which would externalize the perfection inherent in it. The *ijmā'* of the *'ulamā'* did see eye to eye with Āzād on a number of religious and political points; but for the *ijmā'* of the people, the novel concept popularized by Iqbāl (for which Āzād prefers to use the classical term *sawād-i a'ẓam*), Āzād shows an uncompromising indifference.[1]

Unlike Iqbāl, Āzād's intellectual training had been basically traditionalist. When in 1905 he came into contact with Shiblī,

[1] *Taẕkira;* Humayun Kabir, ed., *Abu'l Kalam Azad; a Memorial Volume* (Bombay, 1956); S. M. Ikrām, *Mawj-i kaws̱ar* (1958), pp. 283–5.

the latter had already emerged in revolt against the loyalism and radical modernism of the Aligarh movement. Opposition to Aligarh and all that it stood for was therefore the springboard of Āzād's intellectual activity. This opposition externalized itself in various directions. Basically it tried to substitute an enlightened fundamentalism for a highly speculative modernism.

Āzād completed his education between 1907 and 1909 in the Arab lands, Egypt, Syria, Iraq, and the Hijāz. This reinforced traditionalist and fundamentalist trends in his religious and political thinking. It was during these years that he came into contact with the disciples of Jamāl al-dīn al-Afghānī and Shaykh Muḥammad 'Abduh. Between 1912 and 1930 Āzād edited off and on the two weekly journals *al-Hilāl* and *al-Balāgh*. In these journals, in a style which was highly arabicized but nevertheless forceful, passionate, rich, and decorative, interspersed with Persian and Urdu verses, Āzād wrote on religious and political themes. The two journals were in a way a twentieth-century fundamentalist-liberal response to the challenge of Sayyid Aḥmad Khān's nineteenth-century journal, *Tahẕīb al-akhlāq*. Instead of uncompromising rationalism Āzād tried to offer humanism, and in the place of pure speculation, a synthesis of traditionalism and modernism. And this last element shows the unmistakable influence of Sayyid Aḥmad Khān, whom he so fiercely denounced.[2] Like Sayyid Aḥmad Khān, Āzād rejects *taqlīd*, and turns to seek the answer to all basic problems, the laws of the universe, man's relationship with God and with man, the values of life, ethics, and norms of political morality in the Qur'ān itself. And in the study of the Qur'ān he rejects the bulk of the classical Muslim exegetes: 'When the commentators found that they could not rise to the heights of the Qur'ānic thought, they strove to bring it down to the level of their own mind.'[3] He rejects the classical theory of

[2] *India Wins Freedom* (1959); Humayun Kabir, p. 71.

[3] For Āzād's exegesis of the Qur'ān and the later studies of it see his *Tarjumān al-Qur'ān* (*TQ*) and *Bāqiyāt-i Tarjumān al-Qur'ān*, ed. Ghulām Rasūl Mihr (1961; Eng. tr. of pt. 1 of vol. i by S. A. Latif, *The Tarjumān al Qur'ān*, i: *Sūrat ul-Fātiha* (Bombay, 1962); also A. A. A. Fyzee, 'The Essence of Islam', *Univ. of Toronto Quarterly*, xxix (1960), pp. 181–97; Ashfaque Husayn, *The Quintessence of Islam* (Bombay, 1958); J. M. S. Baljon, *Modern Muslim Koran Interpretation, 1880–1960* (1961), *passim.*

the *iʿjāz* of the Qur'ān, and regards its method of statement and argument as essentially natural and 'germane to the character of its content'. Thus was it received and understood by the Prophet's contemporaries; but the expansion of the Islamic empire and incorporation into Islam of Byzantine and Sāsānid cultural and religious traditions introduced into the science of exegesis extraneous elements and interpretative methodologies. Terminology and concepts of Greek and neo-Platonic philosophy came to be applied to the Qur'ānic exegesis in which 'the idea came to the fore that the Qur'ān should support and endorse every new discovery in scientific knowledge'.[4]

The Qur'ān has to be studied from within itself, in its own right, and not in response to an extraneous pressure, for self-sufficient understanding and not for explanations or endorsements or rejections, extraneous pressures, motives, or criteria. The essential relevatory objectives of the Qur'ān are four. It aims to present the attributes of God in proper perspective. It emphasizes the principle of causality of life, nature, and the universe. It believes in the life hereafter as a vitalistic and ethical principle. And, finally, it prescribes the norms and rules of the good life.[5]

Waḥy does not communicate anything strikingly novel to man. It interprets on the basis of knowledge and faith his inherent urges. The tragedy of man has been that he tends to lose himself in his preoccupation with the created phenomena, and does not always seek behind them the Divine Creator; 'for God has thrown such attractive veils over His own creative beauty'.[6]

Relationship between God and man envisaged in *waḥy* consists of the radiation of three divine attributes towards all creation and all humanity. These attributes are: *rubūbiyyat*, *raḥmat* (benevolence), and *ʿadālat* (justice). *Rubūbiyyat* is a 'process of tender or careful nourishment providing from moment to moment and stage to stage all that one needs to gain the fullest possible development', which has been subject to a plan, an

[4] *TQ*, i. 40–42 (Latif, p. xxxvi).

[5] Ibid. p. 57 (Latif, pp. 6–7).

[6] Ibid. pp. 58–62 (Latif, pp. 7–14).

order, and a law: 'whatever is needed for the existence and sustenance of every being is provided at the appropriate time and in the appropriate quantity in order that the entire machinery of existence might run smoothly'. *Rubūbiyyat* thus fulfils the necessities of what Sayyid Aḥmad Khān had described as the 'laws of nature', or in theological terminology 'the habits of God'. A single principle of uniformity and harmony is applied by *rubūbiyyat* to help the development of all phenomena of nature. It has an outward as well as an inward aspect, the latter being especially pertinent to man. Divine activity of creation unfolds itself; *takhlīq* (creation), giving the created object a proper *taswiya* (mould), assigning to a specific *taqdīr* (role), and giving it *hidāyat* (guidance) in that role.[7]

Taqdīr (destiny) is therefore nothing but the assignment of a role which is conditioned by the outward and inward capacities or limitations of a creature or a created object, by its nature and by its demands for growth and development. A law of compatibility adjusts the creature to his environment. Adaptability to the environment and the urge of growth in a creature receives further protection by *hidāyat* conveyed through the prophets. The evolutionary concept of Āzād's doctrine of *hidāyat* is in harmony, in relation to sequence and to conclusion, with Iqbāl's vitalistic evolutionism, and to some extent with Sayyid Aḥmad Khān's equation of *waḥy* with the laws of nature. Āzād also follows Sayyid Aḥmad Khān in acknowledging the Qur'ān's repeated emphasis on the role of reason, which can study and interpret a scheme of creation that reveals two underlying principles. To begin with there is a single harmonious principle of life which links and holds together all creation; everything is linked to everything else, everything is fitted into the essence of creation for a scientific purpose, and nothing is created in vain. Secondly, the law which determines the interlinking and interdependence of all created objects is the law of causation.[8]

[7] Ibid. pp. 65–66, 74–76 (Latif, pp. 20–21, 28–30); cf. Muḥ. 'Abduh, *Tafsīr al-fātiḥa* (Cairo, 1911), pp. 66 ff.; Baljon, p. 62.

[8] *TQ*, i. 77–93 (Latif, pp. 31–46).

If reason aids man in his physical adjustment in his environment, *waḥy* helps him and guides him on a higher plane, his ethical and spiritual life. The Qur'ān bases its argument for the life hereafter on the analogy of the visible, mundane system of *rubūbiyyat* in the actual world. An object like the human being, who is made to appear the best of objects on earth, and for whose development so much has been carefully provided, is certainly not meant to be a thing which has no better purpose to serve than to strut on earth for a while and disappear for ever.[9]

Closely linked with *rubūbiyyat* is the other divine attribute, *raḥmat*. *Rubūbiyyat* nourishes beauty in creation; *raḥmat* maintains it with balance in growth leading to perfection. The balance is maintained by a law of ebb and flow, of constriction and expansion, of destruction and construction; 'even so, the process of destruction in the universe only subserves the demands of a beauteous construction'. In shaping beauty, nature in its creative flow encounters obstruction and overcomes it. 'It is this urge for perfection which sometimes has to produce convulsions or catastrophes, although these are not in reality evidences of destruction. In fact there is no [absolute] destruction anywhere in life. All that happens is proof of construction.' And construction is aimed at creating and externalizing the value of beauty. 'In fact, the very nature of the universe is constituted of beauty. Even as elements were created to give a form to the universe, even so it was invested with the qualities of colour, light, and shade, and of rhythm and beauty.'[10]

This emphasis on the value of beauty is a novel note in Islamic exegetical literature. Āzād has based it on the Qur'ān, 32: 6–7 and 17: 44. But it seems quite possible that it might be a synthesis of the Ṣūfistic heritage and the psychological acceptance of the criteria of classical Greek and modern western aesthetics. Enshrined as one of the supreme values in Āzād's reading of the scheme of the universe, the value of beauty softens and mellows his religious thought to a considerable extent.

The balance which maintains the value of beauty in all creation

[9] Ibid. p. 93 (Latif, p. 47). [10] Ibid. pp. 93–101 (Latif, pp. 47–53).

also controls the evolutionary process by putting brakes on natural selection and by imposing gradualism. This in turn is a source of checks and balances in man's individual, moral, and social life. This gradualism is also the law that governs the process of evolution by a chain of elimination and conservation. The struggle for existence to which man is subjected is a stimulating challenge for him to achieve perfection through a greater zest for life.[11]

The alternation between night and day, the process of ebb and flow, light and shade, action and inaction is the universal pattern which circumscribes man's activism in his search for perfection: 'It is the difference between night and day that has divided life into two parts. The light of the day is to help man engage himself in life's activities, and the darkness in the night to urge in him the need of rest.'[12]

Parallel with the law of alternation is that of duplication. Life fulfils itself by duplication through reproduction and multiplication. Like most animal species, human beings are created male and female. 'This arrangement is devised to induce love between them and peace of mind, so that through their joint co-operation, they might with confidence bear and counter the trials of life.'[13] This is a refreshing departure from Āzād's early anti-feminism towards a more liberal view of man-woman relationship.

All these balances, gradualism, alternation, and duplication are symmetrical; and therefore expressive of the aesthetic nature of divine activity which has adopted the principle of setting things in the right perspective, for which the Qur'ānic terms are *taswiya* and *itqān*. The ethical counterparts of this symmetrical balance are the conflicting forces of truth (*ḥaqq*) and falsehood (*bāṭil*). To a certain extent these two conflicting elements are complementary in life: for this reason in certain cases *raḥmat* overlooks or forgives the less serious acts of falsehood. It also allows man time for reflection and atonement. This is also the

[11] Ibid. pp. 107–9 (Latif, pp. 56–58).
[12] Ibid. pp. 110–11 (Latif, p. 59).
[13] Ibid. pp. 112–14 (Latif, pp. 59–61).

logical explanation of the oft-experienced fact that falsehood is sometimes suffered to prevail in this world; and the final triumph of truth over it does not take place until the life hereafter. By this law of causality ethics prepares the way for eschatology; while conversely eschatological warnings are meant to enforce ethical standards in this life.[14]

The bond subsisting between God, the benevolent, and man is one of love. Here Āzād has mainly followed the Ṣūfistic tradition; though modified influences of Christian theology and Vedāntism can also be discovered. Love of God can best be expressed through love of His creatures. This dual function of man's love of God paves the way on the one hand for Āzād's monistic eclecticism, on the other for his humanism. Āzād, however, pointedly emphasizes that the humanism of love preached by the Qur'ān does not go against man's nature; it does not call upon man to love his enemies. The Biblical injunction as opposed to the Islamic reflects the historical contingencies of a situation when Christianity at its inception had no other choice. The Qur'ān rationalizes the Biblical injunctions, extolling forgiveness as a great virtue, but permitting retaliation when unavoidable in the interest of security. In the Qur'ān the ethical element has been modified by law. And this brings Āzād to the final point of relationship between *raḥmat* and law incorporated in the Qur'ān. *Waḥy* faces three categories of men: those who accept, those who refuse to accept, and those who are violently opposed to it. For the first category a positive law is prescribed; for the second a message is given and they are left with the free choice of reflexion, for 'there is no compulsion in religion'; but for the third strong action is recommended to meet violence in thought and deed. *Raḥmat* is also identical with *'adālat*.[15]

In Āzād's exegetical *lexique technique*, *dīn* (religion) is equated with law, implying the reward of heaven or punishment of hell for man's good or bad actions. 'Recompense', 'requital', or justice is the causal consequence of man's conduct. *'Adālat* is necessary

[14] Ibid. pp. 117–25 (Latif, pp. 64–72).
[15] Ibid. pp. 141–3 (Latif, pp. 84–85).

for the maintenance of equilibrium in life, and is therefore the extension of the element of balance or beauty from the physical laws of the universe to the sphere of human ethics.[16]

Hidāyat, whether instinctive, rational, or revelational, is ancillary to the attribute of *rubūbiyyat* and complements *'adālat* by giving humanity a rational or moral code. People in every age or at one time or another in their history have received *hidāyat* through a prophet. The divine message received through the prophets is in its essence the same and implies the basic unity of all religions. Belief in God and righteous living in accordance with that belief is common to the essential creed in all human faiths. The unity of man is the primary aim of all religions. 'The message which every prophet delivered was that mankind were in reality one people and one community, and that there was but one God for all of them, and on that account they should serve Him together and live as members of but one family.' 'However numerous the groups into which you have divided yourselves, you cannot divide God into as many pieces. The one God of all remains one, and is one.' The teaching of all religions is two-fold, the essential faith and the law. The former is common to all religions; the latter particularized in the case of each faith.[17] This distinction which Āzād makes between *dīn* and *shar'* (religious law) in Islam is the starting-point of the more radical distinction between *dīn* as revealed faith and *mazhab* (legalistic jurisprudence) made in his wake by Ghulām Aḥmad Parwīz.

Āzād takes the traditional view, crystallized by Shāh Walī-Allāh in India in the eighteenth century, that the process of human history has been one of devolution, and not of evolution. Messages revealed through prophets have been corrupted by their followers. Later prophets, culminating in Muḥammad, have restored the earlier messages.[18]

The element of faith which is common to all religions is perceptible in the monotheistic concept of God in almost all religions.

[16] Ibid. pp. 89–90, 204–10 (Latif, pp. 84–95, 147–52).
[17] Ibid. pp. 213–39 (Latif, pp. 229–36).
[18] Ibid. pp. 240–1 (Latif, pp. 161–2).

Āzād makes a rather dubious use of his piecemeal knowledge of anthropology to argue that primitive man was monotheistic. In the processes of prehistory and history a retrogression in belief occurred in almost all societies. With the help of the *waḥy* received by prophets from time to time, humanity again recovered the lost ground bit by bit, progressing stage by stage from polytheism to monotheism; and finally, within monotheism, from the concept of awe and terror to one of love of God. Committed unswervingly to the Islamic creed, Āzād takes the first step in modern Islamic India towards a theological discipline of comparative religion, in examining the concepts of the deity in Chinese religious philosophies, in Buddhism, Hinduism, Zoroastrianism, Judaism, Christianity, and in Greek and Platonic thought. Āzād is principally interested in the comparative study of Hinduism, where his conclusions reflect interest in the writings of modern Hindu speculative exponents of their faith such as Rādhākrishnan, but not in the studies of purely scientific Hindu scholars such as Dās Gupta. He finally sums up the final essence of Hinduism as a 'monotheistic polytheism' which tries to meet demands both of the unitary and the polytheistic urge.[19]

There is at least one eschatological analogy which Āzād tries to suggest between Hinduism and the Semitic religions: a common angelology, by equating Hindu *devas* with Semitic angels. The 'Aryan concept' regards *devas* as definite entities with the power of initiating action; the Semitic concept, moderated by monotheism, reduces its angels to mere intercessors with God. Compared with all the other religions, Indic or Semitic, the perfection of a transcendental concept of God was achieved only in Islam.[20]

'The fact is', Āzād argues, 'that prior to the Qur'ānic concept, the mind of man had not risen high enough to discard the veils of anthropomorphic similitudes and directly behold the splendour of divine attributes.' There are passages in the Old Testament, like Numbers 12: 5–8, which still show remnants of earlier anthropomorphic involvements. In the Qur'ān (7: 139) the same

[19] Ibid. pp. 153–76 (Latif, pp. 99–115).
[20] Ibid. pp. 171–82 (Latif, pp. 115–27).

situation has been made use of to underline the transcendentalism of God, though there are certain passages in it which offer difficulties and have misled the Ash'arites, though not Ash'arī himself. Āzād follows Ibn Taymiyya and Ibn Qayyim in accepting the classical theological principle of *tafwīẓ* (resignation) with reference to the 'anthropomorphic' verses of the Qur'ān, believing in what has been stated by God, but suspending judgement concerning it and offering no interpretations.[21]

Almost all the Qur'ānic attributes of God imply beauty. He describes himself by beautiful names. And even when a name implies terror or majesty, it is to emphasize justice which is an act of balance and therefore of beauty.[22]

Āzād's exegetical eclecticism is in the last analysis inalienably centred and rooted in Islam. The religious universalism he advocates is the Ṣūfistic model transplanted into modernized traditionalism. In comparative religion his range is more extensive than that of Sayyid Aḥmad Khān, his attitude more polemical towards Judaism and Christianity; unlike him he also deals, and more sympathetically, with the 'Indic' religions, Buddhism and Hinduism. Long before he came under the influence of Gāndhī he was unmistakably feeling his way towards a pluralistic religious coexistence in India, and this must have helped him in developing his political views on composite Indian nationalism after 1920. He had no difficulty in converting the *ijmā'* of the *'ulamā'*, especially of Deoband, to his view. But the *ijmā'* in the modern sense, of the élite and the masses of the Muslims in the subcontinent, rejected his political views, even though a section of the élite respected his religious thought.

But in religious thought he put the clock back, undoing much of the work of the Aligarh modernists and Iqbāl. Unlike them he was not interested in the problem of the reform of Muslim law. He did not concern himself with the validity or historicity of *ḥadīṣ*. On the question of *ijtihād* his position was ambivalent, inclining more towards conservatism than modernism. In spite

[21] Ibid. pp. 185, 190–3 (Latif, pp. 127, 132–3).
[22] Ibid. p. 193 (Latif, p. 135).

of his preoccupation with the quest for an idealized theocratic but modern state, Iqbāl had placed man at the centre of the scheme of things, in charge of the dynamism of creativity and action, at the centre of the universe as God's vicegerent on earth. Despite his eclecticism and humanism, Āzād reasserted God's suzerainty as the provider, the benefactor, the judge, the guide, the beautiful; and left very little for His man to achieve except greater faith in God and an impeccable, balanced, and tolerant moral life.

CHAPTER TEN

COMPOSITE NATIONALISM

IT is in relation to Muslim Indian politics that the thought of Āzād swings poles apart from that of Iqbāl. Both pay tribute to the religio-political ideas of al-Afghānī, but whereas Iqbāl substitutes instead a multi-national concept of neo-pan-Islamism which rejects the theory of the caliphate as irrelevant to modern times, Āzād remains the chief theoretician of the caliphate movement in Muslim India. The accent in Iqbāl's conception of the universe is on the role of man in it, leading to political, social, and moral views asserting man's position of responsibility and stressing the values of power, drive, and creativity. Āzād switches the emphasis back to the role of God and regards man's responsibility as primarily ethical.

Finally, in terms of Indian politics, Iqbāl emerges as the theoretician of a Muslim state; Āzād conversely champions composite nationalism as the political counterpart of religious universalism, and as a political substitute of the older 'universal' pan-Islamism. There are no polemics against one another in the writings of either Iqbāl or Āzād; but much of the political controversy between Jinnāḥ and Āzād represents the battle between these two opposed socio-political standpoints in contemporary Islam in the subcontinent. The *ijmā'* of the Muslim people accepted the view of Iqbāl and Jinnāḥ; that of the *'ulamā'*, especially of Deoband, agreed with Āzād. Iqbāl's political thought became the main inspiration of the Pakistan movement; that of Āzād the rallying point of Muslim 'composite nationalism' in India, especially after 1947. This polarization of influence has not been rigid. The magnetism of Iqbāl's verse exercised a powerful influence on 'nationalist' Muslims and even liberal Hindus, including Jawāharlāl Nehrū. Conversely, Āzād's religious thought and exegetical analysis shaped the course of the more extravagant exegetical modernism of Parwīz, and scholarly editions of Āzād's works have been published in Pakistan.

Āzād's theory of Muslim participation in Indian nationalism begins with a generalized humanism. The only link binding man and man is that of humanity and a common life on earth; all other relationships are artificial and unreal. The social contract implicit in Islam is essentially human, whereas the Arab concept of *ʿaṣabiyya* is a hangover from the days of pan-Islamic tribalism. Islam recognizes no affinity other than that of human brotherhood, rejecting all the other criteria of social groupings such as race, country, colour, or language.[1] These early views of Āzād are interesting because of his later standpoint. At this early stage he had rejected *country* (i.e. nationalism) as a valid criterion of group loyalty, along with colour and language, but not religion. His views were then not very different from those of Iqbāl, and could broadly be described as an idealistic extension of pan-Islamism into idealized humanism.

In 1905, during the Hindu agitation on the partition of Bengal by Lord Curzon—a decision which was meant to provide an opportunity for the economic betterment of the Muslims of East Bengal and Assam—Āzād had come into contact with the Hindu Bengali terrorist leaders, Shyām Sundar Chakrawartī and Arbindo Ghosh. He claims in his later writings that he planned to join them as he regarded their anti-imperialism as parallel to similar movements in other Muslim lands. He even claims that in 1912 he founded *al-Hilāl* to propagate his nationalistic, anti-imperialist stand.[2] But his actual writings in the early files of that journal contradict him; and as a matter of historical fact it can safely be asserted that his participation in the Indian nationalist movement, as distinct from pan-Islamic anti-imperialism, did not begin until 1920 when on his release from jail he met Tilak and Gāndhī for the first time.

In 1912, in answer to a question as to which of the three political choices was the most feasible for Muslims—traditional

[1] *Maẓāmīn*, pp. 159–7.

[2] *India Wins Freedom*, pp. 5–7.

and non-committal conservatism, or participating with the Hindus in constitutional agitation, or revolutionary anarchism in alliance with Hindu extremists—his answer in *al-Hilāl* was that he could recommend only a fourth course, the Qur'ānic *ṣirāṭ-i mustaqīm* (straight path). A Muslim who sought a solution for any action or belief in any other political party or school of thought ceased to be a Muslim, and could be regarded as a political polytheist for seeking a solution alien to the all-embracing doctrine of the Qur'ān.[3]

In 1913 he had rejected political co-operation with the Hindus in so many words. 'The position of Islam is so exalted that its followers must not follow Hindus in determining their political policies.' The *ṣirāṭ-i mustaqīm* of Islam was defined by Āzād as one based on exclusive monotheism, submitting to no authority than that of one God: fulfilling the divinely-ordained mission of the Muslims whom God had exalted as the *khayr al-umam* by developing communal uprightness, self-respect, and a sense of power and strength; adhering to the principle of balance and equilibrium. Muslims were the harbingers of peace; they could take up arms only in defence. They should therefore abstain from creating chaos or unrest, and should not wantonly disturb the Pax Britannica in India. The Islamic polity was not totalitarian or monarchical but parliamentary. Muslims should therefore strive to achieve a free democratic government by peaceful and constitutional means.[4]

From the rigidly traditional position of regarding the Islamic *umma* as an exclusive community which cannot integrate itself with any other political group, Āzād departed in 1920 when the Khilāfat movement was at its height, and Muḥammad ʿAlī was carrying the Muslim élite and the masses close to the Congress. As the theoretician of the Khilāfat movement, Āzād sought to find a basis for a political alliance with the Indian National Congress, which had an overwhelmingly Hindu membership. He sought its sanction in the Qur'ān (40: 8–9), and worked out

[3] *al-Hilāl* (Calcutta), 8 Sept. 1912; *Ṣubḥ-i ummīd*, p. 44; *Maẓāmīn*, p. 14.
[4] *Ṣubḥ-i ummīd*, pp. 45–49.

a theory that after the first world war India consisted of two other communities with actual or potential political power: the British, who were inimical, and the Hindus, who were friendly to the Muslims. He then turned to the *sīra* for a precedent for integrated alliance with a non-Muslim community. He found that in the covenant between Muḥammad and the people of Medina, including Jews and pagans, concluded in 622, Muslim as well as non-Muslim parties were described as a single community (*umma wāḥida*). The covenant, though in practice it ceased to function in relation to Jews and other non-Muslim elements in Medina, still retained, in Āzād's view, validity as a precedent for other situations and in other lands in the subsequent history of Islam, and was especially pertinent to India.[5] Later Ḥusayn Aḥmad Madanī and the *'ulamā'* of Deoband used the same arguments.

Compared with that of Muḥammad 'Alī and other Khilāfat leaders, Āzād's conversion to Indian nationalism was final and irrevocable. In 1923 a rift developed between Muḥammad 'Alī and the Hindu leaders of the Congress. Āzād identified himself until the end with the Congress. To the vast majority of Muslims his continued participation in the Congress was deplorable, especially when, after the Pakistan resolution of the Muslim League in 1940, he allowed himself to be elected President of Congress year after year, to embarrass the League in its demand for a separate homeland for the Muslims.

Āzād had two main arguments against the demand for Pakistan. First, he favoured the role of a powerful diaspora for the Muslims in India rather than the quest for a separate homeland which he considered as parallel with Zionism. Secondly, he considered the partition of India as harmful to the Muslims of the subcontinent in the long run. Though opposed to Pakistan, he was opposed also to a unitary government for the whole of India. In 1946 he favoured a federal constitution with a weak centre in charge of defence, communications, and foreign affairs, and

[5] *Khuṭbāt*, pp. 42–44.

provinces holding residuary powers and in charge of all the other subjects.[6]

The Jamʿiyyat al-ʿUlamāʾ-i Hind, the religio-political organization of Muslim divines founded in 1919, held similar political views. Rashīd Aḥmad Gangohī, one of the founders of the theological seminary of Deoband, had condemned Sayyid Aḥmad Khān's Islamic separatism on the grounds of his 'heretical' views: and as early as 1888 had approved with certain qualifications the association of Muslims with the political movement of the Hindus.[7] His disciple, Maḥmūd al-Ḥasan, committed himself more firmly to an alliance with the Congress, approaching the problem from an anti-British, pan-Islamic point of view. He applied the Gāndhian principle of non-violent and peaceful resistance to the Muslim theory of *jihād*, especially when conditions did not allow an armed struggle. But Muslim participation in the movement of Indian political freedom should be strictly in accordance with Muslim juristic precepts; it should avoid all action leading to chaos or excess; and it should support Hindu nationalism only in so far as it was commendable but should cease to do so if the Hindus adopted a wrong or harmful policy. Maḥmūd al-Ḥasan was especially apprehensive of the economic exploitation of Muslims by Hindus, despite their political liberalism.[8]

By 1927 the Jamʿiyyat al-ʿUlamāʾ-i Hind had fully committed itself to Āzād's covenantal theory of composite Indian nationalism; and Āzād's views were reiterated by Anwar Shāh and by Maḥmūd al-Ḥasan's successor at Deoband, Ḥusayn Aḥmad Madanī, who after his early education at Deoband lived in the Hijāz from 1900 to 1920.[9] As with Āzād, the principal irritant in Madanī's views on Indo-Muslim politics was the loyalism of the Aligarh school. This loyalism had gathered support from some of the *ʿulamāʾ* who favoured the *status quo* on two grounds. First,

[6] *India Wins Freedom*, pp. 140, 185, 214, 223–4.

[7] Madanī, *Naqsh-i ḥayāt*, ii. 71; Muḥ. Miyān, *ʿUlamaʾ-i Ḥaqq*, i. 191–2.

[8] Maḥmud al-Ḥasan, Pres. Address of Jamʿiyyat al-ʿUlamāʾ-i Hind (Delhi, 1920), i. 191–2; text of his *fatwā* of 1338/1920 in Madanī, ii. 253–5, 259.

[9] Anwar Shāh, Pres. Add. of ann. sess. of Jamʿiyyat al-ʿUlamāʾ-i Hind (Peshawar, 1927); Madanī, *Muttaḥida qawmiyyat awr Islām* (Delhi, n.d.).

that a *de facto* contract existed between the British government and the Indian Muslims who had chosen to continue to live under British protection and to refer their law suits to British courts. Secondly, that the contract could not be broken by Indian Muslims either unilaterally by rebellion or by aiding a foreign Muslim power like Turkey. Against this view Madanī argued that even if the existing political and legal situation could be accepted as a valid *de facto* contract, it was no longer binding on the Muslims as it had been repeatedly violated by the other contracting party, the British government in Britain and the British administration in India. Among the 'violations' of the *de facto* contract Madanī enumerated the illegal annexation of Awadh in the 1850s; the double standard of British policies on the question of racial tolerance; official promises of reform or greater self-rule which were not fulfilled or only partly fulfilled under intense political pressure; and failure to meet such contingencies as famines in India.[10]

Islam, he argues, cannot reconcile itself to a status of national slavery. If non-Muslims occupy a Muslim land, which India was under the Mughals, it becomes the obligatory duty of Muslims of that land and of others to strive and regain independence. This *jihād* in India has to be non-violent: and it can be fought only in alliance with the Hindus, who constitute the majority community. In independence thus gained Muslims and non-Muslims would be co-partners in creating a society and an administration which, though not modelled entirely on the conception of an Islamic state, would comprise effective and influential Muslim elements in it.[11]

Up to this point modern Islamic separatism in India, as represented by Iqbāl and Jinnāḥ, which also stood for independence from British rule and was even prepared to consider the chances of tactical alliance with Hindu nationalism, could accept much of Madanī's political thought, with certain variations of emphasis. But between 1937 and 1947 Madanī made several statements

[10] *Naqsh-i ḥayāt*, i. 152, 155–206, 308–70; ii. 73–130.
[11] *Maktūbāt* (1956), pp. 20–21, 45–47.

denouncing the concept of a separate Muslim state. Iqbāl took strong exception to a statement by him in 1937 which had reiterated his identification of a nation with the land it inhabits, irrespective of religious differences. In Iqbāl's view the theological weakness of Madanī's argument was its anachronism. Nationalism was a modern western, not an Islamic religious or political concept. The propagation of nationalistic views in Muslim countries had shattered the unity of the world of Islam. Love of one's country, which was really one's environment, was a natural but not necessarily a political instinct. In a nation comprising several communities, like India, religion was bound to die away, yielding to a unity of secular atheism. Iqbāl also rejected Madanī's distinction between *qawm* (nation) and *millat* or *umma* as mere philological quibbling in the context of the political situation existing in India in 1938. The *qawm* and the *umma* were philosophically identical. Muslims constituted one *millat*, and the non-Muslims taken collectively another. Before his call to prophethood, the people among whom Muhammad lived no doubt constituted a *qawm*, but as his *umma* began to be formed, the status of people as a *qawm* became a secondary one.[12]

In his reply to Iqbāl, Madanī argued that a *qawm* had several connotations: race, religion, country, profession, &c. A group could be co-national with another group in one sense, and separate from it in another. There were references in the Qur'ān bracketing the prophets and their enemies and friends as belonging to the same nations. 'Nation' may be a modern western term also, but in the Qur'ānic sense of the term *qawm*, Indian Muslims were co-nationals with other Indian groups and separate from them as a religious community. A person could be an Indian and a Muslim at the same time with no primary or secondary priorities, just as he could be one person's son, another's father, and another's brother. India was the physical and Islam the spiritual focus for the Indian Muslims. For life in this world the physical aspect had priority; the spiritual for inner

[12] 'Islām awr qawmiyyat', *Iḥsān* (Lahore), 9 Mar. 1938; *Selected Speeches and Writings* (1944), pp. 204–16.

perfection. The covenant of Medina concluded by the Prophet with the Medinan Jews and other non-Muslims was the contractual basis of composite Hindu-Muslim nationalism in India. Islam was a resilient religion; it allowed its followers to enter into a relationship of peace, treaty, pact, coexistence, trade, business, and social intercourse with people of other persuasions. 'It is not rigid and narrow-minded like Hinduism.'[13] Islam had also, potentially, an institutional resilience. It could work through political and administrative institutions, commercial corporations, trade unions, and parliamentary bodies.

But the blueprint of a free India which Madanī presented was rather different from that of the Indian National Congress. Madanī favoured a democratic constitution, with a head of state having regal powers. There should be religious seminaries for the education of Muslims, paid for by a special taxation of Muslims, who should also receive modern education in national institutions. Finally, Islamic law alone could secure real peace in the world. Naturally, it would not be promulgated in a 'composite' free India, nor would Islamic injunctions prevail. But India's secular or Hindu phase would only be a transitory one, for it is the duty of the Muslims to get the universal validity of their religious law acknowledged by the non-Muslim elements in due course by persuasion.[14]

Between 1940 and 1947 the *'ulamā'* of Deoband and the Jam'iyyat al-'Ulamā'-i Hind vehemently opposed the Pakistan movement.[15] Seldom before in the history of Islamic India had the *'ulamā'* taken a stand so contrary to the political instinct of the intellectual élite and the masses of the people. It contributed, however, to the development of the Deoband school of 'nationalist hagiography', in which the nationalist 'throw-back' is a political projection of the present into the past, but which unearthed a large number of forgotten archives, manuscripts, and little-known tracts, and also threw light on the role of the *'ulamā'* in India before, during, and after the 'Mutiny' of 1857.

[13] *Maktūbāt*, pp. 20–21; *Muttaḥida Qawmiyyat awr Islām*, pp. 21–26.
[14] *Muttaḥida*, pp. 44–51, 67.
[15] Ibid. pp. 53–65.

A more secular-minded group of Muslim intellectuals also stood for composite nationalism. In 1920, at the height of the Congress–Khilāfat alliance, Muḥammad ʿAlī, disillusioned by the loyalism of Aligarh, had promoted the creation of a complementary Muslim National University in the same town. This, the Jāmiʿa-i Milliyya-i Islāmiyya, was inaugurated that year in the mosque of Sayyid Aḥmad Khān's Anglo-Oriental College by the Deoband *ʿālim* Maḥmūd al-Ḥasan. In its struggle for survival it chose at the outset a policy of aloofness from all political parties, but its chief leaders during the years of its infancy were the nationalist Muslim leaders of the Congress, Abu'l-Kalām Āzād, Mukhtār Aḥmad Anṣārī, and Ḥakīm Ajmal Khān. It refused to take a grant in aid from the British government in India, but accepted financial support from the princely states of Hyderabad, Kashmir, and Bhopal, and later from the Delhi municipality. Its staff consisted of the devoted scholars Ẕākir Ḥusayn, who later rose to be India's Vice-President, Muḥammad Mujīb, and ʿĀbid Ḥusayn, who set a pattern of plain-living and high-thinking which was Gāndhian in origin but Muslim by adaptation. Most of them had broad sympathies with the Indian National Congress; and Ẕākir Ḥusayn became alienated from the Muslim League and the Muslim consensus in the later 1930s as the president of the controversial Wardha Committee on Education set up by the Congress, which presented a report that was generally considered to have gone a long way to create an educational policy oriented in the direction of Hindu revivalism. Ẕākir Ḥusayn's position could perhaps best be summed up in his own words: 'Indian Muslims love their country as much as any of their compatriots, . . . but they would not accept the complete loss of their cultural identity. They would like to be good Muslims as well as good Indians.'[16]

[16] *Taʿlīmī Khuṭbāt* (1955), pp. 240–8.

CHAPTER ELEVEN

THREE THEORIES OF ISLAMIC SOCIALISM

AFTER the first world war, the Russian revolution made a certain limited impact on the modernist thinking in the Indo-Pakistan subcontinent. The doctrinaire emphasis of communism on the equitable distribution of wealth appeared to Iqbāl to a limited extent as sharing the concept of social justice enshrined in the teachings of the Qur'ān. There was, however, from the outset a rejection of communistic atheism, which he defined as imperfect or negative Islam, rejecting, like Islam, the false gods of material wealth, exploitation, usury, and injustice, but failing, unlike it, in a faith in and submission to one supreme God. As we have seen, Iqbāl regarded communism as the attestation of the first, negative half of the *kalima*.[1] As it failed in the attestation of the second half, it was repugnant, unsatisfactory, and incomplete compared with a socialistic formula which could be developed within Islam. He described Karl Marx as an 'unenlightened Moses, an uncrucified Christ', 'whose writing has almost the inspiration of a scripture without the illuminating flash of the divine revelation.'

This keynote with certain variations led to various theories of Islamic socialism from the 1920s to the present day in India and Pakistan.

It is difficult to assess the precise extent of Iqbāl's influence on 'Ubayd-Allāh Sindhī, who was the only political thinker of any considerable calibre to come directly in contact with Russian communism at an early stage. Born a Sikh, he was attracted to Islam and was converted to it at an early age, and joined the theological seminary of Deoband as a disciple of Maḥmūd al-Ḥasan in 1889. In 1912 he was put in charge of a Deoband enterprise at

[1] See above, pp. 158–9.

Delhi, where he came in contact with the Aligarh leader Wiqār al-Mulk and remained a supporter of combining the traditions of Aligarh and Deoband. In Delhi he also met the future leaders of the Khilāfat movement, Anṣārī, Ajmal Khān, and Muḥammad 'Alī.

In 1915 he was selected by Maḥmūd al-Ḥasan to proceed to Kabul as an anti-British *agent provocateur*. He joined there the 'government-in-exile' inspired by Turco-German agents. After the Allied victory he visited Russia in 1920 and Turkey in 1922, when the Caliphate movement in India was at its peak. Then followed years of exile and scholarship spent in Mecca, whence he returned to India in 1938 with the permission of the British government, granted thanks to the efforts of the Indian National Congress which was in office in several Indian provinces.[2]

In the tradition of Deoband, Sindhī accepted composite nationalism as a political solution for the revolutionary struggle to overthrow the British rule in India, but to a far more restricted extent than the theologians of that school. Though nominally a member of the Congress, he had scant respect for that organization, because of the Hindu revivalism it preached, and for Gāndhī's leadership. Hindu capitalism, which dominated the Congress, appeared to him as the antithesis of Islam, which he regarded as basically and inherently socialistic. After 1941 he favoured an alliance between the Congress and the Muslim League, and wished to see the Congress develop into an 'Indian International Congress', regarding India as one country but not the Indians as one nation. Taking his cue from the 'party line' of the Indian communists at that stage, he developed his own theory of linguistic nationalities in India.[3]

The same dichotomy coloured Sindhī's view of Islamic history in India. He championed the theocratic rule of Aurangzeb, and at the same time had a qualified admiration for the eclecticism of Akbar, rejecting in it the element of heresy that brought about

[2] *Khuṭbāt*, p. 114.
[3] Ibid. pp. 89, 114–16; cf. Muḥ. Sarwar, *Mawlānā 'Ubayd-Allāh Sindī* (1943), pp. 354, 363; Sindhī, *Shāh Walī-Allāh kī siyāsī tahrīk*, p. 230.

the 'corrective' theological response of Shaykh Aḥmad Sirhindī's movement. Rightly guided, Sindhī argues, Akbar's eclecticism could have led to the conversion of the entire subcontinent to Islam.[4]

As a convert to Islam, Sindhī retained and developed in his theological thinking an element of spiritual symbiosis. He regarded not only Judaeo-Christian but Hindu scriptures as true revelation, but their interpretation by their followers as wrong and erroneous. Within Islam he was attracted to Ibn al-ʿArabī's ontological monism, which he emphasizes as a distinct heritage in the thought of Shāh Walī-Allāh. The essential universality of Ṣūfī humanism could resolve the ethical conflicts between Hinduism and Islam. He accepted the theories of the influence of the Vedānta on Ṣūfism, especially on its monistic doctrines, but contended that whereas Hindu mysticism was unable to rid itself of idolatry, Ṣufism regarded its pantheistic image-worship as repugnant. Vedānta was circumscribed to the cultural-national limits of Hinduism; Ṣūfism was universal and rejected all distinctions between lands, races, and peoples.[5]

All humanity is bound by a unity—the unity of thought. The Qur'ān represents this intellectual unity as do other scriptures followed by other faiths. The Qur'ān is therefore meant for all peoples and not exclusively for Muslims. Islam is potentially the religion of all humanity; and the Qur'ān as the final scripture of all religions is applicable to the spiritual and material requirements of all human beings in given epochs or climes according to their social or economic problems.[6]

This modernist approach, though arrived at syncretically, derives support from Shāh Walī-Allāh's views and also marks the influence of Aligarh on Sindhī's essentially orthodox Deobandī theological thought. He declared himself in favour of accepting much of the technological and material content of the

[4] *Shāh Walī-Allāh*, pp. 150–1, 299; Sarwar, pp. 150–1, 291–316; Saʿīd Aḥmad Akbarābādī, *ʿUbayd-Allāh Sindhī awr unke nāqid* (1946), pp. 247–8; for an orthodox rejection of Sindhī's views cf. Masʿūd ʿĀlam Nadwī in *Maʿārif*, Sept. 1944, p. 18.

[5] Sarwar, pp. 39, 97, 131–6, 143–4.

[6] Ibid. pp. 44, 86, 242–7.

western civilization, as well as western military institutions. He favoured Muslims enlisting in large numbers in British Indian armed forces to learn modern military techniques, if only to use them eventually against their masters. The 'universal revolution promised by Islam' could only be achieved in the present age by absorbing into it the materialistic values of western civilization.[7]

Curiously enough, the communist revolution in the USSR was also seen by Sindhī as close to Islam. Like Iqbāl he also advocated the necessity of the propagation of Islam in the Soviet Union to transform their godless revolution into a God-fearing one. 'Muslims will have to evolve for themselves a religious basis to arrive at the economic justice at which communism aims but which it cannot fully achieve. Atheistic communism can bring to the Muslim masses only an emancipation of an imperfect and alien variety.'[8]

In search of a theory of Islamic socialism Sindhī turns to Shāh Walī-Allāh, the common fountainhead of Deoband orthodoxy and of Aligarh modernism, and fathers on him a social philosophy which is largely his own creation. He regards Walī-Allāh as a revolutionary because of his supposed criticism of the Muslim feudal order in the early eighteenth century.[9]

Much of the basis of Sindhī's concept of an Islamic socialist theocracy is, however, derived piecemeal from Walī-Allāh. Faith is the first stage of action. Action is dynamic; it implies impact. Dynamic action aimed at a social and revolutionary end is *jihād* in Islamic terminology. *Jihād* is a holy war which can be fought on many fields, by a variety of weapons—sword, pen, the human heart, or fearless expression. Marxist revolution is the atheistic counterpart of the theistic *jihād*. Unlike the Aligarh modernists or Shiblī, Sindhī offers no apologetics on the question of *jihād*. Instead, he takes the opposite stand, acknowledging and approving it as an aggressively corrective measure, a view directly traceable to Walī-Allāh. In fact Sindhī confesses that his

[7] *Siyāsī taḥrīk*, pp. 134–5; Sarwar, pp. 60–62, 120.

[8] *Khuṭbāt*, pp. 20–21; Akbarābādī, p. 254.

[9] Sarwar, pp. 164–8.

conversion to Islam from Sikhism was motivated by his appreciation of two values of the Islamic faith, absolute monotheism and the doctrine of *jihād*.[10]

Jihād therefore is the basis of the organization of Islamic socialist revolution. This aim can also be achieved by peaceful means. The importance of victory through peace is especially significant; for Islam preaches victory by defensive as well as offensive means. Defensive war needs no apology, but offensive revolutionary war is a matter of great responsibility, especially when it is waged to bring about a social revolution among a section of mankind. Revolutionary offensive can be individual, national, or international. Victory of the Islamic social revolution on a social scale is identified by Sindhī with the ideal envisaged in Walī-Allāh's concept, *itmām-i niʿma*, i.e. fulfilment of God's blessing on earth. *Jihād* is a total obligation binding on all without any mental reservation, and whoever subjects it to his personal convenience is a hypocrite.[11]

The difference between the movement of social revolution preached by Islam and communism is (as Iqbāl had pointed out) the latter's denial of the existence of God and therefore of any fundamental moral basis for the revolution itself. Consequently Soviet communism has become imperialism in non-Russian areas like Central Asia or the Trans-Caspian regions. Walī-Allāhī theistic socialism would give the peasant and the labourer a much fairer deal in life than a purely materialistic communist state.[12]

The Qur'ān promotes the concept of the formation of a *jamāʿa* which is not very different from the concept of a revolutionary political party in these days. The *jamāʿa* has to be monolithic and bound by an overriding discipline. Such an Islamic party actually came into existence during the caliphate of ʿUmar I (634–44), and continued during the caliphate of ʿUthmān (644–56), with whose assassination, which was a result of indiscipline and sedition, it disintegrated. The origins of the Muslim 'party of

[10] *Khuṭbāt*, pp. 20–21; *ʿUnwān-i Inqilāb*; Sarwar, pp. 53–58.
[11] *Khuṭbāt*, pp. 26–59. [12] Sarwar, p. 110.

revolution' could of course be traced earlier to the Medinan phase of the life of the Prophet, whose role was twofold, that of the divinely-inspired messenger of God, and of the political leader of a revolutionary party which was in the process of formation. In this second capacity he did not assert himself as a totalitarian or absolute dictator, but chose the parliamentary principle of consulting the senior members of the political party. Its programme was to sow the seeds of a social revolution that would destroy the monopoly of the merchant hierarchy of Mecca and eventually overthrow the neighbouring imperialisms of the Byzantines and the Sāsānids, to uplift the indigenous masses of peoples with an incentive which was not purely economic but which was aimed at the realization by human effort of the will of God approving dynamic and classless society. The record of humanity and tolerance of the Muslim revolution under ʿUmar and ʿUthmān compares by all moral standards very favourably with the inhumanity of atheistic communist revolution in Russia under Lenin and Stalin.[13]

The expansion of the Muslim state under the two caliphs at the expense of the Byzantine and Sāsānid empires was obligatory on the grounds of political and economic morality. These two empires were tyrannical and decadent, grinding the miserable masses of humanity for centuries. The time had come for revolution from outside to overthrow their political and economic structure which was based on the privilege of the few.[14]

The concept of the Islamic *jamāʿa* as a revolutionary political party helps Sindhī to define apostasy as an act not of religious but of political treason deserving of the canonically prescribed punishment of death.[15]

The main difference between the communist and Islamic economic philosophies, according to Sindhī, is that while both agree that the process of the distribution of wealth should be 'from each according to his ability', Islam would prefer it to be 'to each according to his need' rather than to 'each according to his work'. In other words Sindhī would like to see Islamic socialism

[13] Ibid. pp. 60–64, 128. [14] Ibid. pp. 121–2. [15] Sarwar, pp. 68–69.

on the lines of a western welfare state. And he does not rule out the desirability of socialism by evolution in a democratic society, and actually recommends this process for the areas which now constitute Pakistan.[16]

Sindhī's writings reveal, like those of Iqbāl, a confederal and multi-national and not a unitary concept of pan-Islamism. The Jumna, Narbada, Sind Sagar Party which he founded shortly before his death attracted hardly any membership, but its blueprint is interesting as the projection of his thought in relation to Indian politics in the early 1940s. The party claimed to be organizationally within the Indian National Congress, but its sphere of operations was confined to north-west areas comprising territories far beyond the Muslim League's concept of West Pakistan and including, as in Raḥmat 'Alī's blueprint, Ajmer, a Muslim centre of pilgrimage in the heart of Hindu Rajputana, the valley of the Jumna (where Muslims were in a numerical minority but culturally prominent), and any other parts of India which might like to accede to this territorial nucleus dominated by Muslim culture and therefore the ideal homeland for the development of Walī-Allāhī socialism.[17] The party stood for the attainment of independence through non-violence, and for raising the standard of living of the peasant and the artisan. It envisaged free India as a confederation of multi-national states, each a linguistic and cultural unit. It, as well as the theological school, Bayt al-Ḥikma, which Sindhī had started, encouraged the synthesis of western and Islamic cultures, and even approved a western style of living. The principal emphasis of both institutions was on uniformity in thought, ethics, and politics, based on Sindhī's interpretation of the teachings of Walī-Allāh.

In 1942 Marxism seems also to have made its first tangible impact on at least one or two of the more traditional *'ulamā'* of Deoband. Ḥifẓ al-Raḥmān Sihwārwī tried to evolve a concept of Islamic socialism within the traditional structure of the *sharī'a*. Almost inevitably he also took his cue from Walī-Allāh's argument that a 'pious' economic order is indispensable for

[16] Ibid. pp. 66, 103.

[17] *Khuṭbāt*, pp. 180–1, 236–41.

the exteriorization of an Islamic religious or ethical order.[18]

Sihwārwī's argument begins from the pragmatic position that economic inequality is a natural enough variety of social life, recognized as such by the Qur'ān, which prescribes checks and balances against it by stressing every individual's right to full employment, and by recommending to society an ideal of economic justice and equilibrium. The economic equality emphasized in the Qur'ān is that of opportunity. For this reason concentration or monopoly of wealth in the hands of the few is legally forbidden. The institutionalization of *zakāt* has to be interpreted to signify that no one is entitled to keep to himself more than what he needs for his own and his family's maintenance. The rest of the profit he accumulates and the property he owns should be donated by him to the public exchequer for social welfare.[19]

The Qur'ān therefore seeks to create an economic order in which the rich pay excessive though voluntary taxes to minimize differences in the standard of living, perpetually aiming to blur class distinctions though a combination of private enterprise and unlimited generosity. If this is the correct interpretation of the theory of *zakāt*, why then did God permit men to be born unequal, in affluence and in poverty? The answer Sihwārwī offers is that the given situation of privilege or under-privilege of birth is a test God has prescribed for the affluent to honour their social obligations through self-denial. Likewise a person gifted with greater talent in business or with intellectual acumen earns not only for himself but for the entire community.[20]

Capitalism in the sense of the exclusive monopoly of the means of production or of wealth in the hands of the few is repugnant to the Qur'ān. On the other hand production of wealth by the talented few for the welfare of masses of people has an ethical basis, and as such excludes media of financial exploitation such as usury, or unearned profit, as in speculation or gambling.[21]

This does not mean that the underprivileged or poorer or less enterprising members of society have a right to live as parasites

[18] Sihwārwī, *Islām kā iqtiṣādī niẓām* (Delhi, 1942), pp. 1–5.
[19] Ibid. pp. 40–43. [20] Ibid. pp. 50–51. [21] Ibid. p. 54.

on the effort, income, and charity of the enterprising élite. As wealth and talent is a divine test for the rich, poverty and economic inequality is a test for the poor and the have-nots who are urged to strive, earn, and work their way up the economic and social ladder. Islamic socialism is therefore a pincer movement of hard self-denying generosity by the rich and ceaseless effort and work by the poor to bridge the gulf which divides the classes.[22]

The political structure of Islam similarly negates the concept of privileged authority. The leader of the theocratic Islamic state is not a monarch or a dictator or even the president of a republic. He is designated as 'caliph' with connotations of man's role as God's vicegerent on earth. A caliph is entitled to the loyalty of the community only as long as he adheres to the injunctions of the Qur'ān and the *sunna*. He is also bound to obtain the consensus of a consultative body representing the mature opinion of the community. It is obligatory for him to have the determination to act firmly in accordance with the divine injunctions and the opinion of his consultants. This ideal role was fulfilled by the first four orthodox Caliphs and by the Umayyad ʿUmar ibn ʿAbd al-ʿAzīz.[23]

The control and organization of economic structure in the Islamic state falls under the legal jurisdiction of the caliphate, which may appropriate lands or arbitrate between the landlord and the peasant. It can fix a maximum ceiling on private ownership, interfere in affecting redistribution of wealth, enforce taxation according to the *sharīʿa*, outlaw usury, gambling, or other forms of unfair exploitation, promote incentives to trade, industry, and other means of production of wealth.[24]

In the context of modern economics, Sihwārwī recommends that co-operative institutions could be given a trial as an alternative to capitalist banking which is rooted in prohibited usury. He sees in Islam a sanction for the ownership of movable and immovable property. But the limit and extent of private ownership are restricted. Such sources of communal wealth as mines or means of communication should be controlled by the state.

[22] Ibid. pp. 65–68. [23] Ibid. pp. 83–90. [24] Ibid. pp. 106–7, 270–84.

Industry can be privately owned, but the economic relationship between the capitalist and the working classes should be firmly controlled by the state to eliminate all chances of exploitation and to ensure labour welfare.[25]

The economic theory of Islam is totally opposed to fascism. With Marxism it shares five elements: prohibition of the accumulation of wealth in the hands of the privileged class, organization of the economic structure of the state to ensure social welfare, equality of opportunity for all human beings, priority of collective social interest over individual privilege, prevention or abolition through social revolution of the fossilization of class-structure consisting of the exploiters and the exploited, haves and have-nots, or rulers and ruled. Islam disagrees with Marxism on two issues. It sanctions private ownership within certain limits, and it does not recognize an absolutely classless basis of society; accepting the pragmatical reality of class structure in human societies, Islam tries to control it by enforcing the principle of equality of opportunity for all. Class structure, accepted in Islam as the given data of economic reality, is thus subjected to fluidity and impermanence by the prohibition of the accumulation of wealth.

It is remarkable that, unlike Iqbāl and Sindhī, Sihwārwī does not touch on the point to which Islam is most sensitive to communism, its atheistic materialism. Its rejection is implicit in his theological approach. He is concerned almost exclusively with the economic aspect of a traditionalized socialist theory, with a detachment from the religious and metaphysical aspects of the controversy. Needless to say the theory he presents is frequently inconsistent; its generalized totality is contradicted by the realistic treatment of details resulting in such dichotomies as his view that institutionalized *zakāt* is theoretically an obligation of the individual conscience, but he advocates its enforcement by the state. The Deoband *'ulamā'*, especially Muḥammad Miyān, retained a tinge of 'Walī-Allāhī socialism' in their nationalist ideologies in independent India after 1947.

[25] Ibid. pp. 270–99.

The socialist writings of Sindhī and Sihwārwī belong to the decades before the emergence of Pakistan. The third major theory of Islamic socialism was developed by Khalīfa ʿAbd al-Ḥakīm, one of the semi-official theorists of Islamic modernism, in Pakistan in 1953, eleven years after the publication of Sihwārwī's work. At a stage in Pakistan's history when it was leaning towards the United States, a greater emphasis on purely Islamic values is evident, and socialistic theory can be observed as veering towards an idealistic welfare state concept:

> Between Islam and atheistic, totalitarian Communism there can be no compromise so far as the ideological basis of the two is concerned. If Islam can make no compromise with ideological communism it would repudiate with equal force the racialism and colonialism of imperialistic Western powers . . .
>
> Dialectical Materialism is only a further instalment of Mechanical Materialism of eighteenth-century Europe. Mechanistic Materialism denies the reality of mind, and subjects all phases of life to physical determinism. This deterministic trend assumes a new form in Dialectical Materialism, the inevitable continuum of thesis, anti-thesis, and synthesis. The moral, social, and ideal *Weltanschauung* of Islamic theism, which it shares with other great religions, stands in contradistinction alike to western mechanistic or Marxist dialectic views of matter, existence, and society.[26]

The Marxist theory of being regards matter as without purpose and subject to certain inviolable laws. 'Where there is no purpose there can be no ought and no obligation. . . . This movement is neither moral nor immoral; it is amoral.' Marxist ethics, at its very best, can concern itself with what it calls the 'concrete human situation'. In its content or outlook eternally valid moral intuitions, which the great religions emphasize, do not exist.[27]

Movements of economic and social reform in newly-liberated Muslim countries have borrowed or preferred to borrow in varying degrees elements from Marxist socialism as long as they are not repugnant to or in conflict with the basic theistic structure of Islam. At the same time remnants of or devious substitutes for

[26] Khalīfa ʿAbd al-Ḥakīm, *Islam and Communism* (1953), pp. x–xi, 50–64.
[27] Ibid. pp. 66, 75.

European imperialism are driving some Muslim peoples to look to Russia politically, though not ideologically, for help and sympathy.[28]

The ideal of social justice towards which Muslim society is groping its way is not communistic, 'but socialism of the Islamic pattern with a background of spiritual values'. Islamic democracy is based on the conviction of the basic unity of all humanity. Islam has a firmer record of integral brotherhood of a cosmopolitan fraternity on the one hand, and of tolerance and the provision of equality of opportunity and equality before law of all non-Muslim citizens in a Muslim state 'than any other civilization of mankind'.

> The ultimate object of Islamic democracy is the freedom of individual self-realization . . . For Islam the state is not a super-individual entity or deity to be glorified and worshipped; it is only a means to enable the individuals in peace and security to exercise their freedom in ways that appear to them desirable. . . . An Islamic State would neither be a totalitarian nor a *laissez-faire* state.[29]

The shift in Islamic socialist thinking of the 1950s, epitomized by Khalīfa 'Abd al-Ḥakīm's work, is towards left-of-the-centre liberalism. An Islamic state should harness the freedom of thought, action, and enterprise, as in western democracies, to the guiding principle of the equality of opportunity for all. Geographically the Islamic world stands between the west and the communist east. The record of its civilization bears witness to the capability of evolving a golden mean. If Marxism is the antithesis of the capitalist thesis, then Islam stands in relation to both as the dialectical synthesis.[30]

If this synthesis is Islamic socialism, what then is the premiss of its sociological development? Ḥakīm identifies it with the Qur'ānic term *taqdīr*, which for him is the data of life or the raw material which man has to mould as best as he can. Nature has uniformities as well as diversities; equalities as well as inequalities. Any society that attempts to create a dead level of equality, as communism professes to do, is bound to fail as it

[28] Ibid. pp. 124–5, 152. [29] Ibid. pp. 157–88. [30] Ibid.

would contravene the fundamental laws of nature. Capitalism is, on the other hand, unethical and inhuman for the opposite reasons. It seeks to reinforce, fortify, and perpetuate natural inequalities by producing and stabilizing artificial inequalities. Both these extreme solutions are repugnant to the ideal Islam; as are also authoritarian or hierarchic or monopolistic institutions borrowed by the historical Islam, including monarchy, landlordism, priestcraft, usury or commercial or financial monopoly. Islam need not borrow a socialistic philosophy from an extraneous source or even evolve it. Ideally interpreted and externalized into society and government, Islam *is* socialism in its own right.[31]

All these theories have created a make-believe mythology of communism as well as of Islam, which is unscientific and contrary to the sequence and logic of history. They have read into Islam affinities with Marxism that have never been there. Sindhī and Sihwārwī have both attributed to Walī-Allāh ideas that would have shocked that divine in the early eighteenth century context.[32] In their obsession with western imperialism, none of them except Sindhī, to some extent, has realized the dangers of communist imperialism. And they have done less than justice to the institutions of freedom, democracy, and liberty of conscience in western democracies.

[31] Ibid. pp. 207–31, 251–63.
[32] Mas'ūd 'Ālam Nadwī, in *Ma'ārif*, Sept. 1944, p. 18.

CHAPTER TWELVE

MAWDŪDĪ: ORTHODOX FUNDAMENTALISM

By far the most dynamic and well-organized challenge modernist Islam has been facing in India, and especially in Pakistan, is that of the revivalist writings and preachings of Abu'l-Aʿlā Mawdūdī and his well-knit, monolithic, almost totalitarian religio-political organization, the Jamāʿat-i Islāmī.

Born in 1903, Mawdūdī began his journalistic career in 1929, editing first the *al-Jamāʿat*, the organ of the orthodox Jamʿiyyat al-ʿUlamā'-i Hind, and then starting in 1932 the *Tarjumān al-Qur'ān*, an exegetical journal propagating his revivalist fundamentalism in religion and politics, a movement which he and his party describe as the 'Islamic Renaissance'. He claims to have attracted the attention of Iqbāl in 1937, when he was planning to write on the codification of Muslim jurisprudence. The proposal seems to have come to nothing because of Iqbāl's illness and death in 1938. Despite Mawdūdī's claims, there is very little in common between his and Iqbāl's religious and political ideas, and he merely touches the fringe of the extensive area of Iqbāl's thought. In effect, the core of Mawdūdī's teachings is exactly the opposite of Iqbāl's.

Between 1937 and 1947 Mawdūdī opposed first the Indian nationalist stand of Madanī and of the Deoband '*ulamā*', and later the Pakistan movement, denouncing its secular-minded leadership. In 1941 he founded the Jamāʿat-i Islāmī, assumed its leadership, and has firmly retained it under the disguise of an 'elective' procedure. After the creation of Pakistan he migrated from Pathankot in India to Lahore and denounced the struggle for Kashmir as un-Islamic, for which he was imprisoned in 1950, though later, in 1965, he endorsed the Kashmir war as a *jihād*. In 1952–3 he aligned himself with the former anti-Pakistan group, the Aḥrār, and the orthodox *'ulamā'* in their agitation demanding discriminative legislation and executive action against the heterodox messianistic Aḥmadī sect; and as the agitation led to mass disorders, martial law was proclaimed in Lahore in February 1953 and Mawdūdī was sentenced to death. He was, however, freed, and the martial law administration ended by the intervention of the orthodox-minded prime minister, Khwāja Nāẓim al-dīn, and the then secretary-general (later prime minister), Chawdharī Muḥammad 'Alī.[1] During the military régime from 1958, the Jamā'at-i Islāmī was banned, like other political parties, and like them it was revived under the 'Second Republic' in 1962. As usual the party and its leader aligned themselves with other opposition groups, infiltrating their ranks and influencing their political programme in the direction of Islamic orthodoxy. After a brief imprisonment in 1964, Mawdūdī emerged to support the candidacy of Miss Fāṭima Jinnāḥ for election to the office of the President of the Republic in opposition to Muḥammad Ayyūb Khān, though in his writings he had persistently asserted that a woman could not legally be appointed as the head of an Islamic state.[2]

The starting point of Mawdūdī's *Weltanschauung* is that the Qur'ān refers to man's insignificant and humble position in the universal scheme, although it also refers to his being the most exalted of God's creatures. Man, therefore, is in a difficult and anomalous position. Weak, frail, and vulnerable as he is, he has been entrusted with the great and hazardous office of the vicegerency of God on this planet. He has been commanded to live in and make use of this world. This is a destiny from which he is not allowed to escape by becoming an ascetic. He must mould human society according to the immutable, everlasting, divine law of *waḥy*. This world is therefore the world of action, i.e. of the exteriorization of divine commands to control and apply to human society. The hereafter is the world of judgement. Islam

[1] See below, p. 241.

[2] *Islamic Law and Constitution* (*ILC*) (1960), *passim*; for his volte-face see files of the Pakistan press, especially *Dawn* and the *Nawā-i Waqt* (Lahore), Oct.–Dec. 1964.

subordinates man's actions in this world to the considerations of divine judgement in the hereafter.[3]

Islam's conception of man and his relationship with the universe is the only one which can be called natural. 'As the whole creation obeys the law of God, the whole universe, therefore, literally follows the religion of Islam . . . for Islam signifies nothing but obedience and submission to Allāh, the Lord of the universe.'[4] As long as the Islamic community adhered to this natual law, it remained pure, its culture was pragmatic and ethical. Later, as elements borrowed from other religions seeped into the Islamic culture, its moral purity declined; good living and elaborate architecture flourished; and the way of life became increasingly un-Islamic. Nevertheless, at the core of Islamic culture throughout the world something which was essentially Islamic continued permanently in Islamic societies, and has revealed itself in moments of crisis in Islamic history.[5]

The entire organization of Islamic society is concentrated in the person of God. Religion is therefore identical with obedience, and 'Islam' with submission to His will, which has generated 'natural laws'. It is for man's rationality, itself the product of a physical principle, to adjust itself to these laws. Thus alone can harmony of thought and action be achieved by the individual and by society.[6]

The intellectual basis of human morality is *īmān*, which in its essential sense can be religious or worldly. But religious *īmān* alone is capable of incorporating in itself the terms and requirements of this-worldly *īmān*, and not vice versa. A worldly culture based on a religious *īmān* is therefore more comprehensive and all-embracing than a purely secular culture derived from unguided human rationality.[7] Islamic society is based on *īmān* in Islam, which is explained by Mawdūdī in traditional theological terms, based on the five articles of faith laid down in the Qur'ān including the sovereignty of God, the belief in prophethood,

[3] *Islāmī tahẕīb* (1960), p. 33.
[4] *Towards Understanding Islam* (1960), p. 3.
[5] *Islāmī tahẕīb*, pp. 63–66.
[6] Ibid. pp. 87–89.
[7] Ibid. pp. 115, 123.

God's angels, and the Day of Judgement.[8] God therefore is not only the creator, the provider, the nourisher; he is also the only absolute ruler and legislator for human society. The Prophet of Islam, with whose advent the 'era of polyprophetism' in human history ends, is God's chief representative among men; and the Qur'ān is the only source of basic law God has prescribed for human society. To be a member of Islamic society one has to acknowledge and accept the infallibility of the revealed law. Anyone who holds that an individual or collective human judgement could alter, modify, select, or reject any part of divine injunctions is guilty of an effort to supersede and abrogate the revealed law, and has therefore no place in Islamic society and is not qualified for the citizenship of an Islamic state.[9]

Islamic culture is based on a covenant between God and his creature, man. Its norms are set for all times. They are valid for all humanity, irrespective of national frontiers, race, colour, or language. This extensive potential of enfranchisement is there not to multiply the number of nominal converts to Islam, but to give an opportunity to all human beings to make submission to their master and to order their lives according to His prescribed laws. Islamic universalism is not lax. It is strictly disciplined in moral code as in faith, enabling man to lead the good life in this world in preparation for the hereafter; and in this discipline Islam combines in itself all the virtues which are found individually or in isolation in other religions or cultures.[10]

Kufr (unbelief), the opposite of Islam, is tyranny, rebellion, ingratitude, and infidelity. The inevitable consequence of this revolt is a failure to realize the ultimate ideals of life. An unbelieving scientist would have no moral checks and balances and could expose the entire human race to destruction and annihilation. An ideal Muslim scientist should not lag behind any unbeliever in scientific inquiry into the practical problems of the social and physical sciences, but the objectives of his inquiry

[8] For his angelology see *Tafhīm al-Qur'ān* (1943) and *Islāmī tahzīb*, pp. 181–9.

[9] *Islāmī tahzīb*, pp. 139–41; *Understanding Islam*, pp. 93–137.

[10] *Islāmī tahzīb*, pp. 340–7.

would be different, essentially ethical and beneficent for human society. True belief in the unity of God and in the *kalima* inculcates broadmindedness, self-respect, and self-esteem, combined with modesty and humanity, virtue and uprightness, patience and perseverance, courage, inner peace, and contentment. It saves man from envy, greed, and meanness. Most importantly, it binds man to obey and observe God's law.[11]

Like Abu'l Kalām Āzād and Parwīz, Mawdūdī distinguishes between the revelational religion, *dīn*, and the traditional (for which he prefers to use the term *sharīʿa* rather than *mazhab*). Unlike them his concepts of 'revelational' and 'traditional' religion are different, and he emphasizes the validity of both. *Dīn* is based exclusively on the word of God, and since all His books and messengers must have given the same message without contradicting each other, it is also the element common to all religions, though corrupted in faiths other than Islam by later interpolations or interpretations. The *sharīʿa*, which is the traditional religion and divinely-amended customary law, and which prescribes ritual worship, codes of morality, and distinctions between right and wrong, differs in the teaching of every prophet to suit 'the conditions of his own peoples and times'. Though in this conclusion Mawdūdī inadvertently opens for himself a vista of the historical growth of religion and the role of religion in history, he ignores the reality of movement in history, which transforms the role of traditional religion. Instead he emphasizes the validity of Islamic canon law as unalterable and immutable for all time to come. Here he endorses the standpoint of the traditionalist *ʿulamā'* regarding the six collections of *ḥadīs̱* as the supreme source of canon law, and in agreement with them, though less dogmatically, he also pays a glowing tribute to the founders of the juristic schools of law.[12]

On *jihād* he has written extensively, again from a purely traditionalist point of view. 'In *jihād* one takes away or gives life solely in the cause of Allāh. In the same way, in rendering God's

[11] *Understanding Islam*, pp. 19–20, 105–11.

[12] Ibid pp. 152–3.

rights one has to sacrifice many of those things which man has in his control, like animals, wealth, etc.'[13]

The ideal society which he envisages in the Islamic state is one based on the strict segregation of the sexes, women being restricted to an inferior role.

> To preserve the moral life of the nation and to safeguard the evolution of society on healthy lines, free mingling of both the sexes has been prohibited. Islam effects a functional distribution between the sexes and sets different spheres of activity for both of them. Women should in the main devote to their household duties in their homes and men should attend to their jobs in the socio-economic spheres.

Cinema, theatre, and fine arts are forbidden: 'Islam does not approve of such pastimes, entertainments, and recreations as tend to stimulate sensual passions and vitiate the canons of morality.'[14]

Between 1937 and 1939 Mawdūdī actively turned to political polemics, which were first directed against the nationalist '*ulamā*' of Deoband and the Jam'iyyat al-'Ulamā'-i Hind; there was virulent attack and counter-attack on both sides.[15] He assailed the 'composite' nationalist theory of these '*ulamā*' on the same ground as did the Muslim League, that however well-intentioned their nationalism was, it exposed Muslim India to grave dangers of religio-cultural absorption into Hinduism. Later, in independent India, Mawdūdī's party reversed this stand.[16]

In 1939 Mawdūdī's political polemics altered their target. The threat of the disintegration of Islam in India through the misguided alliance of the Deoband '*ulamā*' with the Indian National Congress had receded into the background with the resignation of the Congress governments in the provinces at the beginning of the second world war. The masses had been swayed and by 1939

[13] *al-Jihād fi'l -Islām* (1929); *Understanding Islam*, p. 167.

[14] *Understanding Islam*, pp. 182–3.

[15] *Musalmān awr mawjūda siyāsī kashmakash* (1937–9), i–iii; A. S. Raḥmānī, *Jama'āt-i Islāmī ke da'we*.

[16] Mawdūdī and A. H. Iṣlāḥī, *Da'wat-i Islāmī* (1956); Mawdūdī, *Siyāsī kashmakash*, iii. 4–5.

rallied firmly behind the leadership of Jinnāḥ and the Muslim League, which Mawdūdī furiously denounced as thoroughly ignorant of the sciences of religion and exclusively motivated in their political programme and orientation by the worldly socio-economic interests of the Muslims. The separatist Muslim nationalism of the secularized élite seemed to him in no way less dangerous than the 'composite' nationalism championed by Āzād and the Deoband *'ulamā'*. Between the survival of the irreligious Muslims of India, or for that matter the Muslims of Iran and Turkey, and their complete extinction, there was no difference as far as he was concerned.[17]

From 1939 to 1947 Mawdūdī continued to attack and argue against the Pakistan movement. A 'homeland' for the Muslims was something very different from the *dār al-Islām*. He did not stand for the political freedom or self-determination of Muslims, but for the rule of Islam, for a purely Islamic, traditionalist-fundamentalist theocracy. Pakistan as envisaged by the Muslim League and Jinnāḥ would be a pagan state and its rulers would not be Islamic but Pharaohs and Nimrods. To call Pakistan an Islamic state would be as misleading as to call an institution of ignorance (presumably the Muslim University at Aligarh) a Muslim university, or a bank in the new state an Islamic bank while Islam forbids interest and therefore the very institution of banking, or to call its society modelled on paganism (presumably of the west) an Islamic society, or its forbidden creations in music, painting, and sculpture Islamic arts, or its 'atheism and heresy' as 'Islamic philosophy'.

> Not a single leader of the Muslim League from Jinnāḥ himself to the rank and file has an Islamic mentality or Islamic habits of thought, or looks at political and social problems from the Islamic viewpoint. . . . Their ignoble role is to safeguard merely the material interests of Indian Muslims by every possible political manœuvre or trickery.[18]

Muslims, Mawdūdī argues, do not constitute a national entity but a *jamā'at*. Islam cannot accept the position of being just a political party; it claims for itself the unique role of being the

[17] *Siyāsī kashmakash*, iii. 6–7.

[18] Ibid. p. 25.

only political party and can brook neither rival nor compromise. It looks at problems in a universal perspective and not in terms of individuals, nations, or classes. Its objectives are permanent. It rejects a national or historical framework of operations, and does not confine itself to the given cultural or traditional data of any particular people. It draws upon the capabilities of *all* outstanding human individuals (who must logically be either Muslims or accept Islam) at a given moment in history and mobilizes them into a movement of *jihād* for an Islamic revolution. It will also be their duty to work out a theory of Islamic law and constitution in an Islamic theocracy thus achieved and organized.[19]

This became the proclaimed stand of Jamāʿat-i Islāmī. Its objectives were to invite all mankind generally and (the so-called) Muslims especially to submit to God (literally *islām*), to purify their lives of all 'hypocrisy and contradiction', to become sincere Muslims; so that the entire Muslim society in an Islamic state might take 'one spiritual form'. Human society, including all Muslim states in the modern world, was being run by evil, wicked, vicious, and sinful leaders; the Jamāʿat-i Islāmī stood for a revolution to overthrow them and to transfer theoretical and practical leadership and governance of the community into the hands of the pious and the truly faithful. The leadership that should rule over the Muslims should be spiritually single-minded, of impeccable morality, and by its exemplary conduct 'should prove itself superior to the present rulers by the qualities required for leadership or government'. The propaganda organization of the Jamāʿat should follow a programme of gradualism, rationalism, and efficiency; its members should propagate the party's programme among their friends, neighbours, and business contacts. Like all fascist parties, its organization was highly centralized, pyramidally converging on a single *amīr* (leader), obedience to whom was binding upon Muslims.[20]

Mawdūdī's acceptance of the principle of gradualism in politics became the main theoretical argument in favour of his party's

[19] Ibid. pp. 30–31, 40–41.
[20] Ibid. pp. 101–12, 171–84; *Daʿwat-i Islāmī*, pp. 39–69.

policy of political manœuvre, compromise, and opportunism. The members of his party had been theoretically forbidden to participate in the administration of an irreligious government; in practice they infiltrated into its ranks to exercise pressure from within; instead of mobilizing for the *jihād* it had proclaimed as its revolutionary motive, it entered the arena of parliamentary politics, aligning itself with various parties but always remaining in opposition, choosing its allies on considerations of strategy and hardly ever of piety; and it participated vociferously in the see-saw struggle for constitution-making in close alliance with non-fundamentalist traditionalists.

Mawdūdī's political thought starts from the premiss that the principal source of constitution and law is the Qur'ān and that the ultimate legal and constitutional authority vests in God alone, though a measure of freedom of choice, strictly limited and circumscribed by revealed injunctions, has been allowed to man. Islamic society is an ideological society, bound by a contract of absolute *islām* (submission) to the divine injunctions. The *sharī'a*, in this context, is the legal codification of this contract. If an Islamic society decides to enact its own constitution, or borrows legal or constitutional elements from an extraneous source, it breaks its contract with God and forfeits its right to be called 'Islamic'. The prescriptions of the Islamic *sharī'a* cover the individual and the collective life alike; they constitute an organic whole and cannot be applied or discarded in bits and pieces.[21]

The *sharī'a* as a source of law is partly unalterable and partly flexible. Qur'ān and *ḥadīs̱* are its unalterable sources; its flexible element rests on the *ta'wīl* (interpretation) of the Qur'ān and *ḥadīs̱*, and on such traditionally accepted juridical sources as *qiyās*, *ijtihād*, or discretionary approval (*istiḥsān*). To be a jurist one has to be a scholar of Arabic language and literature. In this apparently liberal-traditionalist gesture to the flexibility of Islamic law, Mawdūdī has tried on the one hand to placate the traditionalists, on the other to attract the liberal modernists,

[21] *ILC*, pp. 47–48, 50–54.

but his own exegetical interpretation of the Qur'ān is so literalist that it leaves hardly any scope for *ta'wīl* in the modernist sense.[22]

It is an article of faith with Mawdūdī that Islamic laws are not antiquated or out of date. He does not believe in the historical evolution of mankind. But he does believe, like the traditionalists, in historical continuity in the sense that the Islamic community, and the society based on the teachings of the Qur'ān and the *sunna* of the Prophet has been continuously in existence since 'the very first day of the advent of Islam', and in the sense that Muslim people living in various parts of the world share a single and identifiable religious and cultural personality, the same 'beliefs, modes of thinking, ethical standards and values, acts of worship and mundane affairs', and a common way of life. Like some modernists he sees in the early Islamic institution of tribal or intertribal *shūrā* (consultation) the nucleus of an ideal parliamentary system; and in the legal principle of *ijmā'* not so much a sanction for the commendable but fallible consensus of the jurists, but the mature opinion of the community's learned élite during a period 'in which the political system of Islam has been in operation'.[23]

In 1948 Mawdūdī decided to support the principle of 'gradualism' in islamizing law and constitution in Pakistan, whereas earlier in the decade he had condemned the Muslim League for advancing this same principle. His objective remained, however, 'nothing short of demolishing the entire structure erected by our British masters and the erection of a new one in its place', and to erase the effects of the 'poisonous content and the thoroughly materialistic bias of modern secular education'.[24]

The first step in this gradualist islamization would be to 'Muslimize [convert to Islam] the state [i.e. Pakistan] which is still based on and working according to the same secular bases [*sic*] on which it did during the British period'. For this the first prerequisite would be to acknowledge and restore the sovereignty of God over the state so that the 'Government of Pakistan shall

[22] Ibid. pp. 61–63, 75–80. [23] Ibid. pp. 85–95. [24] Ibid. pp. 101–4.

administer the country as His agent'; to restore the basic Islamic *sharīʿa* law, and to repeal all others which are derived from extraneous sources or are repugnant to it. Accepting the *Realpolitik* of gradualism, Mawdūdī also altered the technique of his operations. In addition to the planned revolution through an organized religious party, he decided to achieve his ends by the given parliamentary procedures of election through the emotionally religious and excitable masses of people. 'Howsoever deficient the general mass of our voters may be in respect of formal education, they certainly possess the sense to decide as to what type of people can be relied upon for a certain purpose.' The 'theocrats' could then safely entrench themselves and work out a plan for 'a thorough reform of all the departments of our national life for which all the resources of the state will have to be utilized'. All media of education and mass communication would be used 'for creating a new Islamic consciousness'. Secular-minded civil servants 'who have been incorrigibly affected by the decadent, sinful and corrupt system of life', whom Mawdūdī likens to 'a fibre of discordant colour which will not fit into our pattern', would be replaced. And the 'Hinduistic and Western semi-feudalistic and semi-capitalistic foundations' of the state, together with its political system, would have to be demolished.[25]

In visualizing this utopia Mawdūdī differs from the traditionalist *ʿulamā* in acknowledging the shortcomings of *fiqh* to meet the challenges of modern times, as it does not deal with constitutional, international, and criminal law as separate disciplines. These, he suggests, could be modernized to a certain very limited extent by the study and selective use of the modern sciences of economics and finance, and by the evolution of an Islamic law of evidence, penal code, and civil and criminal codes of procedure. For this purpose he recommends the formation of an Academy of Law in Pakistan, and the reform of traditional legal education. He envisages a reformed judicial system in which there would be no place for practising lawyers, whom he calls legal parasites. Instead he would like to revive the discarded

[25] Ibid. pp. 107–9.

mukhtārī system of eighteenth-century Anglo-Muhammadan law.[26]

Unlike *fiqh*, the political philosophy of Islam is eternally perfect, and therefore incapable of any further evolution or change. Unlike the communist countries or the western democracies, where 'slavery' is perpetuated, Islam repudiates slavery by asserting that the master-slave relationship is applicable in a political and social context only to the relations between God and man. Mawdūdī frankly equates his concept of Islamic polity with a theocracy run by man only as the agent and representative of God. For this concept he coins the term 'theo-democracy', the leaders of which must accept in their totality the clear-cut injunctions of the *sharī'a*, even in regard to institutions the abolition of which would be most repugnant to the westernized intelligentsia. These injunctions enforce the abolition of banks, insurance, and interest, the segregation of the sexes, veiling of women, retention of divorce laws favourable to men but unfavourable to women, and cutting off the hands of a criminal for theft. The sphere of activity of the 'Islamic theo-democracy' is 'coextensive with the whole of human life'; and Mawdūdī is forced to confess that 'considered from this aspect, the Islamic state bears a kind of resemblance to the Fascist and Communist states'. But unlike these two modern systems, Mawdūdī argues that 'the Caliphate granted by God to the faithful is the popular vicegerency and not a limited one' and rules out a dictatorship, a theoretical view which is contradicted by his entire concept and practical programme for the takeover by an organized party led by a supreme *amīr*, even though 'elected' by the party rank and file.[27]

The Islamic state is, according to Mawdūdī, writing in 1959, a national state, a view which is a departure from his earlier lip-service to universalism, and a final repudiation of pan-Islamism. It disclaims all responsibility for the protection or guardianship of Muslims living abroad, a confirmation of official, though not emotional, policy in Pakistan. Mawdūdī seems to have adopted

[26] Ibid. pp. 110–26.

[27] Ibid. pp. 147–52, 154–5, 157–60.

this view to strengthen the position of his party in the political life of Pakistan, as well as a concession to the view of the orthodox *'ulamā'* with whom he forged an alliance in 1953. This freed him once and for all from his earlier profession of universalist humanism by proclaiming that since the Islamic state is an ideological state, its citizens must necessarily fall into two categories, Muslims and non-Muslims. 'This differentiation is essential in view of the ideological nature of the state'. Of course he would not submit the protected non-Muslims to the humiliations and tortures of a medieval European ghetto, but would provide, in his 'theo-democratic' system of *apartheid*, equality between Muslims and non-Muslims in civil and criminal law, applying to the non-Muslims their own personal law as in historical Islam. They would be allowed to worship freely in their own towns and cities but would not be permitted to organize 'public processions of the Cross' in 'purely Muslim cities'. The non-Muslims might repair but not erect temples and churches. They would pay *jizya* (which the Islamic state would collect mildly, not tyrannically), which would exempt them, whether they wished it or not, from military service, as the defence of the state against its enemies was the responsibility of the Muslim population only. In regard to normal taxes and free enterprise in agriculture, trade, and industry there would be no discrimination against them. No non-Muslim could be the head of the state or hold a 'key post' or be a member of the *shūrā* (parliament) of the Islamic state. But non-Muslims could propose codification or amendment in their own personal law; and they might submit representations, objections, and suggestions to the Muslim government or parliament. In freedom of expression or conscience non-Muslims would have equality with Muslims. In education they would have to accept the system of the country but would have the right to make arrangements for imparting knowledge of their own religion to their children in their own schools and colleges or even in the national universities and colleges, and they would not be compelled to study Islam.[28]

[28] *Islām awr jadīd ma'āshī naẓarīyāt* (Lahore, 1959), pp. 295–319.

Coming to the question of the economic structure of the Islamic state, Mawdūdī quotes Harold Laski to support his argument that the capitalist framework of free enterprise, private property, and the profit motive is bedevilled, unlike the Islamic framework, by an 'inhuman evil', usury, which dominates its financial structure. Communism as an alternative to capitalism has a worse record. The economic progress of Russia compares unfavourably with the west. A balance-sheet of communist achievements would show certain gains, for example in the sphere of social welfare and co-ordinated state planning, but they are overshadowed by the tyranny and inhumanity of totalitarianism, by corruption, the replacement of a commercial by a bureaucratic oligarchy, and the total loss of individual freedom. This is the price the Soviet citizen has to pay for his daily bread and social security.[29]

The capitalist system has not been able to solve its problems either, despite the sharpness of the communist challenge. There is still unemployment and poverty amid plenty. In short, its trade-cycle is still firmly governed by the usurious banker.[30]

What economic path should the Muslim society in India and Pakistan take, situated as it is in the midst of ancient Hindu paganism, Mughal feudalism, and the impact of modern western culture? For it Islam alone can offer the best solution, a golden mean between capitalism and Marxism. Islam distinguishes clearly between the right and the wrong means of production of wealth. It prohibits the exploitation of one man by another and frowns upon the accumulation of wealth, as it enjoins its followers to give away whatever exceeds his normal necessities.[31] The moral philosophy of Islam, Mawdūdī asserts, is exactly the opposite of capitalism. Usury and interest are categorically rejected in the Qur'ān as offensive to God. The Muslim law of credit without interest is a calculated moral risk. Donations or charitable foundations in capitalist society are in fact a means of

[29] Ibid. pp. 63–83.
[30] Ibid. pp. 100–4.
[31] Ibid. pp. 112–20; argument based on Qur'ān, 4:5; 3:45; 2:27.

extended commercial publicity, whereas Islam enjoins charity to be anonymous. Muslim charity is controlled by the state in the form of an obligatory *zakāt* which is set aside exclusively for social welfare. The institution of *zakāt* in Islam corresponds with modern co-operative movements, national insurance, and national provident fund. It is meant to take care of the needy, the aged, the widow, the orphan, and the sick. The accumulation of wealth in the hands of a few is further discouraged by the Islamic law of inheritance, which tends to distribute and divide it in a wider and wider group.[32]

In Islamic society it is the individual who forms the basic unit. The contract is between God and individual men and women; and not between the deity and an ethnic group. Therefore the individual remains at the centre of the Islamic economic system, and totalitarianism or state control, as in a communist society, is repugnant to Islam which cannot accept even evolutionary socialism that may develop in a capitalist society. The law of private ownership has been the law of nature since time immemorial, and Islam, being the religion of nature, cannot accept any other law. Mawdūdī is therefore opposed to agrarian reform, though he advocates a 'classless' relationship between landlords and peasants. He regards the Muslim law of inheritance, dividing and subdividing property, as conducive to equalization. He is opposed to rapid industrialization: and favours a gradual replacement of men by machines to avoid the problem of unemployment. Competitive enterprise and equality of opportunity should be the keynote of industrial and commercial life. The government's role should be confined to mere guidance of the industrial policy. Industries and trades should be subjected to *zakāt* to forestall the accumulation of wealth in the hands of the few.[33]

Zakāt in the Islamic state should guarantee social insurance and ensure every citizen the minimum of the necessities of life; and for this reason it should be levied on income and accumulated capital alike.

[32] Ibid. pp. 122–33.

[33] Ibid. pp. 141–7, 151–7.

The Jamā'at-i Islāmī's political platform in India is slightly different from that in Pakistan. Rejecting the Indian National Congress's emphasis on secularism, nationalism, and democracy, Mawdūdī offers his familiar substitutes: submission to God, humanism, and the 'vicegerency of God'. He advises Hindus to search for these principles in their scriptures as they are the revelational essence of all religions. If they fail to find them there—and it is possible that in the course of centuries some of the original 'revealed' truth of Hindu religion may have been lost—Mawdūdī invites them to find it in the Islamic concept of theo-democracy. Hindus will find it identical with their own 'lost revelational heritage' which they might recognize, test, and adopt for their own welfare.[34]

[34] *Da'wat-i Islāmī*, pp. 9–25, 35.

CHAPTER THIRTEEN

PARWĪZ'S EXEGETICAL NEO-MODERNISM AND OTHER LIBERAL TRENDS

GHULĀM Aḥmad Parwīz (b. 1903) is in a number of ways the exact antithesis of Mawdūdī. Both are fundamentalists in the sense that the foundation of the religious, political, and economic systems they propose for Islamic society in Pakistan is based on their understanding of the Qur'ān. But there the resemblance ends. Whereas Mawdūdī is an externalist, Parwīz has built up an entirely new and fantastic exegetical *lexique technique* to explain Qur'ānic chapter and verse in modernist terms.

The central political and economic problem, for a solution of which Parwīz turns to reinterpret the meaning of the Qur'ān, is the backwardness, decadence, and enslavement of Muslim lands, which even after gaining their independence, are not only weaker than the non-Muslim states but are at the mercy of and exist due to the courtesy of the greater powers. All the Muslim countries have one factor in common: political and economic backwardness, though they live in varied geographical zones, in different climates, and have different ways of life. What then is the cause of their common backwardness? The fundamentalists or the traditionalists will attribute it to a falling away from 'real' Islam. The Ṣūfīs will ignore it by belittling this world's power and glory. Both these views are rejected by Parwīz as inaccurate in the light of the logic of history. The universe evolves according to certain physical laws which condition life and the entire human situation on this planet. They affect non-Muslims and Muslims alike, irrespective of any spiritual difference between them.[1]

Of all the modernists since Sayyid Aḥmad Khān, Parwīz

[1] *Asāb-i zawāl-i ummat* (1952), pp. 6–28.

comes perhaps closest to the western outlook in suggesting that a high standard of living and sovereign political, social, individual, and economic freedom are the ideals of worldly life. The standard of living depends upon the measure of freedom a society and its individuals enjoy. On this in turn depends man's mastery of the forces of nature. In placing his emphasis on this-worldliness, Parwīz ruins a sound point of view by creating a far-fetched and untenable exegetical terminology. He attributes different meanings to terms like *dunyā* (this world) and *ākhira* (the hereafter), used eschatologically in the Qur'ān; *dunyā* is merely the immediate present and *ākhira* the future of human generations on this planet. He does not deny faith in life after death as a cardinal principle of the Islamic creed, but merely gives a double meaning to the term *ākhira*, in order to switch one of these meanings from an eschatological to a worldly context, so as to emphasize economic progress. *Taqwā* (piety) is not merely worship of God, but the adjustment and application of man's creative effort to the possibilities of the production of wealth which God has potentially invested in the nature of material things. There is no dichotomy between material achievement in this world and spiritual attainment in the next. The people who made any such distinctions are the 'dividers' (*al-muqtasimūn*).[2]

According to Parwīz, in the theological history of Islam *dīn*, the fundamentalist data of religion as revealed in the Qur'ān, is to be distinguished from *maẕhab*. *Dīn* has a single basis, a concept of the unity of all creation, of all life and all physical law. These unities derive from the unity of God. *Dīn* is also the organization of human effort where present and future merge into a single dynamic oneness. The fundamentalist orthodox society under the Prophet and the four orthodox Caliphs followed that pattern. But the monarchical rule of the Umayyads and the 'Abbāsids eroded the Qur'ānic organization of Islamic society, when the Qur'ānic terms *dunyā* and *ākhira* were given their popular eschatological meanings. The monarch and the theologian worked in close co-operation and strengthened one

[2] Ibid. pp. 29–52; *Why Do we Lack Character?*, pp. 1–20.

another's position. The Qur'ān ceased to be the primary source of law and was confined to liturgical reading. Prescribed religious rituals were treated as self-sufficient exercises, with reward promised in the next world. Doctrines of fatalism and pre-determination were inculcated among the people to make mis-rule and anarchy acceptable. *Aḥādīs̱* were shamelessly invented, and this in turn affected the classical science of *tafsīr*. Qur'ānic verses were twisted to fit in with a spurious *ḥadīs̱* here and a *qiyās* there. The belief in the inherent evil nature of this world achieved its culmination in Ṣūfī quietism. All this helped directly or indirectly to strengthen monarchical absolutism. Most crippling was the *maẕhab*'s imposition of the doctrine of *taqlīd* and denial of the use of reason to understand the significance of Qur'ānic eschatology.[3]

Conformity which relates *taqwā* to rewards in the next world tends to make life and nature, which are beautiful, seem immoral and ugly. Belles lettres, music, art, good living, are all frowned upon as frivolities or as obscene. But the Qur'ān itself has interdicted very few things and has left the rest to the discretion of individuals and society. It is the juristic *maẕhab* which has imposed a ban on aesthetics. This has led to hypocritical compromises in Islamic culture. Music is frowned upon but incorporated as a recognized mystical ritual. Painting is condemned, but a modern theologian has no objection to being photographed. Love inspired by a woman's beauty is considered to be a passport to perdition, but this very passion is sublimated in divine love, and the entire imagery of wine, woman, and song is transferred to mystical poetry.[4] This emphasis on aesthetics is derived from Āzād and stands in contradiction to Mawdūdī's extreme puritanism.

Islamic social ethics, Parwīz continues, also reflect a lack of mental balance. They have incorporated determinism, obedience to absolutism, and tyranny, and there is a large catalogue of things permitted and things prohibited.[5]

[3] *Asbāb-i zawāl-i ummat* (1952), pp. 52–82.
[4] Ibid. pp. 90–97.
[5] Ibid. pp. 98–102.

The root cause of the decline of Islam is, then, the suppression of *dīn*, the open and simple revealed religion, by the juristic and traditional *mazhab*, and the mental and spiritual fossilization it has imposed. This is the root of the decline of Muslim empires. This is the cause of the precarious economic and political existence of Muslim states today and of the societies that live in them.

Parwīz, then, repeats the familiar modernist apologetic argument, voiced by Sayyid Aḥmad Khān, Iqbāl, and almost all others, that the Qur'ān has invited the Muslims to reflect on the mysteries of God's creation, for the scientific study of the forces of nature. But instead of becoming scientists, our savants have preferred to become librarians of medievalism.[6]

In order to survive in the modern world, with its organization and basis of scientific power, the Muslims will have to give up the traditional *mazhab*—juristic religion—of their own invention. This would leave two courses open: either secularism, which would be spiritual death, but even that would be better than the agony of lingering death they are suffering from; or return to *dīn*; for the Qur'ān has promised revival and renaissance to any community which has not totally lost its ability to reform[7]

So far the views of Parwīz can be called modernist; but his involvement with his own far-fetched theories makes his work largely a curiosity among religious cross-currents in Islam in the subcontinent. In dressing up modern concepts in Qur'ānic terminology he develops a fantastic exegetical *lexique technique*. *Rabb* (God the Provider) also signifies to him a universal divine law of *rubūbiyyat*, which is the development of the latent faculties of a creature of God. The entire terminology of the Qur'ān is thus given a far-fetched meaning and interpretation to suit the political or economic requirements of present-day Islamic society.[8] Borrowing from Abu'l-Kalām Āzād the conceptual framework and much of the original idea of a universe nourished by a system of divine providence or nurture (*niẓām-i rubūbiyyat*),

[6] Ibid. pp. 110–15.
[7] Ibid. pp. 128–32.
[8] *Lughāt al-Qur'ān* (1960–1).

16

Parwīz turns it to his own account by giving it a utopian and ideal significance in so far as human society is concerned. Some of the detail features of his concept of the system of *rubūbiyyat* can be traced to Bergsonian evolutionism filtered through Iqbāl. The evolutionary process of *rubūbiyyat* requires co-ordination as well as balance. It has an ideal and an end which man can achieve through *islām*, or submission to God. The Qur'ān is as much opposed to the Ṣūfistic and Vedāntic view of annihilation of the human self in the Ultimate Self as it is to a materialistic concept of human existence. A materialistic view of life is governed by certain economic factors—by rationalism as a guide to the economic structure of society, by individualism and private enterprise, by inequality in the accumulation of wealth, and by the hardening of class structure. Self-defeating nationalism and Machiavellian statecraft are its social and organizational reflexions. The other-worldly view of life goes to the other extreme. Both are contrary to the divine will.[9]

The Qur'ānic shares with the materialistic world view the desirability of prosperity and plenty in this world. But human society is not merely physical and economic. The order of *rubūbiyyat* envisages the development of man's immortal, moral self, as well as his striving for better living conditions in this world. The human self, Parwīz continues (in the wake of Bergson and Iqbāl), though confined within natural laws, partakes of the divine energy; its attributes are derived from the balanced attributes of God, which are so many aspects or facets of the Absolute Reality.[10]

The existence of these attributes of divine origin in man has a particular aim in view, the creation of permanent values which are eternal truths; whereas the values of materialism are relative and not intrinsic. Of these permanent values, the one to which divine attributes primarily point is God's universal providence. Man's first value-creating objective should be the nourishment and subsistence of all humanity. This value subordinates the

[9] *Niẓām-i Rubūbiyyat* (*NR*) (1954), pp. 3–13, 21–46.
[10] Ibid. pp. 47–67.

individual to the society by its greater emphasis on 'give' than 'take'. A society composed of such individuals would necessarily be a generous and humane one. In this society, the means of production of wealth for social welfare is referred to by the term *infāq* (expending, disbursing) in the Qur'ān. Bergson calls it the 'open society' as opposed to a 'closed society'. The one corresponds to paradise and the other to hell. The 'forbidden fruit or tree' is the 'division between man and man'. The legend of the Fall of Adam therefore symbolizes the story of man's reduction to a life of individualism and personal gain. The lost paradise can be regained in the 'open society', where the interest of the individual is subordinated to social welfare. *Waḥy* guides man in that direction.[11]

Man's potentialities for intellectual or physical labour as well as the means of production he employs are all God's creation and His property. Man is entitled only to the right of subsistence by his labour.[12] Parwīz repeats Iqbāl's theory that land, which is the base of all means of production, belongs to God. Man's right of ownership over it can only be indirect. He who works deserves his wages; and he who by some mental or physical inability cannot, deserves social charity, which is identical with the Islamic concept of *iḥsān*. Intellectual and creative or productive capacities of individual men differ. But this difference was not created by God for permanent class stratification. The differences of individual capacity were meant to be complementary to suit various requirements of labour.[13]

Qur'ānic socialism is very different from Marxism, which has no ideally ethical basis for its social philosophy. Communism can be established only by preaching a doctrine of class hatred. The dialectical materialistic view of historical necessity and causation is exactly the opposite of the Qur'ānic concept of life and history, according to which the divine scheme of existence unfolds itself in a perpetual struggle between good and evil. The struggle

[11] Ibid. pp. 57–110.
[12] Ibid. pp. 123–9, basing his argument on Qur'ān, 28: 78; 39: 40, &c.
[13] Ibid. pp. 130–7.

for existence is therefore basically moral and not economic. In this dualistic moral struggle, good alone can survive by the virtue and logic of its being profitable to the society. Good (*khayr*) is social welfare in all its potentialities. It is therefore the sum total of God's blessings.[14]

The Qur'ānic programme leading to the good life lays down certain basic truths which have to be accepted as an act of faith. These include faith in *waḥy*, in a single law operating in the universe, in the brotherhood of all men, and in life after death, which implies a belief in the law of retribution. The next step is to bring about social evolution in the light of *waḥy* to create the ideal society, the *qiyām-i ṣalāt*, a term which should not be translated as standing for ritual prayer, but should be interpreted in its social context as organizing Muslim, or in a larger context human, society in the service of God. The Qur'ānic injunction of *zakāt* should also be interpreted in terms of social welfare; and in this context the rules of charity prescribed in the Qur'ān for the Prophet's day should be distinguished from those implying universal application for the creation of an ideal welfare society.[15]

For the creation of the ideal Qur'ānic welfare society Parwīz, like Mawdūdī, also envisages the formulation of a party (*jamā'at*) of revolution. But unlike him he envisages it as having a democratic rather than totalitarian structure or objective. Its aim should be to establish the rule of an élite which will strive to make the production and distribution of wealth follow a cycle determined not by the few, by pressures and the profit motive, but by social needs of consumption and rising standards of living. It would neither stifle individual freedom, as do the communist states, nor give it licence to exploit others, but develop the principle of individual and social freedom of thought in the light of *waḥy*. The Qur'ānic revolutionary party would enter into a covenant with society to provide all its members with means of livelihood and social insurance. The very name of God, Allāh, is synonymous with this Qur'ānic society. Needless to say, this rather irreverent socio-economic pantheism has been repugnant

[14] Ibid. pp. 143–51.

[15] Ibid. pp. 159–67.

not only to the *'ulamā'* but also to the vaguely conformist middle classes. But this confused 'theistic socialism' is meant by Parwīz to be the final argument for the rejection of the Marxist philosophy of history.[16]

Parwīz's summary dismissal of all forms of government known to history—of arbitration between the ruler and the ruled, of the tribal system which 'led to priestcraft', of theocracy which helped the emergence of autocratic monarchy, of government as a social contract, of materialistic Marxism, of democracy which has 'failed the west' (according to the certificates issued by Professors Cobban, Ewing, and René Guenon), of fascism which is based on hatred—leaves room for one possible form of good government, which Locke has suggested could only be based on divine law. But then Locke was also wrong in regarding the will of the majority as the source of divine law.[17] Here Parwīz rejects Iqbāl's identification of *ijmā'* with the popular will and his view of the chosen representatives of the people, though he agrees with Iqbāl that divine law cannot be found in Christian institutions. Though they represent opposite poles of exegetical fundamentalism and modernism, there is agreement between Mawdūdī and Parwīz on asserting that divine law must consist of 'permanent values' which man, selfish in essence though not necessarily wicked, is incapable of developing by himself without *rubūbiyyat*. Sovereignty over human societies, as over the universe, vests solely and untransferably in God and cannot be vested in man, even in the prophets, a position which strikes at the very root of *ḥadīs̱* and *sunna* as a source of law. Divine law is inherent as a 'directive' and not as a hard and fast legal code in the Qur'ān. An Islamic state is therefore 'not a substitute for God; it is an agency for enforcing God's laws and discharging those duties towards man which God has assumed'. The caliphate of the four orthodox Caliphs represents an instance of such an agency, and functioned with the assistance of a *shūrā* which helped in the interpretation of the Qur'ānic directives.

[16] Ibid. pp. 147–90, 193–204.
[17] *Quran's Political System* (1956), pp. 3–18.

The Qur'ān does not prescribe a specific method of consultation but leaves it to the requirements of every age or clime. But all legislation in an Islamic state or its consultative assembly or parliament has to be within the bounds of certain unalterable principles defined in the Qur'ān.[18]

This 'Qur'ānic democracy', though much more restricted in scope than the western democracy, is far closer to it than to the theory or practice of any state in historical Islam after the orthodox caliphate. Its ultimate aim is universalist in the sense of extending its concept to the entire humanity. This universalism, leading to the evolution of a world state, cannot be achieved through *jihād*, but by the propagation and voluntary universal acceptance of the principles of Islamic unity.[19]

Most of these ideas were summed up by Parwīz in a series of letters addressed to the members of Pakistan's first Constituent Assembly. As a minor civil servant in Pakistan, Parwīz is also concerned with their role, and feels that employees of the state are like cogs in a single machine, the Islamic state.[20]

The aim of the Islamic way of life in an Islamic state is to aid the development of the system of *rubūbiyyat*. The life of the individual within the society should be governed by constant effort to earn a living by fair and permissible means, to balance income and expenditure, to live plainly and to contribute all savings for the benefit of the needy. Domestic life should be pure. Marriage should be based on choice and mutual attraction and should be maintained on the basis of love, respect, and division of work between husband and wife.[21]

The Muslim community must be a united entity in which sectarianism or even modern party politics has no place. Here again Mawdūdī and Parwīz have a principle in common, though they envisage societies that are the antithesis of each other. Non-Muslims should be treated with complete equality and should

[18] Ibid. pp. 25–30 and *Iblīs wa Ādam* (1954), pp. 104–6.

[19] *NR*, pp. 31–40.

[20] *Fundamentals of Islamic Constitution* (1956); *Islāmī ma'āsharat* (1955), pp. 158–66.

[21] *Islāmī ma'āsharat*, pp. 57–83.

have freedom of belief and worship without any coercion. Here Parwīz's declaration of fundamental human rights is more unequivocal than that of Mawdūdī.[22]

Parwīz's attitude to the Old and the New Testament, though in the tradition of Sayyid Aḥmad Khān, is far more negatively polemical, and he gives much more emphasis to the divergence between Christianity and Judaism and Islam.[23] In Islam he rejects the heritage of mysticism, even of orthodox Ṣūfism, not merely because of its quietism, but as unsatisfactory religious and intuitional experience, because it is anti-rational and so false, misleading, and at variance with the prophetic *waḥy*.

Because of his religious views over 1,000 *'ulamā'* in Pakistan signed a ruling declaring Parwīz an apostate.[24] But this orthodox denunciation is not so significant as the fact that it is modernism itself which becomes the casualty of his exegetical extravagance. He carries to its illogical conclusion the apologetics of Sayyid Aḥmad Khān and Iqbāl. But compared with them, so distorted was his confusion of modernism with exegetical fundamentalism that he tried to change even the concept of the Deity, and was therefore declared an apostate by the *'ulamā'* and repudiated even by the modernist élite.

Slightly closer to the common run of apologetic thought, without much originality, and naïvely demotic is the exegetical modernism of Ghulām Jīlānī Barq. His work is meant especially for the non-westernized middle classes and possibly rural gentry in West Pakistan. The influence of Parwīz is unmistakable, while the methodology of his work is that of a popular textbook, illustrating in terms of elementary science views similar to those expressed and established by Sayyid Aḥmad Khān and Āzād, maintaining that *waḥy* and nature are identical. There are two Qur'āns, the one revealed to Muḥammad in words, the other created as nature. Aspects or elements of nature correspond with and are in fact identical with the verses of the Qur'ān. The one

[22] Ibid. pp. 179–92; *Barq-i Ṭūr* (1956), pp. 35–73, 253–78; *Shu'la-i mastūr* (1958), pp. 45–53.
[23] *Salīm ke Nām* (1953), pp. 14–15; *Iblīs wa Ādam*, p. 319.
[24] *Kuchchh Parwīz ke bāre men* (Lahore, 1963).

leads to the other. Both have components which are arranged in an order without sequence. Starting from this premiss, Barq proceeds to write an exegetically documented textbook, rather naïvely covering biology, astronomy, and geology. Needless to say his approach to and knowledge of these sciences are very superficial.[25]

Like Parwīz, Barq also believes in two Islams, a true one based on *waḥy*, and a false one which is historical and juristic and which has been founded on spurious *ḥadīṣ*.[26]

The failure of individual modernists like Parwīz left the quest of an acceptable and practical interpretation of Islam to suit modern conditions in the hands of official and non-official agencies in Pakistan, which in turn had to strike a careful but rather unstable balance between the forces of conservatism and liberalism in religio-political thinking.

What might be described as semi-official religious modernism is perhaps best illustrated in the writings of Khalīfa ʿAbd al-Ḥakīm, formerly Director of the Institute of Islamic Research at Lahore. His chief work, *Islamic Ideology*, concerns itself with applying the basic principles of Islam to the individual and collective life of the Muslims. According to Ḥakīm, Islam is the religion of harmony. Its injunctions based on eternal verities do not tie man down to any single dogma.

Religion is not only possible, but most of the obstacles to belief in it are unreal and cannot bear examination. 'Science expresses a fundamental human need, so does religion.' Nature is a great 'divine manifestation' and both religion and science deal with it. It is God's volitional creation because He is a creative will. The entire creation is ruled by reason and order which work differently at different levels of existence. Belief in the unseen is a fundamental postulate of Islam. If science has revealed a stage in human evolution when the attitude towards the unseen is free from superstition, the Qur'ān also has put forward a similar claim on behalf of religion. The progress of the spirit is from the seen to the unseen, from the outward to the inward, from appearance

[25] *Do Qur'ān* (1963), pp. 1–28. [26] *Do Islām* (1962).

to reality. Islam believes in the unseen God in order to free human beings from biological and physical limitations. Of all the attributes of God, Ḥakīm's emphasis, like that of Āzād, is on God as *rabb*. In discussing other attributes of God, like *hidāyat*, mercy, and love, he has largely followed Āzād; while in his definition of theism as a combination of the consciousness of divine omnipotence and goodness, Ḥakīm emphasizes the value of power, like Iqbāl, as well as that of rationalization, like Sayyid Aḥmad Khān. In his angelology Ḥakīm is warily traditional, like Amīr ʿAlī; in his eschatology he closely follows Āzād: 'Human life would be a mockery if it started with a body and ended with it.' In ritual prayer, like Iqbāl and most Indo-Muslim modernists, Ḥakīm also sees the principle of democracy, universalism, and concentration on a single direction; it identifies Islam as predominantly a social creed. On the question of *jihād* he takes a less apologetic stand, regarding it as a rational and practical doctrine, and not necessarily defensive.[27]

Most significant in the context of Pakistan are Ḥakīm's views on the nature and concept of an Islamic state. Only in a very special sense can an Islamic democracy be called a theocracy. There are varieties of theocratic states, as there are of secular states. Islam is a theocracy in the sense that religion is moral and morality has a social reference. Islamic theocracy envisages a social welfare state. But with Ḥakīm this concept remains far more traditional than the practice or the policy of the government of Pakistan. He makes accommodation for such traditional elements as the theory of *hijra*, and provision for a special treatment of *ẕimmis*. Like Mawdūdī he envisages fundamental rights and civil liberties for all; unlike him he advocates equality of status between men and women. In an Islamic state tax reforms and other measures should ensure the equitable distribution of social benefits. The dedicated aim of an Islamic state, in spite of the permissibility and occasional necessity of *jihād*, is the pursuit of peace.[28]

[27] *Islamic Ideology* (1953), pp. vii–xxiv, 1–31, 34–39, 54–78, 90, 120–1, 181.
[28] Ibid. pp. 191–212.

It is interesting that unlike the *'ulamā'* of Pakistan who, according to the findings of the Munīr Committee in 1953, are theoretically quite indifferent to the fate of Muslims in a non-Muslim state like India, Ḥakīm tries to find a formula of political life for Muslims in diaspora. In this respect his views are not very different from those of the Deoband *'ulamā'* or Indian, as distinct from Pakistani, modernists.

A Muslim who lives as a citizen of a non-Muslim state has entered into a tacit contract with that government to abide by its laws; and in that contract he cannot jeopardise the essentials of Islam so far as his personal life is concerned. Islam lays great stress on the fulfilment of covenants and treaties, even if they are in some respect unpalatable to Muslims.[29]

[29] Ibid. p. 212.

CHAPTER FOURTEEN

THE DILEMMA OF MODERNISM AND ORTHODOXY IN PAKISTAN

Most of the Muslim *'ulamā'*, led by those of Deoband, were opposed to the concept of Pakistan. But the secular-minded leaders of the Pakistan movement, including Jinnāḥ, fought for the achievement of Pakistan—not merely for the political and economic self-determination of the Muslims of majority provinces but for an indeterminate concept of an Islamic state. This concept constituted the main source of appeal for the lower middle classes and the masses. Only a few *'ulamā'*, Mawlānā Shabbīr Aḥmad 'Usmānī being the most distinguished of them, supported the demand for Pakistan and founded the Jam'iyyat al-'Ulamā'-i Islām, a splinter group of the Jam'iyyat al-'Ulamā'-i Hind which was pro-Congress.

The concept 'Islamic state' had varying connotations according to the religious and political opinions of its proponents. After the creation of Pakistan, its ruling élite was content to see that Pakistan had an external Islamic personality, but that the government was run on lines as close to British Indian secular principles as possible. Under pressure from the traditionalists and the fundamentalists they had to retreat, during the processes of constitution-making, to a position whereby Pakistan became 'a laboratory of Islamic principles', in a continued effort to reconcile the opposing concepts of an Islamic state. In 1948 Jinnāḥ had conceded that the constitution of Pakistan should neither be in conflict with the *sharī'a* law nor entirely based upon it.[1] In March 1949 the Constituent Assembly of Pakistan, elected in July 1946, passed an 'Objectives Resolution' embodying the main principles on which the constitution was to be

[1] *Dawn*, 26 Jan. 1948, quoted by L. Binder, *Religion and Politics in Pakistan* (1961), p. 100.

based. It laid down that 'sovereignty over the entire universe belongs to God Almighty alone, and the authority which He has delegated to the State of Pakistan through its people for being exercised within the limits prescribed by Him is a sacred trust'. It envisaged the principles of democracy, freedom, equality, tolerance, and social justice within an Islamic framework, and provided that Muslims should be enabled to order their lives 'in the individual and collective spheres in accord with the teaching and requirements of Islām as set out in the Holy Qur'ān and the Sunna' and that minorities should be able freely to profess and practise their religions and develop their cultures.[2]

In February 1949 Shabbīr Aḥmad ʿUsmānī, the president of the Jamʿiyyat al-ʿUlamā-i Islām, had demanded the appointment of a committee consisting of eminent *ʿulamā'* and thinkers to advise the Constituent Assembly on the requirements of an Islamic constitution.[3] This demand was met a few months later when the Constituent Assembly's Basic Principles Committee appointed a Board of Taʿlīmāt-i Islāmiyya (Islamic Teaching), which included among a number of *ʿulamā'* Shiblī's successor Sayyid Sulaymān Nadwī. The board advised a constitution of medieval traditional pattern, with some projection of modern requirements into the familiar mythology of an idealized and revivalistic concept of the orthodox caliphate. It recommended that the Head of the State should be a Muslim, with ultimate power; that government should be run by an élite of pious Muslims chosen for their piety by the Muslim electorate; that the committee of *ʿulamā'* should decide what legislation was repugnant to the injunctions of the Qur'ān and the *sunna* and was therefore invalid; that a legislative Assembly, which they identified with the Islamic—in fact ancient Arabian—*shūrā*, or tribal consultative assembly, should be empowered to demand the resignation of the Head of the State in certain circumstances.[4] Most of

[2] Pakistan, Const. Ass. Debates, v/i (7 March 1949), cited ibid. pp. 142–3.

[3] Pres. Address at Dacca Conference, 1949, p. 52 (cited ibid. p. 141).

[4] 'Views of Board of Talimmat-e-Islamia on Certain Items Referred to Them by Sub-Committee on Federal and Provincial Constitutions and Distribution of Powers', app. 4 of the Sub-Committee's Report (1950) (cited ibid. app. A).

the board's recommendations were turned down by the Basic Principles Committee of the Constituent Assembly, but they left a considerable imprint on Pakistan's first (1956) and second (1962) constitutions.

During Liyāqat ʿAlī Khān's premiership (1947–51) the traditional tide was held back with some determination. His own efforts and his government's policy in keeping constitution and legislation secular in the British tradition, while accepting an Islamic veneer, was reflected in the Interim Report of the Basic Principles Committee in 1950, which referred only nominally to the *sharīʿa* provisions. A conference of *ʿulamāʾ* was held in January 1951 at which they were to agree on a series of amendments to the Interim Report. At this conference the fundamentalist Mawdūdī joined hands with the secretary of the Taʿlīmāt Board to outline twenty-two principles which were adopted as the basis of an Islamic constitution. These principles reiterated the suggestions of the board and included a clause to the effect that the state should strengthen the bonds of unity and brotherhood among the Muslims of the world. They also re-emphasized Mawdūdī's principles of the social-welfare responsibility of the state to guarantee the basic necessities of life for all citizens, and of the need of a strong censorship to suppress un-Islamic views.[5]

After Liyāqat ʿAlī Khān's assassination in 1951 a different political situation in Pakistan affected the balance between religion and politics maintained by him. His successor, Khwāja Nāẓim al-dīn, and the finance minister (later prime minister) Chawdharī Muḥammad ʿAlī, were deeply religious men and had cordial relations with the *ʿulamāʾ*, whose influence increased very considerably between 1951 and 1953. The political stability which the Muslim League had provided, as the party in overwhelming majority in all legislatures, was shattered by its crushing defeat in the elections of 1953 in East Pakistan at the hands of a United Front led by the veteran politicians of Bengal, Faẓl al-Ḥaqq and Ḥusayn Shahīd Suhrawardī, and occasioned

[5] Text in Report of the Sub-Committee to Examine Suggestions Received from the Public, in Basic Principles Committee Report, 2 June 1951, app. 21.

by the economic frustration and the sense of unfairness felt by the middle classes of East Bengal, and by the grinding poverty of its teeming millions. After Liyāqat ʿAlī Khān there was no single leader who could command the political loyalty of both East and West Pakistan, although the tradition introduced during his lifetime that of the two supreme offices of the state, the Governor-General and the Prime Minister, one should be held by an East and the other by a West Pakistani, was consolidated. But this tradition in terms of the ambitions of individuals became a source of constant friction and manœuvring for supreme power between the two dignitaries.

The first serious challenge and crisis came in 1953, during the agitation against Aḥmadīs, followers of the messianic sect of Ghulām Aḥmad of Qādiyān, who had advanced claims to prophethood in the late nineteenth century. The agitation had been started by the Aḥrār, a former anti-Pakistan nationalist Muslim group, and soon gained a threatening momentum with the full support of the traditionalist *ʿulamā'*, including Sayyid Sulaymān Nadwī, as well as Mawdūdī and his Jamāʿat-i Islāmī. The agitation based itself on two demands made to the government. First, that the Aḥmadīs, like Hindus or other minorities, should be declared a non-Muslim minority as they did not believe in the finality of Muḥammad's prophethood, and should be treated in all legal matters as *ẕimmis* and not as Muslims which they claimed to be. Secondly, that as no non-Muslim was entitled, according to the *ʿulamā'*, to hold a high office of trust and responsibility, the government should dismiss Muḥammad Ẓafr-Allāh Khān from the office of foreign minister and all other highly placed Aḥmadīs. In January 1953 an All-Pakistan Muslim Parties' Convention appointed a Committee of Action, and threatened direct action if the government did not accede to these two demands. Disturbances were much more serious in the Punjab, where the Aḥmadī minority was quite sizeable and influential, and they were covertly encouraged by the provincial government of Mumtāz Muḥammad Dawlatāna, through the Lahore press and a Department of Islamiyyāt, mainly from motives of political ambition and inter-provincial rivalry and in order to embarrass the central government in Karachi, which was headed by Khwāja Nāẓim al-dīn, an East Pakistani. Under a 'direct action' programme, a civil disturbance movement, which soon assumed the form of mob violence and looting, began in the Punjab. The central government of Pakistan made its policy clear to the '*ulamā*' and to the Punjab provincial government, rejecting both the demands of the agitators, and reiterating that the Aḥmadīs or any other sect could not be declared a minority community if it chose to call itself Muslim and that the Aḥmadīs could not and would not be removed from any key posts they held in the state.[6] The government also imposed martial law in Lahore in February, just in time to save the city from being looted and burned by unruly anti-Aḥmadī mobs.

This showdown in 1953 between a government which still upheld the western concept of *de facto* secularism and the traditionalist and fundamentalist groups of '*ulamā*', who wished to see a theocracy established in Pakistan, has been analysed with consummate acumen by Judges Muḥammad Munīr and M. R. Kayānī in their report on these disturbances (generally known as the Munīr Report). The report squarely faces the problem and the dilemma of the concept of an 'Islamic state' in modern times. If it is an Islamic state as defined by the '*ulamā*' or the fundamentalists, it cannot be democratic in the modern sense. Technically it cannot be sovereign either, if sovereignty is vested in God.

> Absolute restriction on the legislative power of a State is a restriction on the sovereignty of the people of that State and if the origin of this restriction lies elsewhere than in the will of the people, then to the extent of that restriction the sovereignty of the State and its people is necessarily taken away.[7]

The policy of discrimination against non-Muslims advocated by the '*ulamā*' and the fundamentalists, if also adopted in regard to Muslims in India, would completely disqualify them for

[6] *Munīr Report* (1954), pp. 1, 8–109, 125–47, 167–8, 185.
[7] Ibid. p. 210.

public offices in the state, not only in India but in other countries under non-Muslim government as well.[8] The dilemma in terms of the general politics of Pakistan originated from the fact that through political slogans, as through religious persuasion, the common man had been led to believe that Pakistan was an Islamic state. The messianistic ideal of an Islamic state had haunted Muslims, especially in India, for centuries during the phase of economic and political decadence of Islam. The Pakistani Muslim found himself

> standing on the crossroads, wrapped in the mantle of the past and with the dead weight of centuries on his back, frustrated and bewildered and hesitant to turn one corner or the other . . . It is this lack of bold and clear thinking, the inability to understand and take decisions which has brought about in Pakistan a confusion which will persist and repeatedly create situations of the kind we have been inquiring into until our leaders have a clear concept of the goal and of the means to reach it . . .[9]

On the question of attempts to bring about a compromise between modernism and orthodoxy in law and constitution, the report commented:

> Opposing principles, if left to themselves, can only produce confusion and disorder, and the application of a neutralizing agency to them can only produce a dead result . . . And as long as we rely on the hammer when a file is needed and press Islam into service to solve situations it was never intended to solve, frustration and disappointment must dog our steps. The sublime faith called Islam will live even if our leaders are not there to enforce it. It lives in the individual, in his soul and outlook, in all his relations with God and men, from the cradle to the grave, and our politicians should understand that if Divine commands cannot make or keep a man a Musalman, their statutes will not.[10]

During the years of political instability between 1953 and 1956, in the struggle for power between the governors-general and the prime ministers and in manœuvrings for striking a balance and determining a proportionate strength between East and West Pakistan, there were also alliances between politicians and

[8] Ibid. p. 229. [9] Ibid. [10] Ibid.

'ulamā'. These alliances, which were opportunistic as far as political parties or leaders were concerned, served, however, in the direction of rehabilitating the influence of the *'ulamā'* in constitution-making.

The second Constituent Assembly, elected by an *ad hoc* electoral procedure, passed the first constitution of Pakistan in 1956, which was again a compromise between modernism and orthodoxy. The law and administration of the state as envisaged in the constitution remained modern, even broadly secular. But the constitution theoretically endorsed the concept of an Islamic state. The name of the state was the 'Islamic Republic of Pakistan'. The preamble affirmed that 'sovereignty over the entire Universe belongs to Allah Almighty alone, and the authority to be exercised by the people of Pakistan within the limits prescribed by Him is a sacred trust'; it settled for a compromise formula, accepting the modern view that the state would be a democracy 'based on Islamic principles of social justice'; it repeated the formula of the Objectives Resolution, that while the Muslims should be enabled to order their lives according to the Qur'ān and the *sunna*, the religious and cultural rights of minorities would be safeguarded, and they would enjoy the same fundamental rights as Muslims. There were two clauses containing Islamic provisions. Clause 204 envisaged the formation of an Institute of Islamic Research 'to assist in the reconstruction of Muslim society on a truly Islamic basis', and the right of parliament to legislate for the collection of *zakāt* from Muslims. Clause 205 made the greatest concession, not only to the traditionalists but to the Mawdūdī group as well, in reiterating that a commission would be appointed to see not merely that no legislation was passed which would be repugnant to the Qur'ān and the *sunna*, but also that all existing laws should be revised in their light. It is not surprising that this constitution received the qualified approval of Mawdūdī. It, however, firmly held to the principle of complete equality between Muslims and non-Muslims, the only disqualification for the latter being that only a Muslim could be appointed Head of State.

In 1958, in the wake of political anarchy, the constitution was suspended and martial law was proclaimed. The President, Iskandar Mirzā, changed the name of the state by ordinance to the 'Republic of Pakistan', dropping the adjective 'Islamic'. A few months later he was removed, and a martial law administration ruled the country until 1962, under which a presidential cabinet under Muḥammad Ayyūb Khān inherited the problem of determining the relative importance of orthodoxy and modernism. On the whole the military revolution of 1958 was conservative. The westernized army officers at the helm had no pretensions to intellectuality or religious scholarship. The administration was therefore quite sensitive to what it considered to be popular sentiment in the matter of an Islamic pattern of law and institutions and interfered as little as possible with the activities of the '*ulamā*' as long as they were not political. Thus while the politicians were in trouble and in disgrace, the '*ulamā*' were able to consolidate their influence.

The military administration took effective steps only in one major area, the reform of the Muslim family law, where the '*ulamā*' violently disagreed. A Commission on Marriage and Family Laws had been set up under the 'First Republic' and had recommended fairly radical measures for restricting polygamy and easy divorce sanctioned by traditional Muslim personal laws. These were effectuated in the Muslim Family Laws Ordinance of 1961.[11] It provided for the registration of all marriages and the issue of marriage licences. It introduced the institution of an Arbitration Council consisting of one representative each of husband and wife and presided over by an officer who was to act as chairman, with the right of final arbitration if the representatives of the two parties did not agree in dealing with any legal problems pertaining to the marriage. It controlled polygamy to the extent that 'no man during the subsistence of an existing marriage, shall, except with the previous permission in writing of the Arbitration Council, contract another marriage'.

[11] Ordinance No. VIII of 1961; Commission on Marriage and Family Laws, *Recommendations* (1959).

A right of appeal at the level of the District Officer, but not to a higher court of law, was also provided. But violation of the restriction on polygamy entailed the fairly light punishment of simple imprisonment, which might extend to one year with or without a fine; this might to some extent deter the poor, but not the well-to-do. Provisions for the reform of divorce were actually a liberal interpretation of the Ḥanafī law, adjusted to modern conditions. Notice of divorce was to be communicated by the husband to the chairman of the Arbitration Council, which was empowered to take all steps necessary to bring about a reconciliation. The wife had the right to obtain divorce if the husband in any circumstances contracted a second marriage.

The Commission on National Education set up by the martial law administration submitted its report,[12] with a very liberal approach in relation to Islamic principles, in 1959. It defined the Islamic way of life as one governed by the principles of truth, justice, benevolence, and universal brotherhood, and accepted it as one of the tenets of the future educational pattern in Pakistan. The report also contained a small section on religious education which laid down that the 'inspiration to be drawn from religion with its sublime moralizing effect has special significance in Pakistan'. 'Several religious faiths are practised in our country', the report continued, 'and their teaching should be confined to those who profess them.' 'The great majority of our population being Muslim, the teaching of Islam assumes particular importance.' But the liberal point of view was also fully endorsed:

> Religious education should do nothing which would impair social and political unity in the country. On the other hand, it should strengthen this unity by trying through mutual understanding to bring humanity together. Religion is not to be presented as a dogma, superstition or ritual.

In actual curricula, the study of theology was envisaged as a compulsory subject in classes (grades) I–VII but as an optional subject in classes IX–XII. The policy presumably was to give a child a basic grounding in theology but to leave his mind free to

[12] Published by the Min. of Education (Karachi, 1959).

accept or harmonize extraneous liberal world views as an individual if he wished to do so; or alternatively to remain a traditional Muslim. This policy at the secondary school level was intended to bring about a liberalization of outlook at the university stage, where there would be a discipline of Islamic Studies to 'undertake research and present Islam in its true spirit', for which university teachers should have a thorough knowledge of comparative religion and world history to be able to bring out clearly and forcefully the important role religion had played in the social, economic and political life of mankind. They should be able to interpret Islam and present it as a body of thought that can meet the challenge of modern times and fulfil the requirements of a modern scientific society. This implies that there should be a gradually increasing critical appraisal of Islam as a code of practical life in the light of the holy Qur'ān and the life of the Prophet. The original liberal and rational Islam should be properly interpreted and applied to the problem of modern life.

In this essentially modernist policy, the fundamentalist viewpoint was partly met in the last sentence. The heritage of Sayyid Aḥmad Khān, and Iqbāl's attempt to reconcile religion and science, were also evident in the statement, 'We attach the greatest importance to bringing Islamic learning closer to life, and not the other way round', and:

> As a religion of nature, Islam has nothing to fear from scientific discoveries and inventions. Advancement of scientific thought is but a revelation of the laws of nature leading ultimately to a control of these forces and their utilization for human aims . . . The great task that lies ahead of all Islamic scholars is to bring together knowledge of the fundamentalist Islamic values and of modern sciences.

In 1960 a commission was appointed under the chairmanship of Justice Shihāb al-dīn to collect data and opinions through questionnaires, and to submit its own recommendations for a new constitution on democratic principles. As S. M. Ikrām points out:

> Of course the Commission applied its own mind to various questions

and especially consulted those who were qualified to provide information or assistance, but the fact the public opinion was being represented before the Constitution Commission not by the elected or chosen representatives of the public as was the case with the Constituent Assembly, but through a method which gave maximum advantage to an organization like Jamā'at-i Islāmī, seems to have had a subtle but important influence on its thinking.[13]

The independent liberal thinking of the judiciary in Pakistan, which had created the monumental Munīr Report in 1953, to some extent resisted the impact of these religious pressures. Examining the Islamic provisions of the 1956 constitution, the new Constitution Commission, in paragraphs 192–4 of its report,[14] stressed the dangers of undermining the general law (as distinct from the personal law) of Pakistan, as inherited from British India, by trying to bring it into strict conformity with the *sharī'a*. It pointed out that 'the fact that in most of the Muslim countries the general law has not been brought into strict conformity with the injunctions of the Quran and the Sunnah becomes relevant'. It recognized the difficulty of identifying the authentic *ḥadīs̱* by which *sunna* could be determined in legal terms. To meet this difficulty, the Commission recommended the formation of another commission to study the Islamization of general law, in consultation with similar commissions in other Muslim lands. In internationalizing the entire question of the change of general law in Pakistan in accordance with the *sharī'a*, the Constitution Commission's intention seems to have been to put the problem in cold storage, knowing that most Muslim countries, except theocracies like Saudi Arabia, would be either lukewarm or hesitant to accept such commissions in their lands; and if countries such as Turkey, Iran, and Tunisia did set up such commissions, their recommendations were bound to range from secularism to liberalism. The Constitution Commission of Pakistan was not only playing for indefinite time to postpone the question of the Islamization of the general laws, but also wished

[13] 'Religion in Pakistan', paper read at Conference on Pakistan since 1958 held at Inst. of Islamic Studies, McGill Univ., June 1964.

[14] Karachi, 1961.

to transfer the pressure of the religious and fundamentalist groups at home to an international context. For this reason it seems to have suggested that before changes were introduced in the general laws, a synthesis had to be made between different schools of Muslim juristic thought as well as other legal views in the modern world of Islam. The Commission also accepted the core of the argument of the westernized modernists, from Chirāgh ʻAlī to contemporary times, that on *ḥadīs̱* an international commission should advise

> as to whether instructions given by the Prophet with reference to local conditions should necessarily be followed literally in the various countries regardless of the local customs to which people of these countries have all along been accustomed, or, only the principles have to be adopted.[15]

In several other respects the Commission's report is very conservative. Its conception of a welfare state is revivalistic:

> We have . . . an ideology which enables us to establish a model welfare state, and history shows that such a state had been established in the early days of Islam. If the modern generation doubts the efficacy of Islam, that is due to their lack of appreciation of the universal applicability of the Quranic teachings and a lack of knowledge of the Islamic history. The remedy lies in acquainting oneself with the principles of Islam and with the Islamic history and not in discarding religion. Those, who talk glibly of secularism in Pakistan, overlook the fact that, by a mere change of expression, one's conduct does not change. If there is any chance of our reforming ourselves, it lies only in drawing inspiration from Islam. Liberal secularism of the West which seems to attract the modern generation, is itself based on the traditional discipline which was developed when religion was a force in those countries.[16]

This, according to the Commission, is the justification for the foundation of, and should constitute the terms of reference of, the Islamic Research Institute which was founded in 1962. The Commission also recommended the formation of a Department of Religious Affairs in the Secretariat.

In the second (1962) constitution several of the Commission's recommendations were drastically changed. Most of the changes

[15] *Report*, p. 124. [16] Ibid. p. 121.

related to the establishment of a strong presidential federal government, but some of them had a religio-political significance. In its Preamble the new constitution retained the formula of the old one, in acknowledging the sovereignty of Allāh over the entire universe, but changed the rest of the formula to 'the authority exercisable by the people . . . is a sacred trust'. This subtle change was based on the implication that man in general, and not the Pakistani Muslim in particular, is God's vicegerent on earth. The new constitution also retained the name of the state as the 'Republic of Pakistan', dropping the adjective 'Islamic'.

As a principle of legislation it laid down that 'no law should be repugnant to Islam', and emphasized, as had all previous constitutional documents, equality of protection and treatment for all citizens. Guaranteeing the freedom of religion, it enjoined that 'no law should prevent the members of a religious community or denomination from professing, practising, or propagating, or from providing instruction in their religion'. It also guaranteed freedom of worship for the followers of all religions. Coming to the 'Islamic way of life' in its principles of policy, it took a more orthodox view in relation to Muslims, making the teaching of the Qur'ān and Islamic studies compulsory for them, and envisaging the proper organization of *zakāt*, *waqfs*, and mosques.

Part X of the constitution provided for two basic Islamic institutions to advise Islamic orientations in governmental law and policy. The first of these was an Advisory Council of Islamic Ideology, consisting of five to twelve members appointed for a period of three years each by the President on the basis of their 'understanding and appreciation of Islam and of the economic, political, legal and administrative problems of Pakistan'. The functions of the Council were

> to make recommendations to the Central Government and the Provincial Governments as to means of enabling and encouraging the Muslims of Pakistan to order their lives in all respects in accordance with the principles and concepts of Islam; and to advise the National Assembly, a Provincial Assembly, the President or a Governor on any

question referred to the Council under Article 8, that is to say, a question as to whether a proposed law disregards or violates, or is otherwise not in accordance with, the Islamic Principles of Law-making.

Political parties which were banned under martial law re-emerged in the 'Second Republic' of Pakistan in 1962. Two of these, the Jamā'at-i Islāmī and the Niẓām-i Islām Party, which is moderate and liberal, are based on religious programmes. Other parties in East and West Pakistan accepted under orthodox pressures a conservative stand in relation to the role of religion in politics and agreed to forge tactical alliances with the religious parties in the National and Provincial Assemblies and for electoral purposes. President Ayyūb Khān, who had entered active politics to face the challenge of the opposition parties, accepted the presidentship of the official Muslim League Party which had constantly to yield to religious pressures on points of orthodox orientation. The second constitution was amended by the Constitution (First Amendment) Act passed by the National Assemly on 24 December 1963.[17] It changed the name of the state back to the 'Islamic Republic of Pakistan'. Formulas were added in the Preamble confining 'the authority exercisable by the people' to be 'within the limits prescribed by Him [God]'. The second constitution had provided for Muslims, individually and collectively 'to order their lives in accordance with the teachings and requirements of Islam'. This formula was narrowed down, at the expense of liberalism, by the addition of the qualification that not only all future legislation but also existing laws should be brought in conformity with the Qur'ān and the *sunna*, providing for the traditionalists and fundamentalists the thin end of the wedge of religious conservatism for which they had been struggling at various stages in the history of the constitution-making in Pakistan.

The First Amendment of 1963 had, however, a number of redeeming liberal features. It provided that

subject to law, public order and morality: (*a*) every citizen has the right to profess, practice and propagate any religion and; (*b*) every religious

[17] *Dawn*, 25 Dec. 1963 and 16 Jan. 1964.

denomination and every sect thereof has the right to establish, maintain and manage its religious institutions.

It also upheld the strong policy of secular orientation in education, by providing that no person attending any educational institution should be required to receive any religious instruction which related to a religion other than his own. No citizen was to be denied admission to any public educational institution on the ground of race, religion, caste, or place of birth. Every community or religion was permitted to set up its own private denominational schools at its own expense, and promised recognition by the state.

By far the most significant clause affecting future legislation was the provision that the Advisory Council of Islamic Ideology would examine all laws in force immediately 'with a view of to bringing them into conformity with the teachings and requirements of Islam as set out in the Holy Quran and Sunnah'. While the President of the Republic retained the power to approve the rules of procedure regulating the proceedings of the Advisory Council and selecting its members, his freedom of decision was restricted by the provision that he should cause to lay before the Assembly the annual recommendations of the Council on the question of the Islamization of all present and future legislation.

In this extremely delicate compromise between the advancing pressures of orthodoxy and the tactically retreating position of modernism, the shape of all legislation and the question whether Pakistan was to become a theocracy (or 'theo-democracy' as Mawdūdī preferred to call it), or remain a modern state preserving a hard core of liberal secularism beneath a religious veneer, depended now on two factors. What religious views a particular President held, and how strong he was to withstand political and religious pressures which would influence his selection of the members of the Advisory Council of Islamic Ideology. This made the questions of direct or indirect elections all the more important. Direct elections would necessarily favour a conservative, orthodox candidate because of the emotional appeal he could exercise upon the religious sentiments of the masses.

Indirect elections through a pyramidal tier of Union Councils were more likely to be dominated by the views of the westernized élite and the economic interests of the rising commercial and industrial classes which would favour stability at home and the image of Pakistan as a modern state abroad. This was the principal issue involved in the presidential elections of 1964–5, in which the chief contestants were Miss Fāṯima Jinnāḥ, the sister of Pakistan's founder, Muḥammad ʿAlī Jinnāḥ, and Field Marshal Muḥammad Ayyūb Khān. The allied opposition parties, including the Jamāʿat-i Islāmī, had selected Miss Jinnāḥ because of her prestige as Jinnāḥ's sister and because of the matriarchical appeal she would exercise upon the masses. Her election might have meant a direct elections system and a repetition of the instability of the 'First Republic', as well as the theocratization of Pakistan, in view of the familiar pattern of alliances between politicians and theologians. It was the first risk rather than the second which led to the election of Muḥammad Ayyūb Khān, who might or might not withstand the tide of orthodoxy, but who could be depended upon to maintain internal stability.

The Advisory Council of Islamic Ideology, however, continued to regress from modernism to orthodoxy. In the revision of the Anglo-Muhammadan Penal Code it recommended that whipping might be added to six types of punishments already prescribed. It met the *ʿulamā'*'s demand in recommending that the President might establish a Religious Affairs Authority to organize Islamic institutions of ritual prayer, compulsory charity, and a special treasury (*bayt al-māl*) to collect it, and for ordering the life of the ordinary Muslim according to the do's and don't's enjoined in the *sharīʿa*. It also set machinery in motion for creating a legal research section to expedite revision of the existing laws in the light of the Qur'ān and the *sunna*.[18]

A most disturbing question from the standpoint of the development of Pakistan's economy is that of the future of the banking system, in view of the Qur'ānic prohibition on interest. Abolition of all interest has been one of the strongest points in

[18] Ibid. 22 Jan. 1965; *Nawā-i Waqt* (Lahore), 23 and 24 Jan. 1965.

Mawdūdī's propaganda. Anwar Iqbāl Qureshī, an outstanding economist who worked for some time on the staff of the World Bank and who is now the Economic Adviser to the government of Pakistan, has expressed in his writings views which stem from the fundamentalist stand of Mawdūdī and the traditionalists in recommending a zero per cent rate of interest and an interestless economy, though he bases his arguments on the views of Keynes in rejecting the classical, productive and monetary theories of interest.[19] On this problem, which affects the developing economy of Pakistan and its entire links with the banking systems of the west and the greater part of the world, the Advisory Council of Islamic Ideology are agreed that *ribā* is forbidden. But the Council are in disagreement as to whether institutional credit would also be covered by the *ribā* specified in the Holy Qur'ān. There is, however, unanimity on the point that 'for the fulfilment of the Islamic concept of social justice and human brotherhood, a system of interestless economy should be built up'.[20]

The opposition parties were campaigning for the repeal of semi-modern Family Law Ordinance of 1961; and during the election campaign of 1964–5, even the official Muslim League Party had vaguely agreed to a revision of it. But as the strength of the opposition has been considerably reduced in the elections to the central and provincial Assemblies in 1965, much would depend as to how long and how far Ayyūb Khān and the Muslim League can resist the orthodox pressure on this and other points.

[19] *Islam and the Theory of Interest* (1961), pp. xxiii, 34–40, 45–174.
[20] *Dawn*, 22 Jan. 1965.

CHAPTER FIFTEEN

TRENDS IN ISLAM IN INDIA 1947—64

As a scholar and a theologian, and with the prestige of India's Education Minister, Āzād became the bridge between the nationalist *'ulamā'* of Deoband and liberal modernists, prominent among whom are A. A. A. Fyzee and the scholars of Jāmi'a Milliyya-i Islāmiyya, like Ẓākir Ḥusayn, Muḥammad Mujīb, and 'Ābid Ḥusayn.

Among the *'ulamā'*, especially those of Deoband, a tradition of political hagiography had developed before partition in writings of Muḥammad Ṭufayl[1] and others. After partition this trend was intensified in the work of Ḥusayn Aḥmad Madanī and Muḥammad Miyān. It was a projection of the political focus of the present into the past. The theory of Walī-Allāhī socialism, as propounded by 'Ubayd-Allāh Sindhī, was fully endorsed and his influence claimed even on Ṭīpū Sultan, whose wars against the East India Company were regarded as a composite national effort.[2] *Jihād* was redefined in Gāndhian terms as 'essentially the control of one's passions, forbearance, and defiance of death', and was thus equated with passive resistance and *ahimsā*.[3] It is not intended here to present a comprehensive survey of religious and political thought in India since 1947, but only to select representative instances to illustrate the principal cross-currents.

Sa'īd Aḥmad Akbarābādī, a Deoband *'ālim* who has also received a western education, represents such a synthesis of Deoband and Aligarh as Maḥmūd al-Ḥasan had envisaged in 1912. He describes nationalism (*qawmiyyat*) as distinct and different from the term as defined in western political science, which he

[1] *Musalmānon kā rawshan mustaqbil* (Delhi, 1945).
[2] Akbarābādī, *'Ubayd-Allāh Sindhī, passim*; Muḥ. Miyān, *'Ulamā'-i Hind*, ii. 25–26, 77–78.
[3] Akbarābādi, p. 122.

asserts fosters national prejudice, aims to exploit and look down upon other peoples, and is repugnant to Islam. He would define it as the national characteristic or the customary law of a people, distinguishing it from others, or as 'national temperament'.[4] On the problem of change in Islamic law with the march of history, his starting-point is the same as that of the modernists, that the divine law revealed to a prophet at a given time is essentially within the framework of that day and age, with a latitude and an implicit permission for change in different climes and ages. Like Shiblī, he regards much of the Islamic criminal law as applicable only to the Arab society in the Prophet's age. Among Qur'ānic injunctions a distinction has to be made between those which were specific to the Arab customary law of the time, and those which are applicable to Muslim and human societies in other times. A number of the Prophet's *aḥādīs̱* are also specific to Arab customary law and are not binding on Muslim society in all times. The Qur'ān introduces the principle of gradualism, altering the given corpus of customary law. The same process of gradualism has been adopted by other Muslim lands where law could be so adapted as not to be outright repugnant to the customary traditions of those lands.[5]

On the other hand Akbarābādī rejects much of modernist apologetics on such questions as slavery. Though Islam did not abolish slavery, it completely changed the concept by raising the status of the slave and by recognizing him as a human being entitled to equal rights.[6] But he takes his cue from the modernists, especially Amīr 'Alī, stressing the point that the lot of the slave in historical Islam was better than that of the subject peoples in modern empires.

Outstanding among the 'believing' modernists is A. A. A. Fyzee, an Ismā'īlī Shī'ī and a scholar recognized in the west as in the Islamic world, who though thoroughly trained in western scientific methodology is emotionally and spiritually involved in

[4] Ibid. pp. 135–51.
[5] *Islām awr ghulāmī kī ḥaqīqat*, pp. 49–97, 241–67.
[6] Theory based on Qur'ān, 2:136.

the challenging theme of re-interpreting Islam for the modern world. His emphasis is on the rudiments of 'religious pluralism' in Āzād's thought, and this constitutes the basis of his own modernism. He regards this as the only pragmatic solution for the Muslim minority in India, and for the preservation and progress of Islam in a composite society in that country. Fyzee bases his investigation into the past, and speculations as to the future of Islamic law, on religious pluralism. With the prestige of being one of the soundest scholars of Islamic law in the subcontinent, he prescribes a methodology of critical anlysis in the process of acceptance or rejection of the classical law of Islam. The procedure of legal thinking he recommends is essentially not very different from the one familiar to Indian Islam in varied gradations, from the composite fundamentalism of Shāh Walī-Allāh through the naturalistic rationalism of Sayyid Aḥmad Khān and Chirāgh 'Alī, to the exegetical neo-modernism of Parwīz.[7]

Fyzee's starting-point is the Mālikite premiss that the 'central message of the Qur'ān 'will last longer than its language'. This 'central message' can be determined and oriented by a methodology of evolutionary exegesis, which in turn implies the correct linguistic assessment of a Qur'ānic injunction as understood by the Arabs of the Prophet's age, and its reinterpretation and application to the conditions of modern life according to the needs and appeals to the mind of the twentieth-century Muslim. This is a position not very different from that of the official religious policies in Pakistan. But Fyzee adds to it a final methodological principle, that of exegetical pluralism, and a sympathetic study of the historical background of Judaism, Christianity, and the Indian religions. To stress this principle Fyzee recommends not only a study of modern western and Indian religious humanists, like Barth, Tillich, Kierkegaard, and Rādhākrishnan, but also of the western disciplines of sociological and linguistic research to assess the phenomena of growth and interaction of religious and historical processes. This, he thinks, would

[7] *A Modern Approach to Islam* (1963), pp. 1–24, 98–101.

disentangle law from religion in Islam, in distinguishing subjective ethical norms from objective rules; and should even make the acceptance of secular law possible. The constitutional theory of God's sovereignty over the earth would be impracticable in the modern world. The only workable principle is as laid down in secular constitutions, namely that the people of a country are sovereign in their own dominions. The divorce between religion and law in Islam will help the independent advancement of both. Islamic humanistic values can be developed in the conscience unfettered by imposed legalities.[8] This is a thesis not very different from that of the Munīr Report.

Rejecting the apologetics of the Aligarh school, Fyzee recommends the formulation of exegetical criteria that would differentiate between the 'literal' and the 'poetic' truth of the Qur'ān's cosmological verses. Science and religion have also to be regarded as separate spheres. Religion (personal belief and subjective ethics), law, and science are three distinct entities. It is only in dissolving this historically accumulated confusion between them that Fyzee sees the chance of a newer 'Protestant Islam'.

Compared with Fyzee, the intellectuals of the Jāmiʿa-i Milliyya-i Islāmiyya are secularists and primarily concerned with the establishment of cultural identity between Islam and Hinduism in India. ʿĀbid Ḥusayn regards the basis of a common Hindu-Muslim culture as Vedic; through processes of challenge and response to Islam in medieval India, this developed into a common Hindustani or Indian culture which disintegrated to some extent during the Mughal period of decline and was partly shattered and partly revived, fertilized, and enriched by the impact of western civilization.[9] In free India its problems have not been entirely solved and it is still undergoing the throes and risks of the process of formation. His theory in its historical context partly runs the risk of over-simplification in such assertions as

[8] Ibid. pp. 101–4.

[9] Abid Husayn, *Indian Culture*, pp. 63–64, and *Qawmi tahẕib* (1955), pp. 102–3.

that the Islamic state in India was on the whole a secular state, in the sense that it was neither ideally nor profoundly religious. He is closer to historical truth in applying this theory to the Mughal empire from Akbar to Shāh Jahān, the age in which according to him the 'Hindustani culture' developed.[10]

Western influences, 'Ābid Ḥusayn continues, have served to fossilize much of the religious commitments of the conservatives, both Hindu and Muslim, even though these influences have immunized the westernized élite of both the communities to a large extent. This conservative polarization has influenced even the most outstanding literary representatives of the two communities in the twentieth century, Iqbāl and Tagore, though he claims that in the work of both of them the basic cognition of reality is the same. So is it in the essence of both Hindu and Muslim components of the 'Hindustani' culture.

But even in the now independent India the cultural problem has not been solved. This has been because of the Muslim feeling of being culturally stifled by such measures as anti-Urdu policies in certain provinces. The adoption in the constitution of India itself of Hindi written in the Devanagari script rather than Hindustani, covering both Urdu and Hindi, is a decision which, says 'Ābid Ḥusayn, the Muslims of India must painfully, but loyally, accept, though cultural unity or the monolithic entity of a composite Indian nation will be difficult to evolve when the Muslim minority feels its cultural and economic position made insecure by this linguistic policy. Muslim non-participation in the cultural growth of India will assume the shape of an absolute pessimism, leading to apathy and stagnation, so that in the end they would become an economic and cultural dead weight hanging around India's neck.[11] This conclusion is not very different from that reached by Wilfred Cantwell Smith: 'The [Indian Muslim] community is in danger of being deprived of its language, than which only religious faith is a deeper possession. Nine years of gradual adjustment in other fields have brought no

[10] *Indian Culture*, pp. 64 and 285–6.

[11] *Qawmī tahẕīb*, pp. 306–7.

improvement in this, and little prospect of improvement';[12] or that of Donald E. Smith: 'The partial repudiation of the Muslim contribution to a composite language is a serious lapse from secularism.'[13]

The threat of Muslim stagnation and backwardness does not emanate merely from the government of India or Indian states' governments' linguistic policies. Muslim conservatism, especially that of the *'ulamā'*—who are among the chief elements from which the government of India derives its Muslim political support—is opposed to any reform in Muslim Personal and Family Law. Hindu Personal Law has been reformed and codified, and polygamy and the crushing burden of the dowry system have been checked. But the Muslim Family Law was not touched by the Indian parliament because of orthodox Muslim susceptibilities. The *'ulamā'* of the Jam'iyyat al-'Ulamā'-i Hind do not regard India as *dār al-ḥarb* because the Muslims are still governed by their Personal Law. They regard any attempt to alter it as an infringement of the 'covenant' of composite nationalism which binds them to India and its Hindu citizens. Donald Smith arrives at the conclusion that 'the continuation of such medieval social practices will mean that Indian Muslims will lag far behind their co-religionists elsewhere, not only in Turkey or the United Arab Republic, but in Pakistan as well'; and then he draws the same conclusion as 'Ābid Ḥusayn: 'It is unfortunately possible that Indian Muslims may remain as a community an isolated static unit in what is at present one of the most dynamic centuries in the world'.[14]

[12] Smith, *Islam in Modern History* (1958), pp. 266–7.
[13] *India as a Secular State* (1963), p. 402.
[14] Ibid. p. 422.

CHAPTER SIXTEEN

CONCLUSION

'THE fundamental *malaise* of modern Islam', remarks Wilfred Cantwell Smith with great insight, 'is a sense that something has gone wrong with Islamic history. The fundamental problem of modern Muslims is how to rehabilitate that history.'[1] This feeling has dominated the religious and political thought of Muslim India for over a century, as it has of other Islamic peoples in other parts of the world.

Through British rule, the association of Muslim India with the west has been more intimate and of longer duration than that of any other Muslim people. In this given historical situation the nineteenth-century Muslim intellectuals turned to reinterpret their own history, Sayyid Aḥmad Khān successfully followed the tradition of western scholarship in editing medieval Indian chronicles; but when it came to the sensitive point of defending Islam at its very source against the semi-polemical historiographical approach of Sir William Muir, he lost his balance of historical objectivity and turned to imaginative apologetics equally unacceptable to orientalists abroad and traditionalists at home.

Essentially Sayyid Aḥmad Khān was not a historian; his primary interest was theology. But the movement he set in motion led to an intimate preoccupation with history among some of his outstanding younger contemporaries. Shiblī Nu'mānī and Amīr 'Alī in their mass of scholarship, polemics, and apologetics, arrive at two distinct and different conclusions on the crucial problem of the situation of Islam in history. For Shiblī it is the triumph of Ash'arism and the traditional theology over the Mu'tazilites under al-Mutawakkil and subsequently. For Amīr

[1] *Islam in Modern History*, p. 41.

ʿAlī it was the failure of the Arab advance against Constantinople and in France, which he regards as a tragedy not merely for the history of Islam but for its civilizing mission in terms of the cultural history of mankind. Of the two Shiblī, though much more conservative, is closer to the core of the problem.

For the traditionalists and the Ahl-i Ḥadīs̱ the interpretation of Islamic history has remained relatively simpler in theological terms. The entire process of Islamic history is viewed as a continuous decline from the perfection of the golden age of the Prophet.

With this half-acknowledged sense of the failure of Islamic history the Muslim intellectual in the Indian subcontinent, as elsewhere, faces the problem of the decadence of Islamic peoples in the modern world. Consciousness of this decadence is reflected in Sayyid Aḥmad Khān's intellectual and political orientations, and his programme of attachment to the west and detachment alike from pan-Islamic universalism and potentially aggressive Indian nationalism. Ḥālī too epitomized and popularized sensitivity to the consciousness of decadence. It is interesting to compare his analysis of Muslim decline with that of the *al-Manār* group some years later. Whereas Ḥālī lays the responsibility on the static lethargy of the Muslim community, the *al-Manār* group blames the Muslim rulers who are ignorant of Islam and its laws and who have permitted evil-doing in the administration by substituting laws of human origin in the place of divine laws, the *ʿulamā*ʾ who have neglected the Qur'ān and the *sunna* as the sources of law and have preoccupied themselves with the *furū*ʿ of law and sectarianism, and the quietist and heterodox Ṣūfīs who have made religion 'a sport and a means of entertainment'.[2] This fundamentalist position is reiterated and considerably intensified by Mawdūdī in Pakistan, whose Jamāʿat-i Islāmī is concerned not merely with the intellectual debate of Muslim reformism, but with the political platform of the 'restoration' of 'original' Islam as a cure for the *malaise* of

[2] Muḥ. ʿAbduh, *Tafsīr al-Qur'ān al-Ḥakīm* (1906–27), ii. 89–90; *al-Manār*, i. 606 ff., 722–30.

modern decadence. His party calls itself a party of 'renaissance' and not of reformism. Among modern Pakistani intellectuals most conscious of Islamic decadence is Parwīz, who recommends this-worldly materialism, but whose terms of reference are again fundamentalistic, based on an extremely extravagant interpretation of the Qur'ān.

Nevertheless, modernists of varying backgrounds, Khayr al-dīn Pasha, Ḥālī, 'Abduh, Iqbāl, and Parwīz, see a way out of the morass of decadence only through the application of the principle of change. Almost all of them have the Qur'ānic injunction at 13: 12 as their starting point:

> God changes not what is in a people, until they
> change what is in themselves . . .

Nations are not condemned and destroyed by God only because of unbelief, if they otherwise follow just and progressive laws. Muslims are merely potentially, and by no means necessarily, the 'best among the peoples'.[3]

Much of modernist sensitivity to present decadence is counterbalanced by the complacency of the '*ulamā*', traditionalist and fundamentalist alike. For them 'retrogression' rather than 'decadence' is the key-word. For the Ahl-i Ḥadīs̱ the entire history of Islam is a series of retrograde steps from a given state of perfection. The fundamentalist explanation of this is a continuous drifting away from the early simplicity of Islam through centuries of *bida'* incorporating extra-Islamic elements in Muslim canon law.[4]

The basic difference of approach to the problem by the modernists and the '*ulamā*' has had a paralysing influence on law, constitution, and institutions in modern Pakistan. Modernists there have been finding it difficult to break from the past and accept the modern world on its own terms and according to its own values. '*Ulamā*', on the other hand, and especially the fundamentalist school of Mawdūdī, have also found it difficult

[3] Cf. Rashīd Riḍā, *Ta'rīkh al-ustādh al-imām al-Shaykh Muḥ. 'Abduh* (Cairo, 1908–10, ii. 323–4.)

[4] For parallel arguments in Egypt see *al-Manār*, xxix (1928), 63–64.

to break totally from the present and to take refuge in the past. The result is a confusion in terms of a theory of 'change' required for cultural adjustments and an attempted compromise between stances which are not entirely polarized. Pragmatic necessities of government and politics urge compromises from time to time in constitutions and amendments to constitutions, in double-edged machinery like the Council of Islamic Ideology and other formulae or institutions. These compromises cannot, in any case, bring about the change which the modernists desire in theory, but which they cannot promulgate in practice owing to the conservative pressure of the lower middle classes who are supported by the masses on certain explosive issues and led by the *ʿulamāʾ* of all shades of opinion. And so in respect of Pakistan, as of many other Islamic countries, Von Grunebaum's remark remains relevant: 'Few culture areas have been subjected to so much and so violent change as that of Islam; none perhaps has so consistently refused to accept the ontological reality of change.'[5]

Much of traditionalist conservatism is rooted deeply in Ashʿarite theology. To some extent modern Islam's lack of resilience and real rather than theoretical or apologetic adjustment to the scientific conception of universe, which is the basis of modern civilization, lies in the Ashʿarite school's denial of the law of causality, which is one of the primary sources of all rational knowledge. Instead of arriving at a law of natural causality, the Ashʿarites have deduced only a law of *ʿāda* (custom). 'It is not law', observes Goldziher, 'but simply the habit laid upon nature by God, that makes certain things follow others; this succession is not, however, necessary.'[6] Sayyid Aḥmad Khān and Chirāgh ʿAlī are perhaps the only Indo-Muslim modernists who have subscribed to the concept of natural laws as superseding the cult of *ʿāda*. For Amīr ʿAlī, as a Shīʿī, it is easy to preach a reform of the Ashʿarite Islam, but his own writings hardly reflect any trace of that reform. Ashʿarism is placed at the very core of Islamic

[5] G. E. Von Grunebaum, *Modern Islam* (Berkeley, 1962), p. 209.
[6] *Muhammed and Islam*, tr. by K. C. Seele (New Haven, 1917), p. 138.

modernism by Iqbāl, while the emphasis on the value of power in his thought is traceable to Ibn Taymiyya.[7]

Walī-Allāhī fundamentalism, though it paved the way for the emergence of modernism by challenging much of the superficial, polemical, or divisive data in Islamic jurisprudence is, when all is said and done, a movement aimed at reorganizing the future in terms of an idealized past. Basically, therefore, it has a great deal in common with Wahhābism which, as Goldziher bluntly observes, 'has its gaze fixed on the past, denying the justification of the results of historical development, and recognizing Islam only in the petrified form of the seventh century'.[8] This verdict is even more appropriate to Mawdūdī's fundamentalism today.

It is significant that Pakistan chose to call itself, under pressure of theological groups allied tactically to political factions, an 'Islamic' state in its first constitution and in the amendment to its second constitution. Tunisia, on the other hand, chose to describe itself as an 'Arab Muslim State' in its constitution. The difference between the concept of an' Islamic' and of a 'Muslim' state is noteworthy. An 'Islamic' state commits itself by definition to continuing and developing the historical process of law as developed by classical jurists. But a 'Muslim' state can be a secular or secularized state, 'the majority of whose citizens are Muslims of varying degrees of observance or non-observance, but attached to Islamic culture and history, to the ethics of the Qur'ān and the many considerable achievements in all fields of human endeavour'.[9] This is precisely the sense which modernists in Pakistan would ascribe to their concept of an 'Islamic state'. But the modernists are confined to a class, i.e. the upper or upper-middle class, and to a particular kind of training and education, i.e. westernized. The creative minority which they constitute is challenged by another creative minority of the lower-middle classes led by the fundamentalists and supported by the

[7] Cf. H. Laoust, *Le traité de droit public d'Ibn Taimīya* (Beirut, 1948), pp. 173–4 and L. Gardet, *La cité musulmane* (Paris, 1954), p. 107.

[8] Goldziher, p. 311.

[9] E. I. J. Rosenthal, 'The Role of Islam in a Modern National State', *Year Book of World Affairs 1962*.

traditionalists, which is closer to the souls of the masses because of the rich, emotional appeal of religion. In the rural areas especially the fundamentalists seem to be consolidating their position. In a survey carried out in 1963 through Pakistani students, 451 villagers from 52 villages in West Pakistan were questioned about the treatment to be meted out to those who did not conform to religious ritual; 45 thought the delinquents should be severely punished; 168 were of the view that they deserved some punishment; 125 held that they should be persuaded by argument and instruction; only 66 were in favour of *laissez-faire*, and only 47 did not express any opinion.[10]

Fundamentalism is by no means the exclusive misfortune of Islam. As Marthelot points out:

> On se plaît, au contraire, en général à dresser la liste des precéptes islamiques en apparance peu favorable au développement économique: certain, en effet, fondementaux, se refèrent à l' affirmation de la Toute Puissance de Dieu; mais laquelle des trois grandes religions, juive, chrétienne ou islamique, n'a pas ce même principe en tête de son crédo? De même l'éthique imposé à la vie économique, notament l'interdiction du *riba*, du prêt à intérêt, n'est-elle pas commune à l'Islam et au Christianisme? Enfin le refus de la novation (*bid'a*), avec cette reprenante idée que le progrès est dans le passé, ne se retrouvait-il pas dans le réflexe souvent enregistré en Chretienté, et pas seulement sur le plan religieux, qui opposait les Anciens aux Modernes.[11]

Yet the report of the Constitution Commission of Pakistan is historically wrong in arguing on this basis that the 'liberal secularism of the West . . . is itself based on the traditional discipline which was developed when religion was a force in those countries (p. 121)'. This view has to be weighed against the point made by Sir Hamilton Gibb, one of the most sincere friends of Islam in the West:

> . . . while the constitution of Islamic society was still based on mediaeval conceptions and its outlook governed by mediaeval ideas, Western

[10] As reported by A. W. Eister, 'Perspectives sur les fonctions de la religion dans un pays en voie de développement: l'Islam au Pakistan', *Archives de sociologie des religions*, xiv (1962), pp. 39–40.

[11] Pierre Marthelot, 'L'Islam et le développement', ibid. pp. 131–8 at p. 134.

Europe had swung right away from its mediaeval moorings and that between the two civilizations, once so uniform in spite of religious antagonisms, the gulf had gradually widened until their common elements and principles seemed insignificant in comparison with their differences.[12]

If not in the Indo-Pakistan subcontinent, elsewhere in the Islamic world there have been categorical rejections of theocracy or, as Mawdūdī would like to call it, 'theo-democracy'. Turkey has been a secular 'Muslim' but not an 'Islamic' state for a generation. Khālid Muḥammad Khālid's views form the very antithesis of the thought and programme of Mawdūdī or even ʿAlā al-Fāsī.[13] He rejects theocracy for its lack of clarity regarding the source and location of authority, for its distrust of human reason, for its appeal to weaknesses of emotionalism, for its hostility to all reform, for its totalitarianism, for its static nature, for its Inquisitorial suppression of all opposition and for its 'brutality which thrives upon the confusion as to the proper limit of authority'.[14]

Idealization of the orthodox caliphate of the first four holy Caliphs of Islam alike by the traditionalists, fundamentalists, and some of the modernists, including Shiblī and Amīr 'Alī but not Sayyid Aḥmad Khān or Iqbāl, is a fundamentalistic trend reflected in historical revivalism. This idealization, common to India-Pakistan and other parts of the Muslim world,[15] is aptly described by Von Grunebaum as the 'classicism of return'; its object is

in part at least, a decrease in cultural complexity; it is a 'retractile' movement advocating consolidation through shrinkage. Such movement characteristically overlooks the fact that the period of apostolic simplicity, which is chosen as authoritative and exemplary, was actually a period of experiential expansion.[16]

[12] *Whither Islam?*, p. 48.

[13] ʿAlā al-Fāsī, *al-Ḥarakāt al-istiqlāliyya fi'l-Maghrib al-ʿarabī* (Cairo, 1948); Eng. tr. by H. Z. Nuseibeh, Washington, 1954).

[14] Khālid, *Min hunā nabda* (Cairo, 1950); Eng. tr. by I. al-Fārūqī, Washington, 1953.

[15] Cf. for instance *al-Manār*, iv. 210, 215–16.

[16] *Modern Islam*, p. 81.

Pan-Islamism and the Caliphate movement of the later nineteenth and early twentieth centuries was a superimposition of *Rāshidūn*-classicism on modern circumstances and was therefore essentially revivalistic. Pan-Islamism itself, like pan-Turanianism and pan-Arabism later, is a modern development influenced by and analogous with such movements as pan-Germanism and pan-Slavism.[17] But something like a feeling of the solidarity of the entire Muslim *umma* is disernible at crucial periods in mediaeval Islamic history. Al-Bīrūnī was conscious of Islam as a cultural unity in comparing it with Hindu religion and culture.[18] Ibn al-Asīr (d. 1234) reflects a consciousness of the Muslim world as a single unity in dealing with the Mongol onslaughts in north-east Persia, which he regards as a calamity suffered by the entire world of Islam.[19] Yāqūt regards the Mongol invasion as an unparalleled calamity for Islam.[20] Ibn al-ʿArabī's (1165–1240) efforts in the direction of a combined effort on the part of the Muslim princes of Syria and Anatolia to repel the Crusaders have an element of what came to be described as pan-Islamism in modern times.[21]

Revival of emphasis on the concept of a universal caliphate begins in Indian Islam with Shāh Walī-Allāh,[22] though he only theorizes about it in the abstract and does not identify it with the Ottoman monarchy, for which he had scant respect.[23] This identification was, however, made in the 1840s by his grandson, Shāh Muḥammad Isḥāq, an immigrant to the Hijāz, and subsequently influenced the *ʿulamā* and the élite of Muslim India from 1870 onwards. The development is paralleled by similar trends in the world of Islam elsewhere. In 1873 Yaʿqūb Beg, the

[17] Taghizade, in *R. du Monde musulman*, xx (1913), pp. 179–220, at p. 192.

[18] E. C. Sachau, introd. to *Alberuni's India* (London, 1910), i. 9–10; al-Bīrūnī, *Kitāb al-ṣaydana*, Eng. tr. M. Meyerhof in *Islamic Culture*, xi. (1937), p. 27.

[19] *al-Kāmil*, ed. C. J. Tornberg (Leiden, 1851–76), xii. 233–5; cf. F. Gabrieli, *Storia della letteratura araba* (Milan, 1951), pp. 232–4.

[20] *Muʿjam al-buldān*, ed. Wüstenfeld (Leipzig, 1866–73), iv. 859.

[21] Miguel Asín Palacios, *El Islam cristianazado* (Madrid, 1931), pp. 93–95.

[22] *Izāla al-khafā* and *Ḥujjat*, ii. 422–9.

[23] *Fuyūẓ al-Ḥarmayn* (1947), pp. 297 ff.

revolutionary leader of Chinese Turkestan, sent his nephew Ḥājī Turāb to the court of the Ottoman ʿAbd al-ʿAzīz, who invested Yaʿqūb Beg with the title of Amīr. On Yaʿqūb Beg's coinage the Sultan's name was engraved on one side and his own on the other.[24] Pan-Islamic and pro-caliphate trends made their first appearance in Tunisia in the 1880s with the French occupation and culminated in the career and activities of ʿAlī Bāsh Hamba and al-S̱aʿālibī during the first two decades of the twentieth century. In this period a conflict between the pan-Islamic and nationalist groups developed in Egypt and was reflected in the controversial articles in *al-Manār* on the one side and *al-ʿĀlam* and *al-Siyāsa* on the other.[25]

Like the Indian Muslim elite, the *al-Manār* group had strongly supported the Young Turk Revolution of 1908; but unlike them it regarded Muṣṭafā Kamāl's abolition of the caliphate and introduction of certain drastic reforms as acts of apostasy. Like the Indian Muslims, the group placed high hopes in the rise of Ibn Saʿūd; but unlike them upheld even the Wahhābī repudiation of such innovations as pilgrimages to sacred tombs.[26] ʿAlī ʿAbd al-Rāziq's advocacy of the abolition of the caliphate is not very different from that of Khudā Bakhsh in asserting that that Institution had been and continued to be a misfortune for Islam and the Muslims and a source of corruption.[27] There is similarity in his argument and that of Iqbāl when he points out that caliphate was not an integral part of Muslim creed; neither the Qu'ān nor the authentic *ḥadīs̱* have anything categorical to say about it; and that the Muslim *ijmāʿ* has 'never been solidly or consistently behind it'.[28] Iqbāl, however, avoids ʿAlī 'Abd al-Rāziq's apologetics in asserting that the Prophet exercised religious but not civil authority, and that as he did not exercise the latter, the question of succession in the form of the caliphate

[24] D. C. Boulger, *Life of Yakoob Beg*, etc. (London, 1878); *The Times*, 16 Mar. 1874.

[25] *al-Manār*, viii, 478; xiv (1911), 36; xxvii (1926–7), 119.

[26] Ibid. xiv. 43; xxviii. 581; C. C. Adams, *Islam and Modernism in Egypt* (London, 1933), p. 185.

[27] *al-Islām wa uṣūl al-ḥukm* (Cairo, 1925), p. 36.

[28] Nuseibeh, p. 153.

does not arise.[29] Iqbāl, Ziya Gökalp, and ʿAlī ʿAbd al-Rāziq reflect in varying degrees an intellectual trend pervading the greater part of the Muslim world in the 1920s, advocating a 'family of Islamic nations, independently organized under civil governments, but all conscious of their heritage of Islamic culture . . . an Islamic Commonwealth'.[30]

The quest for the rationalization of Muslim law antedates the quest for the modernization of the classical concept of Muslim statehood. In Muslim India it began with Sayyid Aḥmad Khān and his colleagues. The two focal points of modernization in the Aligarh system of thought are 'reason' and 'nature'. In so far as its use of reason is concerned, Von Grunebaum's general remark is pertinent: '. . . human reason is charged not so much with discerning unknown areas of facts as with uncovering the insights and the directions implied in the divine or prophetic pronouncements'[31] This is what Shaykh Muḥammad ʿAbduh also affirms by remarking that reasoning has to be applied in examining and explaining the messages of the prophets in the light of the laws of nature as ordained by God.[32] Sayyid Aḥmad Khān's premiss on this problem is even more categorical: 'Between the word of God [scripture] and the work of God [nature] there can be no contradiction'.[33] ʿAbduh, unlike Sayyid Aḥmad Khān, forecasts Iqbāl's distinction between intuitional and dialectical reason by admitting the latter's incompetence in certain theological spheres such as the interpretation of the attributes of God or even full understanding of the nature and quality of human soul.[34]

Through a rationalistic approach to the sources of Muslim law Sayyid Aḥmad Khān and Shaykh Muḥammad ʿAbduh both concentrate on the first one, the Qur'ān; and both, as well as Āzād, do so by a neo-exegetical reorientation of the Muslim scripture. In detail they arrive at very different conclusions, but

[29] ʿAbd al-Razīq, *al-Islām*, pp. 64–65, 69, 79, 84.

[30] Gibb, *Whither Islam?*, p. 364.

[31] *Modern Islam*, p. 19.

[32] *al-Islām wa'l-Naṣrāniyya* (Cairo, 1923), p. 51.

[33] Cf. *al-Manār*, vii. 292; Goldziher, *Die Richtungen der islamischen Koranauslegung* (Leiden, 1920), pp. 352–3; Adams, p. 136.

[34] *Risāla al-tawḥīd* (Cairo, 1926–7), pp. 52–54, 117.

their arguments are strikingly similar. In relation to the second source of law, the *ḥadīs̱*, Aḥmad Khān and Chirāgh ʿAlī's attitudes are sceptical and close enough to the scientific criticism developed later by Ignaz Goldziher and Joseph Schacht, though unlike them the two Muslim modernists do not hesitate to quote a *ḥadīs̱* uncritically when it suits them. ʿAbduh's approach to the *sunna* is more cautious, recognizing a small section of the *ḥadīs̱*-corpus relating to matters of practice as an essential part of the basic data of law.[35] On the whole, Islamic modernism in India followed ʿAbduh's rather than Sayyid Aḥmad Khān's orientation in this respect.[36] *Ijtihād* as a substitute for the third classical source of law, *qiyās*, finds the greatest emphasis in Indian Islam in the writings of the Aligarh group and those of Iqbāl; as well as in Arab Islam in the writings of ʿAbduh, who said that 'there is no limit to what may be done within its limits, and there is no end to the speculation that may be conducted under its standards'.[37] Despite its fundamentalism, the *al-Manār* group emerges as more progressively modernist than Iqbāl in suggesting that civil law, which should be subject to periodic revision, should be separated from religion which is sacrosanct, eternal, and immutable.[38]

Sayyid Aḥmad Khān is alone in his total denunciation of *ijmāʿ* as a source of law. He was conscious of it only in the classical sense, i.e. that of the *ijmāʿ* of the *ʿulamā'*. Outside India ʿAbduh was perhaps the first to see in an extended concept of *ijmāʿ*, as applicable to all Muslims, the seeds of something like modern democracy when he observed that government and legislation by the chosen representatives of the people was entirely in harmony with the spirit of Islam.[39] In the subcontinent the theory of popular *ijmāʿ* as the basis of democracy was developed by Iqbāl. Soon it seems to have gained general currency in the entire world

[35] Ibid. p. 224.
[36] ʿAbduh's *Risāla* was a prescribed textbook at the MAO College as well as in several theological schools in the subcontinent.
[37] *Risāla*, p. 177; Eng. tr. quoted from Adams, p. 131.
[38] *al-Manār*, iv. 859 and *passim*.
[39] Riḍā, *Ta'rīkh*, ii. 71 ff.

of Islam, in most cases developed locally. An Afghan writer, Niyāz Aḥmad Zikriyā, regards the role of *ijmā'* of the *'ulamā'* in classical Islam as a manifestation of delegated power, proving the sovereignty of the people to whom the direct right of *ijmā'* has reverted in modern times.[40]

However liberal or radical the modernist interpretation of the basic classical sources of law may be, as long as the divine word rather than human reason, experience, and requirement is regarded as the ultimate source of law, an Islamic state cannot be sovereign in the modern sense of the word.

> Absolute restriction on the legislative power of a State is a restriction on the sovereignty of the people of that State and if the origin of this restriction lies elsewhere than in the will of the people, then to the extent of that restriction the sovereignty of the State and its people is necessarily taken away. In an Islamic State sovereignty, in its essentially juristic sense, can only rest with Allah.[41]

Nor in the circumstances can that state be democratic or even 'theo-democratic', however broad a meaning may be given to the term *ijmā'*.

The crux of the problem is humanistic. In its larger sense humanism is defined by Pierre Mesnard as 'toute conception théorique, toute attitude pratique qui affirment la valeur exceptionelle de l'homme'.[42] Its starting point in the west is an 'anthropocentrisme réfléchi', an attitude unknown to the classical Islam.[43] In classical Islam, in the totality of the traditionalist and fundamentalist current attitudes and in all Indo-Muslim modernist thought except in that of Iqbāl, God and not man remains the key figure of the universe dominating man's political, social, economic, and cultural life. Iqbāl alone takes a position which is not very different from Jacques Maritain's concept of 'humanisme intégral' which tends

[40] *Les principles de l'Islam et de la démocratie* (Paris, 1958), pp. 41–45.

[41] *Munīr Report*, p. 210.

[42] 'L'humanisme chrétien', *B. Joseph Lotte*, June 1939, p. 7.

[43] L. Gardet, 'Humanisme musulman d'hier et d'aujourd'hui: éléments culturels de base', *IBLA*, 1st quarter 1944.

essentiellement à rendre l'homme plus vraiement humain, et à manifester sa grandeur originelle en le faisant participer à tout ce qui peut l'enrichir dans la nature et dans l'histoire . . . , il demande tout à la fois que l'homme développe les virtualités contenues en lui, ses forces créatrices et la vie de la raison, et travaille à faire des forces du monde physique les instruments de sa liberté.[44]

The humanism of Iqbāl's thought is what Gardet describes as 'humanisme avec Dieu'. Man's vicegerency of God is within certain moral bounds autonomous in the abstract in the thought of Iqbāl, but when it comes to the theory of the government of an Islamic, even a Muslim, state he too harnesses religion with politics. Gardet is right in asserting that, in the view of Iqbāl and Muḥammad Ḥusayn Haykal, if the humanistic renaissance in the world of Islam incorporates anthropocentrism and an absolute naturalism it would do itself considerable damage, for which the west would also be responsible.[45] Thus, Iqbāl's position, though more radical than that of other Indo-Pakistani modernists in asserting the creative autonomy of man, remains fairly close to the consensus, which favours maintaining the traditional balance between spiritual and material values, and endeavours to effect the conquest of nature with this balance.

This delicate theoretical position has not worked out so well in practice anywhere. This is the tragedy of modern Islam. From within itself it has been able to recreate elements of a renaissance, but not of a reformation. Much of the content of Islamic modernism is a westernization of the given data of Islamic juristic law and custom. In this westernization the process of apologetics blurs the historical perspective. As Von Grunebaum describes the psychological logic of apologetics, 'it is a characteristic tendency on the part of the receiving community to interpret heterogenetic change (usually experienced as achievement or advance) as orthogenetic'.[46]

In the modern Islamic world's reactions to the west the oppo-

[44] *Humanisme intégral* (Paris, 1936), p. 10.
[45] In *IBLA*, 1944, pp. 5–6, 38–39; see also his *La cité musulmane*, pp. 273–94.
[46] *Modern Islam*, p. 14.

sites of attraction and repulsion have been working simultaneously and continuously. The west's liberalism is the cause of attraction; its colonialism, neo-colonialism, and parochial insularity the reason for repulsion. 'Comment concilier', comments Muḥammad Ḥusayn Haykal, 'les deux esprits contraires, la liberté et la colonisation? C'est difficile à concevoir'.[47]

Though the initiative for a real reformation of Islam has to continue to come from within it, and has to be thought out and translated into practice by the Muslims, perhaps the west may eventually help. One may conclude on Gibb's optimistic note:

> Islam cannot deny its foundations . . . and in its foundations . . . Islam belongs to and is an integral part of the large western society. It is the complement and counterbalance to European civilization, nourished at the same springs, breathing the same air. In the broadest aspect of history, what is now happening between Europe and Islam is the reintegration of western civilization, artificially sundered at the Renaissance and now reasserting its unity with overwhelming force.[48]

[47] 'Les causes de l'incompréhension entre l'Europe et les musulmans et les moyens d'y remédier', *L'Islam et l'Occident* (Paris, 1947), p. 55.

[48] *Whither Islam?*, p. 376.

GLOSSARY

Note: With a few exceptions, this Glossary is confined to terms used throughout the book and it excludes Arabic words such as *jihād* which have entered the English language.

ʿadālat, justice, a court of law.
ʿālim, sing. of *ʿulamāʾ* (q.v.).
ʿaṣabiyya, group solidarity (a key term in Ibn Khaldūn's interpretation of history).
bāb al-ijtihād, the 'gate' of the use of individual reasoning, which is regarded as having been closed after the completion of the classical system of jurisprudence.
bidʿa (pl. *bidaʿ*), innovation, assumed to be bad unless specifically stated to be good, roughly equivalent to heresy.
dār al-ḥarb, 'land of war', i.e. countries not under Muslim rule.
dīn, religion (used by Āzād and Parwīz in the special sense of fundamental religion).
diya, blood-money.
faqr, poverty, hence a life of poverty with resignation and content; *faqīr*, one who lives such a life.
fiqh, classical Muslim jurisprudence.
fitna, putting to the proof, discriminatory test, hence temptation permitted or sent by God to test the believer's faith; also state of rebellion against the divine law, thus revolt, disturbances, civil war.
furūʿ, lit. branches, the body of positive rules derived from *uṣūl*, the 'roots' and sources of legal knowledge (i.e. Qur'ān, *sunna*, *ijmāʿ*, and *qiyās*).
ghazal, 'song, elegy of love'.
ḥadīṣ, report of a statement or utterance the Prophet is alleged to have said or made, supported by a chain of authorities.
ḥajj, annual pilgrimage to Mecca and Medina.
hidāyat, guidance, particularly divine guidance.
iḥsān, beneficence.
iʿjāz, miraculous style (of the Qur'ān).
ijmāʿ, consensus.
ijtihād, use of individual reasoning.
ihklāṣ, sincerity of intent.
ʿilm al-ḥadīṣ, the science of *ḥadīṣ*.

imām, leader, leader in prayer; in Shīʿite doctrine the hereditary head of the community in line of succession from the Prophet through his daughter Fāt̤ima and his son-in-law ʿAlī.

īmān, faith.

isnād, the chain of transmitters of a *ḥadīs̤*.

amāʿa, jamāʿat, a group, community, assembly.

jizya, poll-tax (imposed on *z̤immīs* in an Islamic state).

kalām, classical Muslim scholastic theology.

kalima, Muslim attestation of faith in the unity of God and the prophethood of Muhammad.

maghāzī, wars or expeditions, specifically those undertaken by the Prophet.

manqūlāt, traditional sciences.

maʿqūlāt, rational sciences.

maz̤hab, religious seat or school of law, used of different schools of jurisprudence.

millat, religious community (especially the community of Islam).

naskh, abrogation of a Qur'ānic verse by a subsequent verse.

qalandar, wandering mendicant dervish, used by Iqbāl in the special sense of a superman in the making.

qawm, people, tribe, later nation.

qiyās, juristic reasoning by analogy.

rabb, lord, God.

raḥmat, mercy.

ribā, lit. excess, variously interpreted to denote interest or usury.

rubūbiyyat, quality of God as *rabb*, Divine Providence.

sawād-i aʿz̤am, a large city (used in the subcontinent in the sense of popular consensus of the Muslims).

sharʿ, *sharīʿa*, holy law of Islam.

shūrā, council, consultation, in modern times used to denote representative government.

sīra, biography, more particularly biography of the Prophet.

sulūk, progress of the mystic towards the attainment of his goal.

sunna, practices and precepts of the Prophet.

tafsīr, exegesis (of the Qur'ān).

taḥrīf, corruption or interpolation introduced in a sacred text.

taqdīr, role, destiny, predestination.

taqlīd, traditionalism, in contrast to *ijtihād*.

taqwā, piety.

ta'sīs, laying a foundation, used by Āzād in the special sense of 'reconsolidation'.

'ulamā', the men of religious learning.

umma, Muslim community.
waḥy, divine revelation.
waqf, pious foundation, mortmain.
zakāt, alms, alms tax.
ẕimmī, protected non-Muslim subject of an Islamic state.

SELECT BIBLIOGRAPHY

I. WORKS IN ORIENTAL LANGUAGES

ʿAbd al-ʿAzīz, Shāh. *Fatāwā-i ʿAzīziyya*, Delhi, 1904.
ʿAbd al-Raḥmān Khān. *Taʿmīr-i Pākistān awr ʿulamāʾ-i Rabbānī*. Multan, 1956.
ʿĀbid ʿAbd al-Karīm. Parwiz Ṣāḥib ke afkār kā sharja-i nasab. *Fārān*, Mar. 1956, 77–104.
ʿĀbid Ḥusayn, S. *Qawmī tahẕīb kā masʾala*. Aligarh, 1955.
Abū Ṭālib Khān, Mirzā, *Masīr-i Ṭālibī*; Eng. tr. by Charles Stewart, *Travels of Mirza Abu Taleb Khan in Asia, Africa and Europe*. London, 1810. 2 vols.
Aḥmad Miyān ʿAkhtar'. *Iqbāliyāt kā tanqīdī jāʾiza*. Karachi, 1955.
Akbarābādī, *see* Saʿīd Aḥmad Akbarābādī.
Āzād, Abu'l-Kalām, ed. *al-Hilāl*, 1912–13.
—— *Masʾala-i khilāfat wa Jazīra-i ʿArab*. (2nd ed. 1920.) Lahore, n.d.
—— *Khuṭbāt*. Lahore, 1944.
—— *Kārwān-i Khayāl*. Bijnore, 1946.
—— *Tarjumān al-Qurʾān*, ed. Ghulām Rasūl Mihr. Lahore, 1961. Eng. tr. of pt 1 by W. A. Latif. Bombay, 1962.
—— *Maẓāmīn*. Lahore, n.d.
—— *Taẕkira*. Lahore, n.d.
—— *Bāqiyāt-i Tarjumān al-Qurʾān*, Karachi, 1961.
—— *Ṣubḥ-i ummīd*. Lahore, n.d.
ʿAzīz al-Raḥmān and Muḥ. Shafīʿ Deobandī. *Fatāwā-i dār al-ʿulūm-i Deoband*. Deoband, n.d.
Bahādur Shāh ʿẒafar'. *Kulliyāt*. Lucknow, 1918.
Barq, Ghulām Jīlānī. *Do Islām*. Lahore, 1962.
—— *Do Qurʾān*. Lahore, 1963.
Chirāgh ʿAlī. *Rasāʾil*. Hyderabad, 1918–19.
—— *Taḥqīq al-jihād*. Hyderabad, n.d.
—— in *Tahẕīb al-akhlāq* (collected reprint). Lahore.
Dayrābādī, ʿAbd al-Mājid. *Muḥammad ʿAlī*. Azamgarh, 1954–6. 2 vols.
Gangohī, Rashīd Aḥmad. *Fatāwā*. Deoband, n.d.
—— *Sabīl al-rishād*. Deoband, n.d.
—— *Zubdat al-manāsik*. Deoband, n.d.
Gīlānī, Mawlānā Manāẓir Aḥsan. *Sawāniḥ-i Qāsimī*. Deoband, 1953.
—— *Tadwīn-i ḥadīṡ*. Karachi, 1956.

* Dates in parenthesis indicate original date of publication.

Ḥālī, Alṭāf Ḥusayn. *Madd-o jazr-i Islām*, known as *Musaddas-i Ḥālī*. 1879.
—— *Ḥayāt-i jāwīd*. Cawnpore, 1901.
—— *Makātīb*, ed. M. Ismā'īl Pānīpatī. Lahore, n.d.
—— in *Tahẕīb al-akhlāq* (collected reprint), iv. 85–108. Lahore, n.d.
Ibrāhīm Mīr Siyālkoṭī. *Ta'rīkh-i Ahl-i ḥadīṡ*. Lahore, 1953.
Ikrām, Shaykh Muḥammad. *Mawj-i kawṡar*. Karachi, 1958.
Ilyās Baranī. *Ma'ārif-i millat*. Aligarh, 1924.
Imdād 'Allāh. *Jihād-i Akbar*. Deoband, n.d.
—— *Ẓiyā al-qulūb*. Deoband, n.d.
Iqbāl, Muḥammad. *Asrār-i Khudī* (1915). Lahore, n.d. Eng. tr. R. A. Nicholson, *Secrets of the Self*. London, 1920. (The introduction, 'Dībācha-i Asrār-i Khudī', appeared only in the 1st ed. It was later reprinted in the 1943 ed. of *Maẓāmīn* (q.v.) and in other collections of his essays.)
—— *Rumūz-i Bīkhudī* (1917). Lahore, n.d. Eng. tr. A. J. Arberry, *Mysteries of Selflessness*. London, 1953.
—— *Kulliyāt*. Hyderabad, 1923.
—— *Payām-i Mashriq* (1923). Lahore, 1942. Fr. tr. Eva Meyerovitch and M. Achena, *Message de l'Orient*. Paris, 1956. German tr. Annemarie Schimmel, *Botschaft des Orients*. Wiesbaden, 1963. A section tr. into English by A. J. Arberry, *The Tulips of Sinai*. London, 1947. Partial tr. into Czech by J. Marek, *Poselsvi z vychodu*. Prague, 1960.
—— *Bāng-i Darā* (1924). Lahore, 1944.
—— *Zabūr-i 'Ajam* (1927). Lahore, 1944. Eng. tr. A. J. Arberry, *The Persian Psalms*. Lahore, 1948.
—— *Jāwīd Nāma* (1932). Lahore, n.d. Eng. tr. S. M. Ahmad, *Pilgrimage to Eternity*. Lahore, 1961. German tr. Annemarie Schimmel, *Buch der Ewigkeit*. Munich, 1957. Italian tr. A. Bausani, *Il Poema celeste*. Rome, 1952. Fr. tr. E. Meyerovitch and M. Mokri, *Le Livre de l'éternité*. Paris, 1962.
—— *Bāl-i Jibrīl* (1935). Lahore, 1942.
—— *Pas chi bāyad kard ay aqwām-i sharq?* (1936). Lahore, 1944.
—— *Ẓarb-i Kalīm*. Lahore, 1936.
—— *Armaghān-i Ḥijāz* (1938). Bijnaur, 1958.
—— *Mazāmīn*. Hyderabad, 1941.
—— *Makātīb* (*Iqbāl Nāma*). Lahore, 1944.
—— *Rakht-i Safar*. Karachi, 1952.
—— *Bāqiyāt*, ed. S. A. Vahid. Lahore, 1954.
Ismā'īl (Shahīd), Shāh. *Taqwiyat al-īmān*. Lahore, 1956.
—— *Manṣab-i imāmat*. Delhi, n.d.

Ja'farī, Ra'īs Aḥmad. *Sīrat-i Muḥammad 'Alī*. Delhi, 1932.
Madanī, Ḥusayn Aḥmad. *Naqsh-i ḥayāt*. Delhi, 1953. 2 vols.
—— *Irshādāt*. Deoband, 1956.
—— *Maktūbāt*. Deoband, 1956.
—— *Mawdūdī ke dastūr-o 'aqā'id kī ḥaqīqat*. Deoband, 1960.
Maḥbūb Riẓwī. *Ta'rīkh-i Deoband*. Deoband, 1952.
Maḥmūd al-Ḥasan Deobandī. Presidential Address to ann. sess. of Jam'iyyat al-'Ulamā'-i Hind. Delhi, 1920.
—— *Adilla Kāmila*. Deoband, n.d.
—— *Maqālāt*. Deoband, n.d.
Mawdūdī, Abu'l A'lā. *Mas'ala-i qawmiyyat*. Pathankot, 1947.
—— *Ta'līmāt*. Lahore, 1955.
—— *Da'wat-i Islāmī*. Rampur, 1956.
—— *Mas'ala-i jabr-u qadr*. Lahore, 1957.
—— *Parda*. Lahore, 1958.
—— *Taḥrīk-i Islāmī kā ā'īnī lā'iḥa 'amal*. Lahore, 1958.
—— *Islām awr jadīd ma'āshī naẓariyyāt*. Lahore, 1959.
—— *Khuṭbāt*. Lahore, 1960.
—— *Tanqīḥāt*. Lahore, 1960.
—— *Islām awr ẓabt-i wilādat*. Lahore, 1960.
—— *Islāmī tahẓīb awr uske uṣūl-u mabādī*. Lahore, 1960.
Muḥammad 'Alī, Mawlānā. *Ifādāt*. Karachi, n.d.
Muḥammad Miyān. *'Ulamā'-i Ḥaqq awr unke mujāhidāna kārnāma*. Delhi, 1946 [?].
—— *'Ulamā'-i Hind kā shāndār māẓī*. Delhi, 1957–60. 4 vols.
Muḥammad Ṭufayl. *Musalmānon kā rawshan mustaqbil*. Delhi, 1945.
Muḥammad Ya'qūb. Sawāniḥ 'umrī-yi Muḥammad Qāsim, in Manāẓir Aḥsan Gīlānī, *Sawāniḥ-i Qāsimī*. Deoband, 1953, i. 23–48.
Muhammadan Anglo-Oriental Educational Conference. *Majmū'a-i resolutionhā-i dihsāla, 1886–95*. Agra, 1896.
Muḥsin al-Mulk, in *Tahẓīb al-akhlāq* (collected reprint). Lahore.
Nadwī, Abu'l-Ḥasan 'Alī. *Ta'rīkh-i da'wat wa 'Azimat*. Azamgarh, 1955–63.
Nadwī, Abū'l-Ḥasanāt. *Hindustān ki qadīm Islāmī darsgāhen*. Azamgarh, 1936.
Nadwī, Mas'ūd 'Ālam. 'Mawlānā Sindhī ka ek nāqidāna jā'iza', *Ma'ārif*, Sept. 1944.
—— *Hindustān ki pahlī Islāmī taḥrīk*. Rawalpindi, 1948.
Nānotawī, Muḥ. Qāsim. *Intishār al-Islām*. Deoband.
—— *Mubāḥiṣa-i Shāhjahānpūr*. Deoband.
—— *Fuyūẓ-i Qāsimiyya*. Deoband.
—— *Taqrīr-i dilpaẕīr*. Deoband.

Nānotawī, Muḥ. Qāsim. *Guft-o gū-yi maẕhabī*. Deoband, *c.* 1930.
Parwīz, G. A. *Mi'rāj-i Insāniyyat*. Karachi, 1949.
—— *Islāmī Niẓām*. Karachi, 1952.
—— *Asbāb-i zawāl-i ummat*. Karachi, 1952.
—— *Salīm ke nām*. Karachi, 1953.
—— *Iblīs wa Ādam*. Karachi, 1954.
—— *Firdaws-i gumgashta*. Karachi, 1954.
—— *Niẓām-i Rubūbiyyat*. Karachi, 1954.
—— *Insān ne kyā sochā*. Karachi, 1955.
—— *Islāmī ma'āsharat*. Karachi, 1955.
—— *Barq-i Ṭūr*. Karachi, 1956.
—— *Jū-i Nūr*. Karachi, 1956.
—— *Ṭāhira kē nām*. Lahore, 1957.
—— *Taqdīr-i umam*. Karachi, 1957.
—— *Man-u Yazdān*. Lahore, 1958.
—— *Shu'la-i mastūr*. Lahore, 1958.
—— *Lughāt al-Qur'ān*. Lahore, 1960–1.
—— *Mafhūm al-Qur'ān*. Lahore, 1961.
—— *Pākistān men Qānūnsazī ke uṣūl*. Karachi, n.d.
—— *Qur'ān ka siyāsi niẓām*. Lahore, n.d.
Pfander, C. G. *Mīzān al-Ḥaqq*. London, 1862.
Raḥmān 'Alī. *Taẕkira-i 'ulamā'-i Hind*. Lucknow, 1914; Urdu tr. Karachi, 1961.
Raḥmānī, A. S. *Jamā'at-i Islāmī ke da'we, khidmat awr tarīqa-i kār kā jā'iza*. Deoband, n.d.
Raḥmat-Allāh Kīrānawī. *Izālat al-awhām*. Delhi, 1862.
—— *al-Baḥs̱ al-sharīf*. Delhi, 1864.
—— *Iẓhār al-Ḥaqq*. 1891.
—— *I'jāz-i 'Īsawī*. Delhi, n.d.
Sa'īd Aḥmad Akbarābādī. *Mawlana 'Ubayd-Allāh Sindhī awr unke nāqid*. Lahore, 1946.
—— *Islām awr ghulāmī kī ḥaqīqat*. Delhi, n.d.
Sa'īd Ḥalīm Pasha. *Buḥrān-i Fikrimiz*. Istanbul, 1917.
S̱anā-Allāh Amritsarī. *Tafsīr-i S̱anā'ī*. 1896.
—— *Āyāt-i mutashābihāt*. Amritsar, 1904.
Sarwar, M. *'Ubayd-Allāh Sindhī*. Lahore, 1943.
Sayyid Aḥmad Khān. *Āṣār al-ṣanādīd* (1847). Cawnpore, 1904.
—— *Asbāb-i baghāwat-i Hind* (1858). Agra, 1903.
—— *Ta'rīkh-i Sarkashī-yi Bijnore*, 1858.
—— *Tab'īn al-kalām* (Commentary on the Holy Bible), Urdu text and Eng. tr. Ghazipur, 1862–5.
—— *Khuṭbāt-i Aḥmadiyya*. Agra, 1870.

Sayyid Aḥmad Khān. *Tafsīr al-Qur'ān*. Lahore, 1880–95.
—— *Izālat al-ghayn 'an Ẕu'l Qarnayn*. Agra, 1890.
—— *Tarqīm fī qiṣṣa Aṣḥāb al-kahf wa'l-Raqqīm*. Agra, 1890.
—— *Lectures* [Urdu], ed. Munshī Sirāj al-dīn. Sadhora, 1892.
—— *al-Taḥrīr fī uṣūl al-tafsīr*. Agra, 1892.
—— *Tafsīr al-jinn wa'l-jānn*. Agra, 1892.
—— *Ibtāl-i ghulāmī*. Agra, 1893.
—— *Akhīrī Maẓāmīn*. Lahore, 1898.
—— *Tafsīr al-samāwāt*. Agra, 1898.
—— *Aḥkām-i ṭa'ām-i ahl-i kitāb*. Lahore, 1899.
—— *Taṣānīf-i Aḥmadiyya*. Agra, 1903.
—— *Khuṭūṭ*, ed. Ross Masood. Badaun, 1931.
—— *Makātīb*, ed. Mushtāq Ḥusayn. Aligarh, 1960.
—— *Musafirān-i Landan*, ed. S. M. Ismā'īl Pānīpatī. Lahore, 1961.
—— ed. *Tahẕīb al-akhlāq* (1869–) (collected reprint). Lahore, n.d.
Shiblī Nu'mānī. *Sīrat al-Nu'mān* (1892). Lahore, n.d.
—— *al-Ghazzālī* (1902). Azamgarh, 1922.
—— *'Ilm al-Kalām* (1903). Azamgarh, 1922.
—— *Shi'r al-'Ajam* (1908–18). Azamgarh, 1920–2. 5 vols.
—— *al-Ma'mūn*. Azamgarh, 1926.
—— and Sayyid Sulaymān Nadwī. *Sīrat al-Nabī*. Azamgarh, 1953–62.
Ṣiddīq Ḥasan Khān. *Kitāb al-mu'taqad al-muntaqad*. Delhi, 1887.
—— *Haṣṣ al-insān*, Agra, 1889.
—— *Tarjumān al-Qur'ān*. 1889.
—— *I'lām al-bashar bi-wujūh al-khayr wa'l-sharr*. Agra, 1890.
—— *Ḥadīṡ al-ghāshiyya*. Benares, 1891.
—— *Iqtirāb al-sā'a*. Benares, 1891.
—— *Ṣalāḥ ẕāt al-bayn*. Benares, 1891.
—— *Tarjumān Wahhābiyyat*. Agra, 1897.
—— *Wasīla al-najāt*. Benares, 1889.
—— *'Āqibat al-muttaqīn*. Benares, 1904.
Sindhī, Mawlanā 'Ubayd-Allāh. *Shāh Walī-Allāh awr unkā falsafa*. Lahore, 1949.
—— *Urdū sharḥ-i Ḥujjat Allāh al-bāligha*. Lahore, 1950.
—— *Shāh Walī-Allāh awr unkī siyāsī taḥrīk*. Lahore, 1952.
—— *Kābul men sāt sāl*. Lahore, 1955.
—— *Khuṭbāt*. Lahore, n.d.
—— *'Unwān-i Inqilāb*. Lahore, n.d.
Ṭayyib, M. *al-Kalām al-Ṭayyib*. Deoband.
Thānawī, Ashraf 'Alī. *Bayān al-Qur'ān*. Delhi, 1916–17.
—— *al-Bawādir al-nawādir*. Delhi, 1945–6.

Thānawī, Ashraf ʿAlī. *Bihishtī Zewar*. Deoband, 1954.
—— *Islām awr ʿaqliyyat*. Lahore, 1957.
—— *Ḥuqūq-u farāʾiẕ*. Multan, 1960.
—— *Ḥayāt-i muslimīn*. Karachi, n.d.
ʿUs̱mānī, Shabbīr Aḥmad. *al-Islām*. Deoband, n.d.
—— *Iʿjāz al-Qurʾān*. Deoband, n.d.
—— *Khuṭbāt*. Lahore, n.d.
Walī-Allāh, Shāh. *ʿIqd al-jīd*. Urdu tr. Delhi, 1925.
—— *Fuyūẕ al-Ḥarmayn*. Urdu tr. M. Sarwar. Lahore, 1947.
—— *Ḥujjat Allāh al-bāligha*. Lahore, 1953.
—— *al-Fawẕ al-kabīr*. Delhi, 1955.
—— *Izāla al-khafā*. Karachi, n.d. 2 vols.
—— *Siyāsī Maktūbāt*, ed. K. A. Niẕāmī. Aligarh, 1950.
Ẕafar ʿAlī Khān. *Bahāristān*. Lahore, 1937.
Ẕafīr al-dīn, M. *Jamāʿat-i Islāmī ke dīnī rujḥānāt*. Deoband, n.d.
Ẕākir Ḥusayn. *Taʿlīmī Khuṭbāt*. Delhi, 1955.
Zubayrī, Muḥammad Amīn. *Ḥayāt-i Muḥsin*. Aligarh, 1934.

2. WORKS IN EUROPEAN LANGUAGES

Abbot, F. K. Mawlana Mawdūdī on Quranic Interpretation. *Muslim World*, xlviii (1958), 6–19.
Abdul Hakim, Khalifa. *Islamic Ideology*. Lahore, 1953.
—— *Islam and Communism*. Lahore, 1953.
Afshar, I. and Mahdawi, A. *Documents inédits concernant Seyyed Jemal al-din Afghani*. Tehran, 1963.
Aga Khan, *see* Sultan Muhammad Shah.
Aḥmad Barelwī, Sayyid. Notice of *Ṣirāṭ-i mustaqīm*, *J. Asiatic Society of Bengal*, i. (1832), 479–98.
Ahmed Khan, Syed. *Essays on the Life of Mohammed*. Vol. i. London, 1870.
—— *The Truth About Khilafat*. Lahore, 1916.
Ali, Mohamed, Maulana. *Select Writings and Speeches*, ed. Afzal Iqbal. Lahore, 1963. 2 vols.
Ameer Ali. *Ethics of Islam*. Calcutta, 1893.
—— *A Short History of the Saracens*. London, 1899. (1961 reprint.)
—— *Mahommedan Law* (1912). 5th ed. Calcutta, 1929. 2 vols.
—— *The Spirit of Islam*. London, 1922. (1961 reprint.)
—— The Modernity of Islam. *Islamic Culture*, i. (1927), 1–5.
—— Islamic Jurisprudence and the Necessity for Reforms. *Islamic Culture*, ii. (1928), 477–84.
—— Memoirs. *Islamic Culture*, v. (1931), 509; vi. (1932), 1–18, 163–82, 333–62, 504–25.

Andrews, C. F. *Zaka Ullah of Delhi*. Cambridge, 1929.

Anwar Shah. Presidential Address to ann. sess. of Jam'iyyat al-'Ulamā'-i Hind. Peshawar, 1927.

Arnold, T. W. *The Preaching of Islam*. London, 1896.

—— *The Caliphate*. London, 1924.

Azad, Abul Kalam. *India Wins Freedom*. Bombay, 1959.

Aziz, K. K. *Britain and Muslim India*. London, 1963.

Aziz Ahmad. *Islamic Culture in the Indian Environment*. London, 1964.

Baljon, J. M. S. *Modern Muslim Koran Interpretation, 1880–1960*. Leiden, 1961.

—— A Modern Muslim Decalogue. *World of Islam*, n.s. iii/3–4 (1954), 187–200.

Barq, Ghulam Jilani. *Islam, the Religion of Humanity*. Lahore, 1956.

Bausani, A. The Concept of Time in the Religious Philosophy of Muhammad Iqbal. *Welt des Islam*, n.s. iii. (1954).

Binder, L. *Religion and Politics in Pakistan*. Berkeley & Los Angeles, 1961.

Blunt, W. S. *The Secret History of the English Occupation of Egypt*. London, 1923.

—— *Diaries*. London, 1932.

Cheragh Ali, Moulvi. *The Proposed Political, Legal and Social Reforms in the Ottoman Empire and Other Mohammedan States*. Bombay, 1883.

—— *A Critical Exposition of the Popular Jihad*. Calcutta, 1885.

Clark, R. *The Punjab and Sindh Missions*. London, 1885.

Dar, B. A. *The Religious Thought of Syed Ahmad Khan*. Lahore, 1957.

Eister, A. W. Perspectives sur les fonctions de la religion dans un pays en voie de développement: l'Islam au Pakistan. *Archives de sociologie des religions*, xv (1963), 35–42.

Farquhar, J. N. *Modern Religious Movements in India*. London, 1924.

Fück, J. S. Muhammad Iqbal und der indomuslimische Modernismus, in *Westostliche Abhandlung R. Tschudi zum 70 Geburstag überreicht*. Wiesbaden, 1954.

Fyzee, A. A. A. *A Modern Approach to Islam*. Bombay, 1963.

—— *Outlines of Muhammadan Law*. London, 1964.

Halim Pasha, Prince Said. *The Reform of Muslim Society*. Eng. tr. Lahore, 1936 (reprinted from *Islamic Culture*, Jan. 1927).

Hunter, W. W. *The Indian Musalmans*. London, 1871.

Husayn, Abid S. *Indian Culture*. Lahore, 1963.

Ikram, S. M. *History of Muslim Civilization in India and Pakistan*. Lahore, 1961.

—— *Muslim Civilization in India*. New York, 1964.

International Islamic Colloquium at Lahore, 28 Dec. 1957–8 Jan 1958. *Proceedings*.

Iqbal, Javid. *The Ideology of Pakistan and Its Implementation*. Lahore, 1959.

Iqbal, Muhammed. *The Development of Metaphysics in Iran*. Cambridge, 1908.

—— *Reconstruction of Religious Thought in Islam*. London, 1934.

—— Presidential Address at ann. sess. of Muslim League, Allahabad, 1930, reprinted in C. H. Philips and others, eds. *The Evolution of India and Pakistan, 1858 to 1947*. London, 1962.

—— Letters to Jinnah, reprinted in *The Struggle for Independence, 1857–1947*. Karachi, 1958.

—— *Selected Speeches and Writings*. Lahore, 1944.

MacDonough, Sheila. *An Ideology for Pakistan; a Study of the Works of Ghulam Ahmad Parwiz*. Unpubl. PhD. thesis, McGill Univ., Montreal, 1963.

Malik, Hafeez. *Moslem Nationalism in India and Pakistan*. Washington, 1963.

Maududi, Sayyid Abul Ala. *Towards Understanding Islam*, Eng. tr. K. Ahmad. Lahore, 1960.

—— *Islamic Law and Constitution*. Lahore, 1960.

—— and others. *Studies in the Family Law of Islam*. Karachi, 1961.

Morley, W. H. *The Administration of Justice in British India*, London, 1858.

Muhammadan Anglo-Oriental College, *Speeches and addresses . . .* Aligarh, 1888.

Muʿin al-Dīn Aḥmad Khān. A Bibliographical Introduction to Modern Islamic Development in India and Pakistan, 1700–1955, app. to *J. Asiatic Society of Pakistan*. Dacca, 1959.

Nadwi, Abul Hasan Ali. *Islam and the World*. Eng. tr. Lahore, n.d.

Pakistan, Commission on National Education, Jan.–Aug. 1959. *Report*. Karachi, 1960.

—— Constitution Commission. *Report*. Karachi, 1961.

—— Sub-Committee to Examine Suggestions Received from the Public. *Basic Principles Committee Report*. Karachi, 1951.

Paret, R. Das islamische Colloquium in Lahore. *Welt des Islam*, n.s. v (1958), 228–34.

Parwiz, G. A. *Fundamentals of Islamic Constitution*. Karachi, 1956.

—— *Islamic Ideology*. Lahore, n.d.

—— *The Quran's Political System*. Lahore, n.d.

—— *Why Do We Lack Character?* Lahore, n.d.

Philips, C. H. and others, eds. *The Evolution of India and Pakistan, 1858 to 1947*. London, 1962.

Punjab, Court of Inquiry constituted . . . to inquire into the Punjab Disturbances of 1953 [Pres.: M. Munīr]. *Report*, 1954.

Qureshi, Anwar Iqbal. *Islam and the Theory of Interest*. Lahore, 1961.

Rosenthal, E. I. J. The role of Islam in the Modern National State. *Year Book of World Affairs, 1962*.

Schimmel, A. *Gabriel's Wing*. Leiden, 1963.

Sheikh, N. A. *Some Aspects of the Constitution and Economics of Pakistan*. Woking, 1961.

Siddiqi, Muh. Zubair. *Hadith Literature*. Calcutta, 1961.

Smith, Wilfred Cantwell. *Modern Islām in India*. London, 1946.

—— *Pakistan as an Islamic State*. Lahore, 1951.

—— *Islam in Modern History*. Princeton, 1955.

Stchoukine, Ivan. *Les miniatures indiennes de l'époque des Grands Moguls au Musée du Louvre*. Paris, 1929.

Smith, Donald E. *India as a Secular State*. Princeton, 1963.

Sultan Muhammed Shah, Sir, Agha Khan. *The Memoirs of Aga Khan; World Enough and Time*. London, 1954.

Wherry, E. M. *Islam and Christianity in India and the Far East*. New York, 1907.

INDEX